# MOVING PICTURES

# MOVING PICTURES

## HOW RUSH CREATED PROGRESSIVE HARD ROCK'S GREATEST RECORD

### WILL ROMANO

**Backbeat Books**

Essex, Connecticut

**Backbeat Books**

An imprint of Globe Pequot, the trade division of
The Rowman & Littlefield Publishing Group, Inc.
4501 Forbes Blvd., Ste. 200
Lanham, MD 20706
www.rowman.com

Distributed by NATIONAL BOOK NETWORK

**Library of Congress Cataloging-in-Publication Data**
Names: Romano, Will, 1970- author.
Title: Moving pictures : how Rush created progressive hard rock's greatest record /
    Will Romano.
Identifiers: LCCN 2022024577 (print) | LCCN 2022024578 (ebook) | ISBN
    9781493062355 (paperback) | ISBN 9781493062362 (ebook)
Subjects: LCSH: Rush (Musical group). Moving Pictures. | Progressive rock music—
    History and criticism. | Rock music—Canada—1981-1990—History and criticism.
Classification: LCC ML421.R87 M65 2023  (print) | LCC ML421.R87  (ebook) |
    DDC 782.42166092/2—dc23/eng/20220523
LC record available at https://lccn.loc.gov/2022024577
LC ebook record available at https://lccn.loc.gov/2022024578

♾️™ The paper used in this publication meets the minimum requirements of American
National Standard for Information Sciences—Permanence of Paper for Printed Library
Materials, ANSI/NISO Z39.48-1992.

# CONTENTS

# ACKNOWLEDGMENTS

Geddy Lee, Alex Lifeson, Neil Peart, Terry Brown, Paul Northfield, Deborah Samuel, Mike Girard, Jason Bittner, Eric Barnett, Kevin Aiello, Uriah Duffy, André Perry and Yaël Brandeis, Ken Hensley, Pete Agnew, Paul DeLong, Robert Di Gioia, Jonathan Mover, Brian Tichy, Jason Sutter, John DeServio, David Greene, Freddy Gabrsek, Marty Morin, Yosh Inouye, David Marsden, Adam Moseley, Bruce Gowers, Dave Krusen, Brian Miessner, Wanda and Ronnie Hawkins, Frank Davies, Mike Tilka, Len Epand, Rick Ringer, Graham Lear, Rick Colaluca, Gerald O'Brien, Dwight Douglas, Rodney Bowes, John Coull, Moira Coull, Alfie Zappacosta, Monte Nordstrom, Mark Richards, Terry Draper, Steve LeClaire, Craig Martin (Classic Albums Live), John Sinclair, Sandy Roberton of Worlds End, Patrick Ledbetter (CIMCO), Blair Francy, Jane Harbury, Dan Del Fiorentino (NAMM), Steve Tassler, Arielle Aslanyan, Lynne Deutscher Kobayashi, David Jandrisch (Musicians' Rights Organization of Canada), Toronto Audio Engineering Society, Morgan Myler (IATSE Local 58), Tim Kuhl, Graham Betts (Pickwick Group Limited), and Natalie Pavlenko (OCAD).

A special thank-you to my wife Sharon, my in-laws and family members, my brother Michael, my uncle Tony, Aunt Gigi, Mom and Dad, Anthony Bernard, Dave Penna, Bernard Scott, Vincent Tallarida, Michael Richford, Ed Perry, Gary Jansen, Mike Harrison, as well as those who've helped to make this project possible: Chris Chappell, Barbara Claire, Laurel Myers, Bruce Owens, John Cerullo (for taking on this monstrosity to begin with), and everyone at Backbeat Books/Rowman & Littlefield. Thank you for the opportunity and your patience.

I dedicate this to Molly, Maggie, and Gilligan. You're forever with me, but I still miss you. Every day. Grateful for the newest member of the family, Scarlet. Grateful for the river.

Thank you, JC.

# CHAPTER 1

# 1981: THE LAST PICTURE SHOW

The obvious question when reading or even writing a book such as this is, why? Why *Moving Pictures*? Why expend the time, energy, and other resources on a single album by a Canadian power trio recognized, by and large, as a progressive hard rock band?

I could simply state the company line, that Rush has racked up dozens of gold records, and more than a dozen platinum in the United States alone. And, according to sales figures tallied by the Recording Industry Association of America (RIAA), Rush is third, behind only the Beatles and the Rolling Stones, for the most consecutive gold or platinum albums by a rock band.

*Moving Pictures* did well in its day and had attained quadruple-platinum status from the RIAA. That was, until April 2021, when the record went five-time platinum, surpassing 5 million units sold in the United States.

All of this stuff looks great as a few lines of a résumé, in a record company press release, or in the biographical information offered on a management or a booking agency website. No one disputes these totals, but numbers often leave us cold and don't always tell the whole story or help drill down to the why—and how.

Why was *Moving Pictures* effective? How did it become so popular?

Follow me as I turn back the clock a few decades.

Close your eyes: Imagine it's 1981.

You have the radio dial set to your favorite rock station in your home, room, basement, car, office, apartment—or wherever. The DJ announces that this is "the new one" from a band called Rush. There's silence for a split second, and then a snarling synthesizer portal opens, and before you have time to react, you're hit with the sonic equivalent of shrapnel—fragments of artillery fire that hit you where you live, changing you forever.

Compression-enhanced sound clamps down on bandwidth of audio, adding a concentrated punch to a funky, murky, groovy, ballsy hard rock anthem. Somewhere, about midway through the track, the sound implodes, or collapses, with short bursts of percussion solos—cymbals crashing, drums thundering—in patterns you've rarely if ever heard in rock music before.

It's unforgettable. A little unnerving. What *is* this thing?

When the four-minute-and-thirty-three-second track comes to a close, our friendly guide, the DJ, returns to tells you that the song is called "Tom Sawyer," and it's featured on Rush's new record, *Moving Pictures*.

You need a minute to process what you've heard: first you were frightened, then exhilarated . . . and now intrigued. Titling the track "Tom Sawyer" seems so anachronistic, so incongruous with the modern sounds that have caught your ears, you can't help but wonder how they were made, the personality profile of the people who made them, and why you feel the way you did.

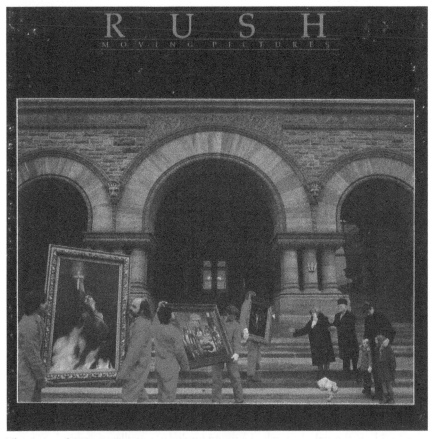

The cover of *Moving Pictures*

The near-perfect marriage of music and lyrics seemed so contemporary, even cutting edge. It's thought-provoking music and kind of kick-ass, too: headbanging sounds for music nerds, poetry wrapped up in intellectual rock—and catnip for esoteric adrenaline junkies.

This was Rush, circa 1981.

Many may have had a similar experience the first time they'd encountered "Tom Sawyer" being spun for listeners over the airwaves. The auditory power of "Tom Sawyer" and its rippling synthesizer vortex chewed a gaping hole in the space-time continuum, creating a new dimension that grabs us by the collar and compels us to listen even today.

And "Tom Sawyer" is but the opening salvo for an album that won Rush so many praises and fans. In reality, the record helped stabilize and bolster their career.

So, when we ask, why *Moving Pictures?*, the answer lies in tapping into the same exploratory energy that fueled the instinct to chase that first scare, that initial thrill. Like watching the best suspense movie you've ever seen, you pursue that "high" in the hopes of recalling the same emotions and reliving the moment of discovery. By examining several factors, or tributaries—or, in movie terms, plotlines—that contributed to the success, making, and appearance of the album, we might discover why *Moving Pictures* remains so vital in the twenty-first century.

Nothing is created in a vacuum, and the three members of the Canadian progressive hard rock band—bassist/vocalist/keyboardist Geddy Lee, guitarist Alex Lifeson, and drummer/percussionist and lyricist Neil Peart—were influenced by a great number of musical genres over the years. These cultural tributaries powered the creative process and funneled into the anatomy of the musical work at question, *Moving Pictures*.

A main thematic tributary coursing through *Moving Pictures*, as its title suggests, is the filmic properties the seven-track album possesses. The overriding principal of music, as Jimmy Page once said of Led Zeppelin's catalog, is "synesthesia," "creating pictures with sound."

Indeed. *Moving Pictures* was conceived as a collection of independent stories, cinematic vignettes, captured by three very different but relatively experienced young men using advanced audio equipment and their inherent creative instincts, which resulted in a complete, coherent work.

Unparalleled in the band's recorded output, *Moving Pictures* boasts multisensory qualities: the famous snarling synth portal we'd discussed ("Tom Sawyer"); the pulse-quickening cyclical patterns corkscrewing through the genre fluid "Vital Signs"; a spine-tingling sci-fi thrill ride thinly masking social commentary ("Red Barchetta"); technically precise musical jousting amid time signature changes ("YYZ"); chilling glimpses of a hellish, torch-lit mob haunting "Witch Hunt"; the wide-screen dual optics of "The Camera Eye"; and a ferocious guitar tone taking a bite out of fame ("Limelight").

Layering tracks, knowing when to use guitar effects (and when not to), various panning techniques used during the mix, and digital production methods, not to mention Rush's sharpened technique and songwriting craft, created a song cycle that's sonically transparent but offers the impression of depth. It's as three-dimensional as Rush's music had ever gotten to date and perhaps ever.

Like cinematographic blocking, the art and science of capturing movement on film, if the action is framed correctly for the lens, the viewer receives a sensation of three-dimensional space. In this case, the band and the production team of coproducer Terry Brown and lead recording engineer Paul Northfield were masters of sonic geometry.

There's a promise fulfilled with the appearance of *Moving Pictures* as both a manifestation of the impact of the counterculture and the impact of film and music *on the counterculture*. Historian, author, and educator Arthur Schlesinger Jr. once noted that the counterculture youth of the 1960s "find in music and visual images the vehicles that bring home reality."

Vaguely hinted at with Rush's previous studio album, 1980's *Permanent Waves*, *Moving Pictures* can be interpreted as a piece of neorealism, the very stuff of influential cinematic movements, compared to the sci-fi and fantasy epics of the band's past. Liminal on its front edge ("Tom Sawyer" and "Red Barchetta"), the album balloons to full-on realism, with tracks such as "YYZ," "Limelight," and "Vital Signs."

Yes, the fictional, fantastical, and phantasmagorical exist in *Moving Pictures*, but so does the personal, which intermingles with these elements, sometimes within the framework of a single song, making for one hell of a thrill ride.

The leadoff track, "Tom Sawyer," acts as a kind of overture, setting the lyrical, musical, and thematic tone for the record. *Moving Pictures* is passage to a new dimension, one in which "Tom Sawyer" cracks the portal open and mythology elevates to the real. This anthem to the modern-day outlier, the nonconformist, whose default position was one of self-reliance, independence, free thought, even defiance, contained as many earth-shattering philosophical implications as groundbreaking sonic properties: it redefines the outlaw motif and the contemporary definition of icono-clast within a difficult-to-pigeonhole musical framework.

Partly inspired by one of America's greatest satirists, "Tom Sawyer" is not only American—it's *friggin'* American. You almost can't get more American than Tom Sawyer and Mark Twain. By extension, the song is the quintessence of North American rock, nay, North American progressive rock.

In Twain's original novel, Tom Sawyer is an irrepressible youth who has others gift *him* for the privilege of painting his Aunt Polly's fence or, after running away and pretending to live life as a pirate, shows up at his own funeral. But Tom does grow up (somewhat) throughout the novel and eventually performs a civic duty, as most adults do. This nod toward personal responsibility was one that Twain generally skirts in the novel, but before our eyes, Tom Sawyer did the responsible thing.

*Moving Pictures*, then, in its own way, reflected a band matured. Indeed. *Moving Pictures* was Rush's last picture show, the record that marked a coming of age in the wake of numerous musical, cultural, and personal upheavals in the mid- and late 1970s. Rush so elevated their game that their music had risen to the realm of the audiovisual.

"Red Barchetta" may be one of the best, if not the greatest, example of the band successfully blending varied emotional content and visual information inside a single song. The sound of the middle section is evenly paced and spaced, like the broken yellow dividing lines of the highway. We're aerodynamically screeching toward an unknown destination.

The third song, an instrumental titled "YYZ," a jazz-rock juggernaut with a hint of Eastern modalities, captures the excitement of the exotic travel but also represents the liberties of modern transportation. Shuttling us to distinctly different composi-tional sections but also looping us through cyclical parts, the song becomes the thing it represents: a journey full of expectation, wonderment, and, ultimately, release and euphoria.

The aura cast around the East and Eastern musical modes gripped the pro-gressive rock and psychedelic rock imagination, inspiring such innovative popular artists as prototypical progressive popsters the Beatles and later Led Zeppelin, who were seduced (if only a smidgen) somewhere along the way by the progressive rock movement.

The Morse code pattern opening "YYZ" is unvocalized language providing a beacon for safe terrestrial travel, which echoes the distant signals of early progressive rock movement. This repetitive, rhythmic cipher rings in sympathy with the blinkin', seemingly extraterrestrial transmission heard at the opening of Pink Floyd's "Astronomy Domine," from 1967's *The Piper at the Gates of Dawn*, and the aquatic radar-like pings of "Echoes" of 1971.

While it speaks to progressive rock nascent stirrings, at the same time, "YYZ" is also part of the rich tradition of the Western world's mid-twentieth century instrumental pop singalong—tracks such as "Tequila," "Walk Don't Run," "Apache," "Telstar," "Guitar Boogie," "Wipe Out," "Green Onions," and, honorable mention, "(Ghost) Riders in the Sky" (often performed as an instrumental).

Dig deeper into the unknown origins of instrumental music, reach back into a dark epoch in which rhythm and sound fused, and Rush's "YYZ" is absolutely monolithic, essential, even primordial. Except Rush wasn't rockin' a lyre in Syria and communicating via cuneiform on clay tablets in dedication to the goddess Nikkal. Rush was redefining instrumental music for generations to come.

What makes "YYZ" so unique is that it somehow remains grounded in Canadian soil—or, at the least, circling Canadian airspace. While on tour with Rush in the mid-1970s, Peart read Richard Rohmer's novel *Exxoneration* from 1974, a fantastical tale of the takeover of Canada by the United States.

"We're proud of Canada," Peart told *RPM* magazine in November 1976. "But nationalism has tenuous bounds. It has to be kept in balance."

Although Peart's stance on nationalism later became crystal clear with "Territories," from 1985's *Power Windows*, what "YYZ" accomplishes is the near impossible: It drapes the Canadian flag over sonic travelogue.

The last song on the original side 1 of the vinyl LP, "Limelight," preaches that self-exile and isolation are preferable to the phoniness of celebrity and fame. Those who continue to live their life and wish to find meaning or lasting relationships or true invention should do so, far away from stage lights.

Despite its title, "Limelight" isn't about the act of performing music per se but how fame intoxicates both the performer and the acolyte alike. Celebrity corrupts, derailing the process human beings possess for rational thought, such as it is.

This converges with and diverges from Rush's earlier song about fame, "Best I Can," from 1975's *Fly by Night*, penned by sometimes lyricist Geddy Lee. In the song, Lee welcomes rock and roll stardom while simultaneously attempting to denounce phonies.

Rush fans in Brazil sing the instrumental lines of "YYZ." (Pictured: the cover of the concert film DVD release, *Rush in Rio*, 2003.)

Ironically, the themes Rush sings about in "Limelight" wind up coming true and further defining Peart's rather pronounced stance on fame and privacy.

In press photos of Rush from the late 1970s, drummer Neil Peart is shown wearing a suit jacket on which he'd pinned a button featuring the image of a bicycle—a symbol of freedom related to the English television series *The Prisoner*, starring Patrick McGoohan as a former British intelligence officer. Judging by many of Peart's statements to the press, the idea of being a "prisoner" of the music business, perhaps even a band, helped contribute to the need to write "Limelight."

"Don't get into a situation you can't control," offered Peart to a reporter for the *Kansas City Times* newspaper, who asked him to provide words of advice for up-and-coming rock musicians. "All you have to do is be aware and use your head."

Whatever pretense the band had toward reclaiming their anonymity in the face of the rock and roll lifestyle was, perhaps, gone forever once *Moving Pictures* was deemed a great success.

Rush easily slipped into their iconic status:

The bespectacled singing bassist, the one the *St. Petersburg Times* had claimed possessed as shrill a voice in pop music as Frankie Valli (the *Montreal Star* went as far as to detect "heinous sounds" emanating from Lee's vocal microphone), was no longer just another front man: he was multitasking, triple-threat Geddy Lee.

Alex Lifeson, the fleet-fingered dude who traded in his vintage-style Gibson guitars for custom Fenders, had transformed himself into a gear and effects guru, a sage of secret and sacred guitar tones.

Neil Peart, a blur of moving arms and swiveling head behind a fortress of red-coated drum shells, was "the Professor," whose acolytes and apostles deciphered his poetic words, committed every piece of his drum gear to memory, and tracked the evolution, in minute detail, of his drum solo throughout the decades.

In his book on Patti Smith's *Horses*, professor and author Philip Shaw forwards an interesting theory, positing that "death and transformation of the rock god is regarded as an essential, even desirable, condition of cultural change."

Consider this: Roger Waters and Pink Floyd were disintegrating right before our eyes by the early 1980s. Although Floyd had reached stratospheric commercial success by the mid-1970s with *The Dark Side of the Moon* and *Wish You Were Here*, Waters had become withdrawn from the public, even from his own bandmates. *The Wall*, released in 1979, was inspired largely by this sense of alienation. Dysfunctional and broken, hardly working together as a unit, Floyd released only one more studio album with Waters.

The old guard was dismantling. While Rush was on tour in 1980, playing music that would appear on the upcoming *Moving Pictures* album, Zeppelin drummer John Bonham died unexpectedly on September 25, 1980. Zeppelin was effectively over, opening up opportunities to younger artists, such as Zebra, who had patterned their approach on the iconic British band's mixed-genre grandeur, and even those who had only briefly flirted with the Zep sound (Billy Squier).

Furthermore, Rush was beginning to taste stardom when former Beatle John Lennon died. On December 8, 1980, the night Lennon was fatally shot outside his New York City apartment building, the Dakota, Rush was in the studio working diligently to complete *Moving Pictures*.

Lennon, who had cowritten with chameleon rock star David Bowie the song "Fame," a number one U.S. hit five years earlier, often struggled to balance his personal and professional lives while preserving a sense of identity. The difficult and painful lesson of Lennon's untimely death at the hands of Mark David Chapman forces us to reexamine notions of celebrity and privacy. Peart's words for "Limelight" were prescient to say the least.

Side 2 of the original vinyl release opened with the eleven-minute-long "The Camera Eye," inspired in part by John Dos Passos's novelistic trilogy *U.S.A.* Lyricist Peart makes a daring commentary about breaking loose of a kind of collective mindset, one in which we're cognizant of the natural wonders around us.

The greed, corruption, criminality, and personal failures we find in many characters of Dos Passos's epic trifold narrative reflect the moral deterioration, a spiritual rot in the first half of twentieth-century America. Although sanitary by comparison, Peart's lyrics force a refocus of humanity and seems to indicate that the people he observes on the streets of two major world-class cities are missing something, too.

"The Camera Eye" is the final long-form composition to appear on a Rush studio record. Although with 2007's *Snakes & Arrows* and 2012's *Clockwork Angels* Rush had seemingly relearned the value of composing lengthier tracks, nothing on these records was in the same ballpark as "The Camera Eye." For this reason alone, it's a milestone and marks a beginning and an end—the alpha and the omega of Rush's progressive rock era.

The following song, "Witch Hunt," also represents an alpha and omega paradigm of sorts. Epitomizing the dangers of mob rule and groupthink, "Witch Hunt" was the last installment of a musical saga titled Fear (then envisioned as a trilogy until a part 4 emerged years later). Despite being part 3 of Fear, "Witch Hunt" was, paradoxically, the first to be recorded. Although fellow Canadian prog/album-oriented rock group Saga had already begun recording portions of their often-impenetrable "Chapters" puzzle-like plotline and doing it out of sequence, very few narrative arcs were handled in a similar way in a rock setting.

Listeners would feel their spine tingle from the creepy crawlies of part 1 of Fear ("The Enemy Within," from 1984's *Grace Under Pressure*) and groove to the hypnotic bounce of "The Weapon," part 2 of Fear—an ode to mass manipulation featured on 1982's *Signals* studio album.

"Vital Signs," the final track to be written for the album, fittingly aligns with contemporary minimalism, New Wave–esque synth sequencing, reggae, and a dash of prog rock. It's unlike nearly anything the band had previously recorded. For that matter, the clarity of vision exhibited in "Vital Signs," particularly on the topic of individuality, has rarely been matched since *Moving Pictures*.

Whereas "Natural Science," from *Permanent Waves*, extols the virtues of honesty and integrity in the face of scientific progress, "Vital Signs" hits similar notes, urging us to preserve what makes us what we are in the cyber present and near future.

As diverse a collection of songs that *Moving Pictures* is, these entries have one thing in common: together, they compose an anthology of mini-movies that have been conceived, coproduced, directed, blocked and framed, written, and starred in by Rush. Finally, Rush blends all these tracks together, as any great film editing team would.

It's not surprising to find that Rush was using film as a kind of creative fuel. Spooling in the background during the making of *Moving Pictures* was David Lynch's Kafka-esque 1977 horror flick *Eraserhead*—hardly an anthem to self-reliance and responsibility.

Although it would be a stretch to claim many similarities between Lynch's psychological and symbolic work—and themes inherent to *Moving Pictures*—the noir aspects of parenthood have some relevance to the birthing process Rush underwent to record a rock album. Other connections may be difficult to report if not avoid: Geddy had recently become a father, and perhaps he saw his fears reflected in Lynch's surrealistic, if at times gruesome, cinematic vision.

"In the official videos for the album you can see a poster up on the wall of *Eraserhead* and that was there throughout the whole of the making of *Moving Pictures*," says recording engineer Paul Northfield. "It was a film that they had seen on their tour bus. They thought it was hilarious. The guy from *Eraserhead* [Jack Nance who portrays the character Henry Spencer] was the mascot for the album."

Sonically and thematically, the songs hang together well. Indeed. Rush seemed to settle into a root key shared by many of the tracks on the record. In 2012, *Guitar Player* magazine pointed out that with *Moving Pictures*, the keys of E and A duke it out.

Doesn't all this mean that *Moving Pictures* is a concept album?

We would have to reply in the negative if the classic rock opera is the model or template. The material on *Moving Pictures* is unlike the plot twists and emotional landmines hidden beneath the surface of the Who's *Tommy*, for instance. By the same reasoning, it's dissimilar to Genesis's *The Lamb Lies Down on Broadway*, from 1974. The record's snaky, mystical narrative was difficult to decipher, but an overriding story arc exists nonetheless.

That isn't to say that *Moving Pictures* fails to deliver a coherent message. It's a time capsule, a snapshot if you will, of the very moment the band ascended to rock stardom. It also denotes the end of a cycle of progressive hard rock albums for Rush, a clarion call for the musical possibilities they'd explore in the 1980s.

Spurred on by the success of *Permanent Waves*, a clear break from the hard-core progressive releases *A Farewell to Kings* and *Hemispheres*, Rush fell in with the flow of change and the pulse of the times.

*Moving Pictures* was created in the first summer of a new decade. Applying terms from lexicon of the *Seinfeld* universe, the time frame from 1980 to 1981 was indeed the "Summer of Rush."

"It was early in their career and being early, it is the best time," says André Perry, in whose studio, Le Studio, in Morin-Heights, Quebec, the band recorded *Moving Pictures*. "I'm not saying the other albums are not as good, but *Moving Pictures* was the peak of their career."

Rush had, of course, been making professional recordings for years prior to *Moving Pictures*, but for many, it is this album that represents their introduction to the band—and maybe for good reason. As the guys had often said, their music provides (and provided) a kind of sound track both with regard to Geddy, Alex, and Neil but also for their fan base.

Enduring Classic: Rush performed *Moving Pictures* in its entirety on the Time Machine tour.

"Given my druthers, I would make out first album *Moving Pictures*," Peart told Martin Popoff for the book *Contents Under Pressure*. "I can't think of a single reason not to do that."

It would be difficult for anyone, much less the band, to argue to the contrary that Rush didn't strive for a level of success. However, fighting to become successful—battling a hostile press, an often-shortsighted label, fickle popular tastes, concert promoter and radio programmer bias, and so on—is only one aspect of the Rush story.

This account details the band's rise to stardom and the band's balancing act of the personal and professional; everyman personas and rock stardom; keyboard technology, technical excellence, and accessible hard rock; and commercialism and progressive rock.

For Rush, it was always a question of balance.

Our world likes black and white. Be one thing, not the other. If you are one thing, you can't be the other. In order to win friends and influence people, Rush performed a delicate and very public balancing act.

When writer Anne Leighton interviewed Geddy Lee for *RIP* magazine in 1989, it was apparent that he was aware that the band's music doesn't fit into a neat categorical box.

"Our sound has changed so much over the years," Lee told Leighton. "It's funny. When you talk to metal people about Rush, eight out of ten will tell you that we're not a metal band. But if you talk to anyone outside of metal, eight out of ten will tell you we are a metal band. . . . But if you have to label us, hard rock suits us better. It's not as limiting as metal, especially if you label it progressive hard rock."

Because of the time period in which Rush gained momentum in the mainstream and because they played amped-up electric guitar (or their concerts were too deafening for critics), they were mistakenly categorized as heavy metal.

Deena Weinstein, in her book *Heavy Metal: The Music and Its Culture*, points out that metal is a style of music in which "intense" vocals rest side by side with heavily distorted amplified guitars, specifically those played with fervor. "There is no doubt that as early as 1971 the term 'heavy metal' was being used to name the music characteristic of the genre's formative phase," Weinstein wrote.

Music scribes began labeling all manner of rock band—from Led Zeppelin and Black Sabbath to Uriah Heep and Deep Purple—"heavy metal" whether they'd earned this tag or not. Others, such as MC5, Iggy and the Stooges, Pentagram, Alice Cooper, and even the Kinks, contributed to metal, but, like Rush, many of the above-named artists were pigeonholed by the industry.

"The best story I have is from the second album, *Salisbury*, for a song called 'Lady in Black', which I wrote during a U.K. tour, and was two chords and a chorus with no words in it," Uriah Heep's Ken Hensley told me before his death in 2020. "It's the biggest single song we've ever had globally. It became a huge hit in so many huge markets, except for America. The most unlikely thing, because it is like a folk song, and the band added a rock touch to it. At first the band didn't want to record it, because they said, 'Nah, that's a folk song. We don't so folk songs.' The producer [Gerry Bron] said, 'Now you do write folk songs, and we'll record it . . . ,' and thank God we did, because it was a launching pad for the band from the second album onwards."

Exactly where the phrase "heavy metal" first appeared in print and why has been the basis of parlor games for the past five decades. Some say it was William Burroughs, the English music periodicals, or the lyrics of Steppenwolf's top-two hit "Born to Be Wild" (not to mention the press it generated in *Creem* magazine), which attempted to capture the physical vibrations of a motorbike or automobile rumbling down the road. *Creem* later used the phrase "heavy metal" in its 1971 review of *Kingdom Come*, a record by New York's Sir Lord Baltimore, coproduced by Eddie Kramer, Jim Cretecos, and future Bruce Springsteen manager Mike Appel and issued via Rush's American distributor, Mercury Records.

So, if the origins of heavy metal are a bit murky, one has to wonder about the wisdom and value of categorizing any kind of music at all.

Weinstein suggests that through the 1970s, bands that were melodic but still rockin', such as Aerosmith and Kiss, were labeled "hard rock" to separate them from other "heavier" acts. Some of this, I would add, may have to do with North America's quickly conglomerating rock radio format. Rush certainly fit the more melodic end of the hard rock spectrum, even though they too used noise/distortion, guitar amplifier feedback, and driving or thunderous beats.

As we—and the music industry—ambled into the 1980s, metal became increasingly synonymous with power, volume, speed, and vocalists honing their voices into sharp growls. If these characteristics ever applied to Rush, then certainly, by *Permanent Waves* and, of course, *Moving Pictures*, the three guys from Canada were moving away from them.

Irony of ironies: *Moving Pictures* became popular just as the New Wave of British Heavy Metal began barking at the moon. Metal's dominance as a musical form throughout the 1980s awakened the collective consciousness. Rush wasn't British, of course, but there may have been some residual appreciation for the band's harder or heavier sides from those who remembered the rip-roaring moments in their repertoire, such as those in "2112," "Bastille Day," and "Anthem."

The fact is that Rush's style circa 1981 was owed less to their contemporary heavy metal cousins and more to the popular sounds of rock a decade and a half prior to the release of *Moving Pictures*.

Rush's raison d'être can be traced back even further, to the realm of the psychedelic power trios—Cream, the Jimi Hendrix Experience, and Blue Cheer. (Some historians and rock fans have included bands such as the Who and Led Zeppelin in this class, as they were power trios fronted by a lead vocalist.)

"I was hugely influenced by Eric Clapton when I was young, at the time of Cream," Alex Lifeson once told me. "Being a three-piece band, that was definitely an influence on us."

But as psychedelia slowly dissipated, new subgenres emerged. Modern compilations, such as the Brown Acid series from RidingEasy Records (in cooperation with Lance Barresi, co-owner of Los Angeles–based Permanent Records) and Darkscorch Canticles, issued through Numero Group, explore shadowy corners of the post-hippie North American psyche, largely accomplishing what Nuggets had for proto-punk vinyl collectors and enthusiasts. Rummaging through rock's dusty attics and basements helps to present a historical bridge between psychedelia and hard rock or, if you like, "heavy metal."

The mere presence of these compilations illustrates a shift in consciousness in the waning days of the Vietnam War, the coming political storm of Watergate, and also in a decline in the use of LSD as a recreational substance. As hallucinogens fell out of favor, casual and habitual usage yielded to harder drugs. With it, a less psychedelic strain of rock emerged, quickly relegating hallucinogenic music to the obsolescence bin and giving rise to hard rock and the hybrid psychedelic hard rock.

Rush's sound aligned itself somewhere along the way with psychedelic hard rock and progressive rock, as evidenced by the extended songs "The Necromancer" and "By-Tor and the Snow Dog," both from 1975. Rush straddled the line between the progressive rock and the psychedelic hard rock sound.

When the great splintering of psychedelic rock occurred, one of the extant off-shoots, progressive rock, began building steam in Europe. From British bands, such as Pink Floyd, the Nice, Yes, the Moody Blues, King Crimson, Family, Van Der Graaf Generator, Clouds, and Jethro Tull, as well as some notable American ones (Frank Zappa and the Mothers of Invention and Touch), progressive rock emerged in the late 1960s and early 1970s—a postmodernist mash-up of classical, rock, blues, folk, studio and electronic experimentation, and much more.

Eventually, Rush learned to mix many of these genres too, perhaps in ways that few of the above mentioned did. Arguably, albums such as *2112*, *A Farewell to Kings*, and *Hemispheres* didn't fit into any category previously established. The music wasn't composed of endless jams or deliberately ambient or spacey passages. Nor was much of it baroque. But there were some massive compositions, sometimes clocking in around twenty minutes and rivaling classical's epic scope, plenty of technical prowess, layers on layers of guitar tracking, and a wilderness of odd time signatures.

Rush's efforts, from 1975's *Caress of Steel* to 1977's *A Farewell to Kings*, the following year's *Hemispheres*, and, to a degree, moments of 1980's *Permanent Waves*, such as "Natural Science" and "Jacob's Ladder," would not have existed without progressive rock and its impact.

Why? Let's take a brief look at prog rock when it had hit its commercial peak, just a few years prior to the appearance of *Moving Pictures*.

If one album is emblematic of everything British prog got right (and mostly wrong), a record that encapsulated the subgenre's transgressions, creative ambitions, liberal use of keyboard technology, meandering concepts, musical beauty, and fusion of technique and melody, it's Yes's sprawling double LP *Tales from Topographic Oceans*—released at the height of prog rock commercial success/excess, late 1973.

Its companion release, Emerson, Lake & Palmer's *Brain Salad Surgery*, unleashed just weeks earlier, wrapped itself in packaging boasting illustrations of sexualized biomorphic torture devices, courtesy of H. R. Giger, and manifesting the counterculture's dark impulses and premonitions.

*Brain Salad Surgery* admonishes us on the dangers of an artificial society, a message that gives us a glimpse of mechanical Armageddon—a prophecy foretold by the counterculture. This apocalyptic view was, no doubt, a partial by-product of the counterculture's preoccupation with soulless machines, fueled by a paranoia of the evils of technology, atomic bomb panic, fear of nuclear fallout, and more than a century of post-*Frankenstein* cautionary tales, warning us of the dangers inherent to poking and prodding nature through so-called advances in scientific research.

Conversely, *Tales* beckoned us to throw off the shackles. The record's often esoteric messaging hinted at the attainment of spiritual enlightenment—a drilling down through layer on layer of learned behavior to unearth ancient, lost knowledge of the divine (i.e., the "song"), something that's been embedded, perhaps even programmed, into our collective memory.

Both *Tales* and *Brain Salad Surgery* fomented in the crucible of 1960s flower power that defined, in their own way, what it meant to be human. Rush's post-counterculture entry *Moving Pictures*, from 1981, also explores what it means to be human by injecting a neorealism and a confessional voice into the band's music that had been only faintly heard in commercial progressive rock prior to the record's release.

*Moving Pictures* procures some of the best elements of these (and other) progressive rock records from England in the early and mid-1970s, including Genesis's *Selling England by the Pound*, Pink Floyd's *The Dark Side of the Moon*, and even the faux narrative and synesthesian qualities of the Beatles' *Sgt. Pepper's Lonely Hearts Club Band*.

By 1981, Rush had begun streamlining their musical approach, abandoning, for the most part, the complicated twenty-minute epics, and, in fact, *Moving Pictures* appeared at a time when the popular appeal of progressive rock from Britain (and North America) had waned and a newer more brash form of heavy metal—speed and thrash—was formulating.

*Moving Pictures* stood at a precipice: not truly progressive rock, not totally hard rock, and not, as we'll see, New Wave, either. It seemed to erase so-called lines between these musical genres while also boasting some of the best aspects of them.

"*Moving Pictures* is a good example of a function of the times," says producer and recording engineer Paul Northfield, who would work with Rush on *Permanent Waves*, *Moving Pictures*, and the live album *Exit . . . Stage Left*, among others. "That album arrived at a time when progressive music, in the Yes era, had peaked and we had gone through the punk era. The thing about *Moving Pictures* is it brought a power to progressive rock, and it was also a period that Rush were simplifying a bit and getting in all the incredible playing but not writing twenty-five-minute songs. That was peaked with *Hemispheres* and *2112*. Now they were focusing and sheer power, as a power trio, with very simple orchestration from very simple keyboard parts."

That's the rub. Despite punk/New Wave's impact in the United Kingdom and the United States and even a small scene in Canada (i.e., Vancouver-based D.O.A., Viletones, the Mods, the Ugly, and the Diodes, among others), progressive rock still held some fascination for the popular psyche.

"Punk got crammed down our throats," explains drummer Paul DeLong, a veteran skinsman who has worked with a variety of artists in the past several decades, including Canadian prog popsters FM. "I liked Joe Jackson and Elvis Costello, but some of the bands that played like amateur garage hacks really bothered me. I guess that was the point, but I didn't like it. I was still going to see Gentle Giant at Massey Hall and listening to fusion. People will always listen to what they want to listen to, regardless of popular trends. The fact that Rush became so huge without hit singles attests to this fact."

"I think that the evolution of Rush was timed perfectly," says Rick Colaluca, drummer for Texas-based thrash metal band, WatchTower. "Like you said, there was somewhat of a void to be filled in the progressive arena, and Rush was right there to meld a heavier sound with progressive elements and take the whole thing to a new level. They were heavy enough to appeal to the hard rock and metal crowd, progressive enough for the music nerds and approachable enough for a much wider audience. That was exploited to its fullest when *Moving Pictures* came out with a genuine radio hit in 'Tom Sawyer.'"

And with Led Zeppelin calling it quits after the untimely death of drummer John Bonham, many of the bands that critics—and the public in general—compared them to were fading.

"In the beginning Rush had more of a Zep thing going on, and then they got deeper into prog and experimenting," says drummer Brian Tichy (Billy Idol, Foreigner, Whitesnake, Steven Tyler, Ozzy Osbourne, and Vinnie Moore). "After that, they tightened it up and got a little simpler and radio-friendly, I suppose. But Rush always had a way of gaining fans that were more 'metal' and 'hard rock' and 'prog.' They wrote music that had those elements underneath their 'Rush Umbrella.'"

Was Rush fated to release *Moving Pictures* when they did?

"Nothing at that time had such a unique blend of songs that had great melodies composed by musicians with such mastery of their instruments," says drummer Dave Krusen (Candlebox, Pearl Jam, and Unified Theory). "I think that's why they resonated with metal heads too. It blew so many people away, how well they did it. There were other prog bands, but Rush had everything going at once."

Punk rock still had its die-hard fans and true believers, but the mainstream public's taste for fast and loud was apparently satiated by metal and its ever-developing variants. Those predisposed to a different and, let's say, European style of rock gravitated toward the minimalistic and industrial sounds of post-punk New Wave. Well, that is, if crossover from punk happened at all.

Rush was reshaping their sound accordingly based on their interpretation of these forms. There's no denying that tastes of rock fans were changing in the late 1970s and early 1980s. But how much of this change can be attributed to zeitgeist, slick marketing, consolidation of radio programming, listener fatigue, labels looking for a higher return on investment, or the industry searching for the "next big thing"?

Whatever the reason, Rush seemed to read the tea leaves correctly. For instance, Human League's megahit *Dare!* would soon dominate the early 1980s. Released in the United States in 1982, "Don't You Want Me" became an international hit—a song framed largely by a LinnDrum, an electronic device that could be programmed to produce unwavering beats.

After Joy Division front man Ian Curtis committed suicide in 1980, the band regrouped as New Order and released their debut, *Movement*, in 1981 on the Factory label. As author Chris Ott points out in his book on Joy Division's debut album, *Unknown Pleasures*, producer Martin Hannett had the technical ability and willingness to experiment with and finesse audio equipment to, in essence, create new sounds from existing tracks, something he did for the guitars and drums for *Unknown Pleasures*.

Through ambience, sound effects, and digital delay, Hannett and the band practically invented a new subgenre, allowing a punk esthetic, luminescent electronic sounds, hard rock, and techno pop to intermingle, which greatly differed from the more in-your-face sound of the band's concert performances.

Rush absorbed what was happening around them, listening to these sounds as well as recorded output of others, such as Ultravox, Japan, and post-Genesis solo artist Peter Gabriel, and even found themselves branching out as listeners and gravitating toward so-called world music—the Caribbean flavoring of reggae and artists such as Peter Tosh and Bob Marley and the Wailers.

The name of the game was short, good, catchy, and, to a degree, electronic. And who could argue? Even something as earthy as dub reggae, a recognized musical form since at least the late 1960s, was shaped by the use of cosmic reverb or space echo.

Rush was one of the few mainstream hard rock bands in North America (if not the only one) left on the board to credibly embrace New Wave and music from around the globe. *Moving Pictures* not only solidified the band's desire to throw themselves headlong into a slimmed-down musical direction but also provided a vehicle to further navigate musical avenues they had only begun to explore a year earlier, such as we hear in the final song on the album, "Vital Signs."

"The world changed from the Punk Era that was pushing, pushing, pushing, and then it was gone," says drummer Jason Sutter (P!nk, Marilyn Manson, and Chris Cornell). "The Clash got popular and so did the Ramones, but that punky sound went into New Wave. The heavy hard rock of Led Zeppelin was over. The Genesis freak-out/Peter Gabriel era eventually led to the Phil Collins era and *Abacab* [1981]. The band switched gears. I think that definitely had something to do with the success of Rush."

Running the risk of scoring superficial points, we should note the band's public persona during the *Moving Pictures* time frame. Peart cut his hair, reverting to his appearance when he first joined Rush. Lifeson's long reddish/blond hair was chopped, perhaps in sympathy with the glam-inspired fashions of New Romantic and New Wave aesthetics. In concert, Lifeson even dons a crimson suit jacket and proverbial early 1980s skinny tie.

If appearances mean anything, then at least two-thirds of the band were desperately searching for an escape hatch from a false paradigm. Indeed. If we dress for the job we want, not the one we have, then Rush did not aspire to metal.

Not saddled with the same baggage as its British progressive rock counterparts, *Moving Pictures* is the sound of liberation. Largely setting aside what Rush biographer Steve Gett called the "Cecil B. DeMille proportioned epics" for a more condensed songwriting approach, Rush found themselves in a different headspace to create. The songs, on the whole, were shrinking in size, but the process of streamlining was quite liberating.

Through songwriting craft, production quality, and a bit of determination and perseverance, *Moving Pictures* became, quite simply, Rush's golden mean: the middle ground between excess and minimalism, progressive rock, hard rock, and synth/techno rock. Yet it simultaneously skirts all of these confining categorizations. It's the alpha and omega of Rush and, by extension, of progressive hard rock.

If we deem all of these things to be true, how did Rush arrive at this point?

# CHAPTER 2

# BIG-SCREEN BEGINNINGS

## THE CAMERA EYE, PART 1

### (Scenes from the Rush Sound Track Reel)

Geddy Lee is silent as he stands at the center of the room. His eyes peer over the rounded rims of his specks, what some would call "John Lennon" glasses, and patiently waits for me to enter and for our interview to begin.

No matter how many interviews you do, you're always a little nervous when meeting people for the first time. You begin to question: How will the interview go? What is the person like? Have I got the correct line of questioning? How attentive am I, today, to ask follow-up? How aggressively do I press certain issues if I don't get the responses I was looking for?

Aside from all of that, it's an odd feeling to meet someone like Geddy Lee, someone you'd seen perform numerous times onstage and in motion pictures or concert films, and then occupy the same space as he does. There's always this nagging feeling in the back of your mind about rock stars and pedestals and all of that crap. That is to say that it's all a bit surreal, as if you should not be sharing the frame with him.

But here we are: This is big screen. Or big-time reality. After a casual greeting, we're sitting at a hotel suite in New York City, where the loquacious Lee was promoting a record and speaking a bit about his career, Rush's next plans, and the band's possible future. He seems at ease, willing to talk, even eager. It's as if that significant gap between the guy in the stand and the rock star standing onstage shrunk.

When the interview was winding down, Lee easily transitioned from shop talk to a few personal topics: some of the music he'd enjoyed and even some of his pastimes.

I remember wearing my Yankees cap, a hat that for some reason I had always misplaced or lost for a time. Somehow, though, I managed to recover it, once even in a bad windstorm. I was glad I had it on that day.

Lee knew I was writing for a New York City daily newspaper and, I believe, had noted my hat before any talk of Major League Baseball arose. It seemed like a natural segue, so we talked Bronx Bombers, their chances for the pennant, and baseball in general, and I found that Lee was knowledgeable of New York sports, which was interesting for someone who made his home in Toronto.

"Mariano Rivera is untouchable in the postseason," Lee said.

We exchanged quips on the relief pitcher's stats, something about earned run averages, I believe, and spoke for a few more minutes. Funnily enough, it was one future Hall of Famer assessing another: Rivera earned a one-way ticket to Cooperstown, and Lee's band, Rush, made it to Cleveland, by hook or by crook.

The meeting was breaking up, and there was little milling around. Then it was over.

This initial meeting with Geddy Lee, all those years ago, are recalled in flashes. They've been strung together, and I've set the button to playback, as if a mini movie reel were spooling in my head: Geddy was and is obviously a rock star. But I was and continue to be struck by how down to earth he was.

Some of the thematic notes of the Rush song "Limelight" certainly resonate. We both had our jobs to do, I suppose, our roles to play: Geddy was promoting a record, and I was, myself, writing about it. But maybe for a brief moment, the veil had lifted, and I saw beyond the rock star. There was something real behind what *Rolling Stone Encyclopedia of Rock* dubbed "Lee's clawing banshee how."

I'm sure Geddy can be charming when he wants to be, trying to win over the press with a relaxed smile, but he genuinely had an interest in talking baseball and one or two other topics. Most of all, I think, perhaps sensing I was a bit nervous to break that fourth wall and stand inside that "performance space," his attitude and approach set me at ease.

And I'll never forget him for that.

Part of what makes *Moving Pictures* a classic is the manner in which Rush and, specifically, lyricist/drummer Neil Peart treat the concept of fame and how it changes people. How did the band make sense of the world around them as they were becoming more popular than they had ever been? What did they think of their fans and the public at large?

These are deep, layered questions that cannot be easily answered. One of the ways to drill down to the core of the issue is to begin a kind of examination, a look at the artist's life in question.

The temptation is to search in their distant pasts for evidence, reasons for how and why they eventually created a record such as Rush's *Moving Pictures*. Some biographers might attempt to chronicle the early years of each band member to forge some symmetry between what these artists were as individuals, growing up in Canada, and what they'd become, in Rush's case, circa 1981, as blossoming rock stars.

Some may try to use Freud, Jung, or Lacan to inspect, psychoanalyze, and dissect their subjects from afar. But looking for biographical and psychological patterns can be tricky, especially since certain events or so-called signifiers can be easily misunderstood and improperly or disproportionally weighed as to their meaning in the overall story.

What I've done is present some meaningful facts about our subject matters in an attempt to understand a little bit about the formative years of Geddy Lee, Alex Lifeson, and Neil Peart and attempt to examine the music they wrote leading up to the album *Moving Pictures*. It's all in service to figuring out how *Moving Pictures* has endured, what makes it work.

Where appropriate, I've also included some personal reflections of my experiences with Rush, which you can find in certain select chapters under the subheadings "The Camera Eye."

The one question that has fueled me through the entire process was, why? Why did Rush feel the need to record an album containing music that they deemed to be cinematic and gather all of these conceptual pieces in one recording document? Maybe the reader and I can try to answer this burning query as we set out on this journey together.

Before heading off into the body of Rush's recorded output, we should start with a little bit of background and give a brief summary of how the band formed.

Alex Lifeson was born on August 27, 1953, aka Aleksandar Živojinović, son of Yugoslavian Serbian parents (Alex's father spent time in a prison camp), left their home country, and emigrated to British Columbia after World War II. The family then moved to Toronto.

Alek was already playing viola but found he wanted something with a bit more oomph. The future Alex Lifeson made a pact with his mother that if he had good grades, he could get a guitar. His first, a steel-stringed Kent, a Japanese import, cost $25, a purchase for which his mother and father needed to secure a loan. The story goes that Alex found a way to amplify the acoustic by repurposing the stylus of his record turntable.

Lifeson told *Guitar One* magazine in 1996 that he'd listen to (or at the least heard) Eastern European music at home when he was young. But once the British Invasion hit the shores of North America, Lifeson had be seduced by the more modern sounds of Cream and the Yardbirds as well as the distortion-filled soundscapes of the Jimi Hendrix Experience and the West Coast/Bay Area psychedelic scene, including Jefferson Airplane and the Grateful Dead. Later, of course, Lifeson was enamored of the guitar playing of the likes of Jimmy Page of Led Zeppelin, Steve Howe of Yes, and Steve Hackett of Genesis.

Gary Lee Weinrib was born in Willowdale, Ontario, Canada, on July 29, 1953, son of Holocaust survivors Manya and Morris. The initial intent of Lee's parents was to settle in New York, but they continued to travel north instead.

"I was born in the suburbs of Toronto," Geddy Lee once told me, "[an] immigrant family that came over [from Poland] after the war. Largely Holocaust survivors. I grew up in an environment that is not exactly modern."

Lee's parents opened a retail store as a means of supporting the family. Lee's Polish mother, with her heavy Yiddish accent, pronounced "Gary" as "Geddy," and anyone who knew him referred to Lee by his new nickname. On Rockline Radio in October 1987, Geddy explained that it was his mother.

By age twelve, Geddy's father had died, and soon, after seeing a neighbor with a guitar, Geddy thought he'd like one himself. Taking money he'd earned from working with his mother in her retail store, Gary/Geddy bought his own six-string—an acoustic with palm trees painted on the face of it. Before long, music had seized his life.

"When I was thirteen, I became obsessed with music," Lee told me, believing that music chose him, not the other way around.

Alex and Geddy met in Fisherville Junior High School, in the Willowdale section of Toronto, and quickly became friends. They seemed to complement each other: Geddy a bit reserved and Alex more extroverted. Each had a sense of humor and a love of music. They hit it off.

Alex would borrow Geddy Lee's amplifier, and the two began playing together at local coffee shops when the pair were in the eighth grade. At first, Geddy and Alex had not been playing together in a band at all. It was Alex and his neighborhood drummer friend John Rutsey, both in their early teens, who had teamed up and formed a band called the Projection. It was short lived, though, having lasted only a matter of months.

Myriad personnel changes throughout the late 1960s and early 1970s make it nearly impossible to follow the comings and goings of the band that would be Rush—that is, without a score card. But one highlight was a gig at a youth drop-in center in Willowdale called the Coff-In at St. Theodore of Canterbury Anglican Church. It was the first time Geddy, Alex, and Rutsey had played together. Their combined earnings for the gig was $10.

Pancer's deli was the next stop—to celebrate. And it was around this time that, legend has it, the name Rush was first used as the band moniker—a suggestion made by Rutsey's brother, Bill.

Ged, Alex, and Rutsey soon graduated to the Yorkville coffee shop scene, including the Upper Crust. They played music of the British Invasion: the Rolling Stones and the Animals as well as Van Morrison/Them, the Yardbirds, and Cream covers and other British blues-rock songs.

"I would pretend I was Eric Clapton, Geddy would pretend he was Jack Bruce, and we'd play 'Spoonful' for twenty minutes," Lifeson told *Guitar One* magazine in 1996.

Eventually, Lifeson had saved up enough money, working with his dad as a plumber's assistant, to buy a Gibson ES-335 and a Marshall amplifier along with a few effects pedals.

Again, personnel shifts marked a very messy period. Surprisingly, Geddy left the band, and by the summer of 1968, Jeff Jones was singing and playing bass. But he too left, and Geddy returned. Rush then added keyboardist/vocalist Lindy Young.

A name change to Hadrian was followed by Geddy leaving again in the spring of 1969. Some sources say he was fired, to be replaced by Joe Perna. Undeterred, Geddy formed the blues band Ogilvie (which later changed their name to Judd). Lindy Young exited Hadrian (formerly Rush) and joined Geddy in Judd, which had been booking gigs with the assistance of young hype man Ray Danniels.

Then a strange twist of fate occurred. Joe Perna wasn't meeting expectations, and Rutsey and Lifeson decided to call it quits, for the time being, anyway. Perhaps because Rutsey and Lifeson realized the error of their ways or perhaps because Judd, keeping active throughout the summer of 1969, had broken up, Lifeson and Rutsey re-recruited Geddy, and he (and the name Rush) was reinstated.

Lee was back, Lindy was off to college, and one of the greatest power trios in rock history had just solidified its lineup. Immediately, the band got to work. Funnily enough, Lee would eventually marry Lindy's sister, Nancy.

John and Alex penned a song titled "Losing Again," which became one of the first (if not the first) tune the band wrote together. All three would contribute pieces or pieces of ideas, bring them to the band, and develop them. Around this time, Geddy had been working on "In the Mood," which was virtually completed when the bassist/vocalist brought it to the guys.

By the early 1970s, other originals, such as "Morning Star," "Love Light," "Garden Road," and "Child Reborn," among others, were composed, some heavier and more complex than others.

In the meantime, Rush continued to play a mixture of originals and covers, including Robert Johnson's "Crossroad Blues" (made famous by Cream via its supercharged revamp "Crossroads"), the Bonnie Dobson/Tim Rose folk classic "Morning Dew," and music by Jeff Beck, Buffalo Springfield, David Bowie, Jimi Hendrix, the Yardbirds, the Rolling Stones, Traffic, and Eric Clapton, among others.

"Years before I joined Wireless, I was playing in a band called Truck, from southern Ontario," says drummer/vocalist Marty Morin, whose former band, Wireless, would be produced by Geddy Lee in the late 1970s. "A number of times Rush would open for us. I remember when John Rutsey was in the band and we would do these summertime shows at, what we call up here in Canada, pavilions. Even back then Rush were a little bit different. They insisted on using their own lights. It may have been just some floodlights screwed to a two-by-four, but they insisted they had to have their lights. I remember Alex Lifeson painting glitter nail polish on his fret hand. They were doing something just a little extra."

In early 1971, someone named Mitch Bossi was added as a second guitarist, but he left after a few months. Despite these comings and goings, the band continued packing crowds in the bars of Toronto, including at a venue called the Gasworks on Yonge Street. And why not? The drinking age in Toronto had dropped from twenty-one to eighteen years of age, significantly impacting who could get buzzed and, more important, who could attend the band's shows.

Although they'd face challenges over the next two years, including witnessing a dip in support and being tossed from a venue for volume, by 1973, Rush had entered Eastern Sound Studio and recorded their first single, "Not Fade Away" (written by Norman Petty and Charles Hardin, aka Buddy Holly), and an original, "You Can't Fight It," composed by Geddy and John. David Stock, a Brit who had worked with Ray Danniels and Vic Wilson's SRO Management company, was the recording engineer.

"Not Fade Away" is a raunchy raver, simmering with crunchy guitars, echo-enhanced vocals, and a Bo Diddley–esque hambone/West African beat. At just under three minutes, "You Can't Fight It" further slips into heavy riff rock, impressing with the briefest of drum solos. Its hypnotic tempo falls somewhere between northeastern punk and British blues rock. It's not difficult to hear why so many observers chose to compare Rush to Led Zeppelin and Uriah Heep.

At the time, Rush had written and performed two other songs, "Fancy Dancer" and "Garden Road," largely blues-rock numbers that, to my knowledge, were not recorded at Eastern Sound.

Truth be told, even prior to the single they'd cut at Eastern Sound, Rush was attempting to shop a semiprofessional demo they'd made at the Sound Horn at Rochdale College. This was the first of the band's unfortunate run of luck with courting Canadian record labels.

Manager Ray Danniels, who had been promoting the band since the early days of 1969 and had already established his own agency, Music Shoppe, tried in vain to score a record deal for Rush in Canada. Due to the lack of response, Danniels and his business partner, Vic Wilson, formed Moon Records and released the band's single with an eye toward recorded a full-length LP one day. Hundreds of copies were pressed.

It was settled: Rush would record a full-length record and make a run at greatness. After one of their numerous gigs around town, the band assembled at Eastern Sound in Toronto and hammered out most of the record in nearly eight hours in the wee hours of the morning, largely to keep the budget costs down.

Unhappy with the sound quality of what they'd tracked at Eastern, they moved on over to Terry Brown's Toronto Sound Studio in the fall of 1973 to record new songs and rerecord others.

Brown had been an engineer in England, his native country, before arriving at the shores of Canada in 1969, just prior to the great recording and creative boom in Toronto and in Canada in general. With business partner Doug Riley, Brown opened Toronto Sound in 1969, and a Toronto recording scene was born.

After a couple of days' work, Rush recorded what would become the debut's stunning opener, "Finding My Way," and the rest of the tracks, including redoing guitar tracks. Mixing and remixing occurred during this time, too.

"They had been recording during the graveyard shift, mixing and recording some extra tracks," Terry Brown once told me in an interview I conducted. "Vic Wilson [partner in Rush management company] called me and said, 'Can you look after the boys?' Do something with them.'"

The record was completed in late 1973, and thousands of pressings were done in March 1974. The cover image by Paul Weldon popped, like an action scene from a comic book. Weldon, an Andy Warhol acolyte and an actual comic-book letterist, fathered what has gone on to become one of the most iconic debut covers in rock history.

In an early Rush press release promoting the band's debut, Lee indicated that there was some interest from Canadian labels but that they'd decided to release their eight-song debut on their own independent label, Moon Records, a division of SRO Productions. Danniels has gone on record as saying the production of the record cost himself and Vic Wilson a combined $9,000—not insignificant for a small operation like SRO catering to a relatively unknown band in the mid-1970s.

Donna Halper, music director at Cleveland's kingmaker radio station WMMS, originally from Boston, was an admitted fan of Canadian rock bands. When friend Bob Roper at A&M Records in Canada gave Halper a copy of the Rush debut, Halper handed the record to DJ Denny Sanders to ask his advice about playing any of the songs on air. Sanders liked the record and agreed that this band Rush had *something* and began spinning "Working Man."

"Finding My Way," "Here Again," and "In the Mood" soon followed, receiving their own public airing on WMMS; the requests kept pouring in.

As the story goes, Halper solicited Ray Danniels and Vic Wilson to ship copies of the Rush debut to a Cleveland-area record store, Record Revolution, owned by Peter Schliewen, known for its imports. Within weeks, hundreds of people bought it. Soon, that number jumped to thousands in and around Cleveland, not including the 5,000 LPs that had already sold in Canada on Moon.

Although Halper's position in Rush lore is well established, we should note that inside the borders of Rush's native Canada, there were early champions of the band, such as DJ Don Shafer ("The Voice") and David Marsden formerly of CHUM-FM in Toronto.

"Don and I have been supporters of Rush since the mid-1970s," says Marsden, who you can find on Internet radio at www.nythespirit.com. "I was at CHUM-FM at the time, when the first album came out and I started playing it before anyone else in North America had been playing it—contrary to the popular story that's out there."

Halper was Rush's connection in the prized United States, however, and Halper knew Mercury Records promo/artists and repertoire (A&R) man Cliff Burnstein, who had heard the band's debut and was impressed with the sound and power of the music. Burnstein, who would later comanage heavyweights such as Metallica (who were themselves Rush fans), urged the label and its director, Irwin Steinberg, to court the band. Mercury had already signed Bachman-Turner Overdrive, another hard-driving Canadian band, so looking to the Great White North was not something Mercury was averse to.

However, there was some (if minimal) interest at other labels, including Casablanca and Columbia. Producer Tom Werman liked Rush, and there was some discussion about signing the band to the Epic record label, but he could not convince the brass to do so. It was Mercury that scored the deal and hammered out a two-record contract worth a reported U.S.$200,000.

Founded in Chicago in the late 1940s, Mercury nurtured a roster of rhythm and blues, blues, jazz, folk, and soul artists, ranging from Bill Eckstine and the Platters to Sarah Vaughan, Frankie Laine, Josh White, Josephine Baker, Buddy Rich, Patti Page, Dinah Washington, and Big Bill Broonzy. This is to say nothing of the symphonic and classical releases the parent label issued through its imprints in the 1950s and 1960s. And in the decade prior to the release of *Moving Pictures*, Mercury had quite a diversified portfolio: Rod Stewart, Bachman-Turner Overdrive, the New York Dolls, the Ohio Players, Uriah Heep, and others.

From the mid-1970s though the mid-1980s, Mercury U.S. and Canada did not shy away from signing and distributing progressive, arty pop, and avant-garde artists, such as Aussie prog band Sebastian Hardie (specifically their *Four Movements* LP from 1975), 10cc's classic 1970s catalog, Cleveland art punkers Pere Ubu, and one of the more eclectic bands to emerge from England's musical underground, Jade Warrior.

Interestingly, not long after (or virtually timed with) the arrival of *Moving Pictures*, Mercury pursued two strains of rock prevalent in Rush's sound circa 1981: New Wave and hard rock. Suddenly, Soft Cell, Tears for Fears, Big Country, Bon Jovi, and Kiss made the cut, and the success of Def Leppard seemed to mirror Rush's own rise to prominence from the late 1970s through the early 1980s.

But let's not get ahead of ourselves.

The Rush that Mercury signed was somewhat dysfunctional, still finding its feet. Rutsey was the band lyricist but either refused to write words for the songs they were recording for the debut or was not confident in what he'd scrawled down on paper. Alex and Geddy were dumbfounded and nonplussed: isn't it better to have something than nothing?

Other than the words for "Here Again," which Alex penned, Geddy was forced to write lyrics to accompany the music—a last-minute activity, spanning two days, just prior to entering the studio.

Performances of the songs "Need Some Love," "Before and After," and "Best I Can" (later recorded *without* Rutsey for 1975's *Fly by Night*) were captured on film in 1974 at the Laura Second Secondary School in St. Catharines. The clip, featured as bonus material included with the *R40* box set, shows Rutsey injecting bombastic fills and performing some nifty moderately fast/mid-tempo shuffles while laying down a solid groove.

Rutsey, at least this night, was the trio's spokesperson—not Geddy or Alex as later fans might have expected. From behind the kit, Rutsey introduced the numbers and the guys onstage, acting in effect as the band's front man. Rutsey seemed to be a natural leader. But as the pressures of being in a band slowly mounted and the members of Rush grew more serious about being professional musicians, Rutsey had less and less in common with his mates.

Nursing a diabetic condition and weary of a touring musician's lifestyle, the constant gigging and late nights, Rutsey was not confident in his future as a live performer. Adding to this, Geddy and Alex had ideas of expanding the band's sound and conquering the world; Rutsey could not see it—or hear it. This set up a conflict, a perfect storm spelling catastrophe for the young band.

Differing versions of the story have circulated for decades, but ultimately, Rutsey's prospective future was incompatible with Geddy and Alex's. According to some sources, Rutsey was asked to leave by comanager Vic Wilson.

A report from the time, appearing in *RPM* magazine on August 24, 1974, confirms that, at least officially, the reason for Rutsey's exit was due to his health. Rutsey had already quit at least once prior to this for health reasons back in the fall of 1973 and was briefly replaced by drummer Gerry Fielding. In retrospect, that Rutsey stayed for the recording of Rush's first full-length album was a natural evolutionary step, one that they'd been eagerly eyeing following the release of their first single.

But Rutsey was gone, and his exit couldn't have come at a worse time. Rush had been booked for a late summer 1974 tour of America (with fall dates following) short one drummer. Rush had played a couple of dates in the United States—at a festival in

Michigan and, of course, their home away from home, Cleveland—but not anything for an extended period of time.

Rush was in desperate need of a drummer.

"Going back to 1968–69, I was playing around Toronto in clubs, and so was a buddy of mine, who was a good heavy, solid drummer, who came from London [Ontario] with me, and . . . our wives worked together, and he said, 'Graham, I have an offer to go audition with this band Rush,'" says veteran drummer Graham Lear (Santana, REO Speedwagon, and Natural Gas). "I did not know that much about them, but I knew they were managed by local Toronto manager and they were gigging around. My friend was with an existing band that was doing quite well and had a first album out. He said, 'They are auditioning for drummers, and I would have to quit the gig I'm doing now and start with them.' I think at the time he was asking for my advice. . . . And the way it looked to me, I advised him to stay in the band he was in. They went on to do quite well, but he didn't stay with them forever."

Most fans know the story of what happened next: drummer Neil Peart had been performing with a band called Hush and was tipped off to Rush, and so he too auditioned.

Once Neil played a fast triplet and flashed his double-kick technique, Lee was pretty much sold. Legend has it that the band jammed on the future Rush tune "Anthem," and once Neil played fast triplets and flashed his double-kick technique, it was unanimous.

Geddy was sold on Neil's poise, drum setup, ferocious playing, and ability to intelligently converse on a range of topics. Alex, however, reserved judgment and had asked Geddy to do the same.

To no avail.

Before the end of the day of auditions, Geddy knew Neil was the right man for the job, and Alex had—or *had to*—come around. Whatever reservations had existed at the beginning of the day evaporated.

Neil joined on July 29, Geddy Lee's birthday.

Peart explained that his outlook on life changed nearly immediately when he joined a rock band that had a recording contract in the United States—and a North American tour already booked. Still, he was skeptical, at least initially. Peart said he had heard these types of promises from band managers he'd dealt with prior to Rush, but their plans never materialized. This would not be, of course, the case with Rush, as he would soon realize.

"Neil gets the gig, and nobody knew him at that point, and nobody knew that Neil was going to come in and become an integral part of the writing," says Graham Lear. "Everything he did on drums, and writing the lyrics, made them what they are today. If my buddy had gotten that gig, and he wasn't a lyricist, per se, would Rush have done what they did? They may never have, even though he was a good musician. An example of how things can change, right? You might not be the right person for every gig; you might think you are. Neil was that third piece in the puzzle that they needed."

Peart, born on September 12, 1952, was raised on a farm near Hagersville, Ontario, but the family later moved to St. Catharines. Peart's father, Glenn, worked at a farm equipment dealer Dalziel; his mom worked at a restaurant.

Peart had taken piano lessons when he was seven or eight years old (some reports have it at ten). Whatever experience he brought forward with him was translated years later to tuned and mallet keyboard percussion and marimba. It was around this time that Peart received a transistor radio, as he told the cameras for his 1996 instructional video, *A Work in Progress*.

Within a few years of seeing the film *The Gene Krupa Story*, Peart would bang about the house with chopsticks until his parents acquiesced and bought him drumsticks and drum lessons at age thirteen, then a drum kit.

The time Neil spent at lessons may have been brief, but they had a profound impact, essentially shaping the rest of his life. Neil explained to *Rhythm* magazine in 1987 that the Gene Krupa–Buddy Rich drum battle was the first record his drum teacher played for him.

By the late 1960s and early 1970s, names such as John Bonham, Mitch Mitchell, Santana's Michael Shrieve, Ginger Baker, Keith Moon, Carmine Appice (circa 1970), Emerson, Lake & Palmer's Carl Palmer, King Crimson's Michael Giles, and Yes's Bill Bruford were considered the vanguard of rock drummers, perhaps the greatest of their generation. Peart was being influenced by all of them. He was also checking out locals who would have a profound impact on his style.

"Around 1970, we had played a lot in Montreal because some of the musicians were from Montreal, but most were from Toronto, and we were doing a one-nighter in St. Catharines, and there was this big tall lanky kid at the entrance when I went to take my gear in," says Graham Lear. "He walked up to me, introduced himself, and said, 'I'm Neil Peart,' and I didn't know who he was. He was just a tall lanky kid, and I was only about nineteen or twenty myself. He would have been about fifteen? Nice kid, but we were late getting in there from Toronto, and I had to set up. He said he would help me with my gear. He helped me set up, and I didn't know who he was."

Lear would have a lasting impact on Peart's style, as would Robin Boers and his use of (what sounds like) triplets in the Ugly Ducklings' single from 1967 "Gaslight." These rhythmic figures were internalized and echoed by Peart throughout his career. For added measure, Boers appears to do his best Keith Moon impression in "Just in Case" (on the York Town label)—a connection to Peart that, in retrospect, seems self-evident.

Another early influence on Rush—and Peart in particular—was the psychedelic soul/rock band Mandala, formed in 1966, later fronted by vocalist Roy Kenner. "One Short Year," from Mandala's 1968 album *Soul Crusade* (Atlantic), written by the group's Italian-born guitarist Domenic Troiano (the Guess Who and the James Gang), boasted an instrumental opening, featuring a rudiment-like march cranked out by Finnish drummer Pentti "Whitey" Glan, perhaps best known for his work with Alice Cooper. It's something that undoubtedly had an impact on Peart: we hear similar rhythmic phrasings years later in "Jacob's Ladder," "The Camera Eye," "Countdown," and "Manhattan Project."

"Whitey was playing funky, quasi-R&B cum Second Line stuff," says Graham Lear (REO Speedwagon, Gino Vannelli, Santana, and Natural Gas). "It was like New Orleans Second Line, Memphis blues stuff, but in a heavier feel that fit with what Mandala was doing. I was blown away by that. Up to that point, we were listening to the Stones and the Beatles around here. It was a big influence on me, so I think it would be an equally big influence on Neil. There was also [John Wetherell], drummer for David Clayton Thomas and the Shays. We were a contingent of Canadian drummers in this area. We were all basically listening to each other, learning from each other."

Peart, a high school dropout, joined the band J. R. Flood, which had been building a buzz doing similar gigs to Geddy and Alex in high schools and Knights of Columbus halls. He'd banged around with Mumblin' Sumpthin', a gig for which he bought a Rogers kit from a local music store via a loan (leaving his dad on the hook); the Majority; and, just before joining Rush, a band called, interestingly enough, Hush. Much of what he played with these groups was blues, rhythm and blues, or soul standards.

But just prior to this, the music mecca of London (and England in general) had generated so many great rock bands that Neil suggested to his bandmates in J. R. Flood that they take a chance and relocate to the United Kingdom. No one would bite, however, and when J. R. Flood was kaput, Neil fled to England.

It turns out that for all his ambition and dreams, Neil did not make very much headway while living across the Pond. Although he joined local bands, such as English Rose, Heaven, and a fusion band called Seventh Wave, he was forced to take a job at Gear, a trinkets and souvenirs shop on world-famous Carnaby Street in London, one of the trendiest spots in London catering to the "in crowd."

Peart escaped the monotony and doldrums of life as a working stiff through science fiction novels and social commentary by the likes of Ayn Rand and Samuel Delaney. Peart bought a copy of Rand's *The Fountainhead* from a newsstand in the British Underground and read it on his commute to and from his job on Carnaby Street.

In addition, in his London apartment, Peart found a closet stacked with fantasy and sci-fi paperback novels. Due to a lack of funds, Peart was forced to live hand to mouth; with little to do with his free time and with auditions and gigs few and far between, Peart escaped into imaginary worlds. Peart would open up a book of fiction, put on headphones, and shut out the outside world, spinning Frank Sinatra and big-band jazz records his dad loved, including the classic live album *Sinatra at the Sands*, starring Ole Blue Eyes with the Count Basie Orchestra and featuring drummer Sonny Payne.

Peart flew back to Canada for the 1971 holidays, but his stay was temporary. He claimed a recidivist status in England for the next year until, by the end of 1972, he returned home for good. His overseas experiment—and his vision of making it in England—ceased. He'd bargained with himself: he'd rather play music he loved part-time than earn a paycheck for music he hated.

Once home, Peart worked with his father at Dalziel Equipment and also part-time at a record store, where he met his future wife, Jackie, who worked their briefly.

Vic Wilson, of the recently formed Toronto-based SRO Management, came by to see Neil at Dalziel and after witnessing him spank the drums asked about his availability for an audition with Rush. Neil was intrigued. Rush had a recording deal, something that had eluded him while in England.

On the day of the audition, Peart rolled up in a Pinto with his drums stuffed inside trash cans. Peart had eighteen-inch Rogers kick drums (considered small by rock standards); he hit hard, and he used the butt end of the sticks. He had short hair. Very un–rock star like.

He fit in with the guys almost immediately.

With everything now in place, Rush hit the road in August 1974 and did their first show in Pittsburgh, Pennsylvania, sharing the bill with Uriah Heep and Manfred Mann's Earth Band. Not only had the band played before a crowd of 11,000 in Pittsburgh (some sources say 18,000 attendees), but the money the band had been advanced went toward acquiring new musical gear. Peart went as far as to call it entering "Fairy Tale Land."

Rush would go on to support Blue Öyster Cult and Rory Gallagher, racking up sales of their debut album.

"Those were the days when record companies and managers and agents, everyone, all worked as teams," former Uriah Heep songwriter and keyboardist/guitarist Ken Hensley told me. "Rush came out with us courtesy of ATI, American Talent International, and Mercury Records, and it was like they put out their baby bands with some of their established ones, and this was supposed to be a vehicle toward exposure. On paper, of course, it is. So, they were working with us, and I do remember going inside the dressing room and chatting with the guys and telling them if they needed anything, basically, let us know. These are genuine, if slightly pompous, thoughts because we ourselves hadn't been on the road that long. We achieved some fairly solid success, but we were not in a position to offer life career guidance to a bunch of guys who were trying to find their way around."

Still, Hensley saw the potential in a young Rush from the first time Uriah Heep had toured with them in America.

"We were in no way going to impede them," says Hensley. "Our crew worked with theirs and . . . we didn't have to tell them to. They just did it. From the point of view of an introduction to the Big Time, I'm sure it worked for them, and the thing that blew my mind was their playing. They are just such great musicians. [Uriah Heep's] focus was never on musicianship. It was on writing and recording powerful songs that people could relate to and delivering them the best way we could live. That succeeded tremendously. But [Rush] were so technically brilliant and did things that we would never think about doing, so it seemed to me that at the beginning, they might struggle a little bit because their music was not so accessible, a little bit noncommercial. Three-piece bands were supposed to be guitar, bass, drums, and nothing but big power chords. They were far form that and bordered on great free-form jazz-rock things, and then they were venture off into musical tangents that were staggering, to me."

Heep was the kingmaker to rock bands in the 1970s, helping to fuel the mete-oric rise of popular talent. "It came back to bite us," Hensley told me, still bemused at it all. "It wasn't just Rush, but in 1973, Kiss opened for Uriah Heep. In 1976, Uriah Heep opened for Kiss. And I think in 1976 or 1975, Foreigner opened for Uriah Heep, and, you know . . . it was like, [we're] a launching pad, here?" [laughs].

Nazareth, sometimes spoken of in the same breath as Uriah Heep because they played on the same bill so often in Europe, had played with Rush around Ontario, Canada, prior to Neil's joining. But by the fall of 1974, Neil had been recruited, and Nazareth was the headliner, again, for a string of dates.

"We were up in Canada, and we were doing a coast-to-coast tour, and the first time, I think it was a big 'uni' in Ontario," Pete Agnew, bassist of Nazareth, tells me. "Huge success up there. That was a big boost. But when you go on tour, you don't always know who is going to be the opening band, especially when we were going away to another country. We didn't pick them; it was the promoter and agency. It was this young band, and we went to this sound check, and they were very shy. They were impressed to be playing with Nazareth, of course, and then they were using the same lineup . . . guitar, bass, and drums. We thought they were brand-new, just kids."

Agnew says that Rush was not much into taking life to the limits on tour, although they did occasionally hang out outside of the venue.

"They were not partygoers," says Agnew. "We were half crazy at the time, and they were a bit more well behaved. We went out shark fishing. . . . We were in Vancouver, and there was a pal who had a boat, and we would go out with him, and we used to get ripped. We would go out in his boat, and we took the boys with us, and I think they were a wee bit worse for the wear when they came back, the three of them."

Nazareth, Uriah Heep, Kiss, Blue Öyster Cult, and Manfred Mann's Earth Band were some of Rush's touring partners from the summer of 1974 through the end of that year. Rush also toured with Kiss and Aerosmith for months and played for thou-sands as a headlining act when their Canadian tour pulled into Massey Hall, Toronto.

Massey Hall was a shrine and, for the band, the shining beacon on the hill of Toronto concert venues. It was the same venue where Geddy had seen one of his favorites bands when he was growing up: Cream. Lee wouldn't be in the audience this time, of course, but would see the place from a different perspective—the stage.

# CHAPTER 3

# ENOUGH ROPE?

## THE CAMERA EYE, PART 2

Admittedly, it comes to me in a blur, with the lens perhaps a bit out of focus. I can't really remember all of the set list or every note the band played, but a few images poke out from the fog of memory. Or maybe this is the way I chose to recall it—as a psychedelic swirl of sound and vision.

I saw Rush on the Power Windows tour, in 1986 at the Nassau Coliseum in Uniondale, New York, and some of the highlights were watching Rush perform songs such as "Grand Designs," parts of "2112," "Mystic Rhythms," "The Big Money," and "Marathon."

The latter two of these certainly jog my memory, largely because of visuals being projected on a big screen upstage of the band, accompanying the performances onstage.

The video for "The Big Money" remains fresh in my mind. The three-dimensional motion graphics used for the video were cutting edge for the day, even if the process was painstaking to complete. But how the visuals fit with the music was fascinating: I clearly remember the computer software–designed Monopoly board, the skyline of the big city behind Neil Peart at the drums, and all of it fusing in my mind as I watched the show in the arena.

I've come to find out that the director of "The Big Money" video was Rob Quartly, who had worked with Corey Hart and a few Rush-related bands (Platinum Blonde, Boys Brigade, and Coney Hatch). If Quartly and Rush wanted to leave an imprint, mission: accomplished. It is one of the few things I can recall from the show.

The concert film projections beaming onto the rear screen, the dancing lasers, the golden flair of crashing cymbals under the concert lights, a cherry-red misty surrounding Peart—all this has fused to create a single audiovisual memory.

Still, this was not the first time Rush had used film or projection imagery at its concerts. Far from it. As early as 1977 and 1978, for instance, Rush had rear-projection imagery on their A Farewell to Kings tour and the Tour of the Hemispheres. Sci-fi scenes were beamed onto a backdrop to tie what audiences were hearing with what they were seeing. One reporter from Texas remarked that the spacecraft shown on-screen looked like that famous fictional starship *Enterprise* from the TV series *Star Trek*.

As we'll see, even prior to *Moving Pictures*, Rush had a history of songs that qualified as cinematic—"By-Tor and the Snow Dog" and "The Necromancer"—but also the later "Cygnus X-1, Book I: The Voyage" and much later "The Pass," "Middletown Dreams," "High Water," "Test for Echo," "Double Agent," "Driven," "Force Ten," and "Lock and Key."

By the mid-1980s, Rush had become masters at visual spectacle. Ten years earlier, however, they were just starting to figure out what it meant to marry sound and imagery.

Rush entered Toronto Sound Studios in January 1975 with their new drummer to record the follow-up to their promising debut. John Rutsey is remembered today for his contributions to the band's debut. Songs such as "Finding My Way" and "In the Mood" have earned a certain stature within Rush lore and the band catalog, and "Working Man" has become something of a concert warhorse for the band. But Rush's history as a progressive rock group really begins with *Fly by Night*, a record completed in a whirlwind ten days.

The opening track, "Anthem," was inspired by the concepts of personal liberty espoused in the work of Ayn Rand and, in particular, the novel that shares its name with the song.

A comprehensive overview of Rand's work (and even criticism of such) might be better saved for a later date. It's enough to say that Ayn Rand wrote *Anthem* in response to the Communist Revolution in Russia and its aftermath. Enough of her ideas on industry, ethics, capitalistic free markets, individualism, and exceptionalism resonated with a young Peart, not to mention Geddy, ensuring that these concepts seeped into the lyrics of tracks such as "Anthem" and, as we'll see, the later "2112" and even the song cycle of *Moving Pictures*.

Like Rand herself, Rush was often unaccepted by the cultural gatekeepers of the day, making their salvo, "Anthem," the greatest opening statement that a reconstituted Rush could have made. It's a microcosm of all that Rush was at that moment while offering tantalizing clues on what was to come.

"Anthem" is an adrenalized roar of self-confidence demonstrating the band's belief in their new material. It races at twice the speed of what we consider the rate of a healthy human heartbeat. It's anxious to make its point, and it can't get there fast enough.

When he was living in England, Peart wanted to play in a Who cover band—or, like Keith Moon, in a band such as the Who. But as time wore on, Peart came to his senses: He wished to continue to be inspired by Moon without aping him. "Anthem" is the first real taste of the controlled hurricane of rhythm that Peart brought to the band.

Peart's performances were not always defined by the difficulty of the individual grooves or sections of the song he was playing, although this is not a hard-and-fast rule. It was the fluidity of putting all these sections together to create a seamless performance, switching rhythmic gears, and timing an important fill. Peart was not Moon (he certainly wasn't as exaggerated), but a certain level of showmanship and bravado rubbed off on the young Canadian drummer.

Some of the hallmarks of Peart's celebrated style are all there: the melodic and idiosyncratic phrasing; coordination between two kicks and the snare, producing thunderous results; various voicings of percussive timbres; control in ratcheting up the intensity without increasing the beats per minute; the use of triplets and other beat groupings; and so on.

During the guitar solo, Peart plays a kind of shuffle-march, and, dare I say, the roving bass line Geddy keeps under Lifeson's blistering solo may not have been possible if not for Peart's input.

"Anthem" has all the bombast, adventurousness, precision, and inventiveness we had come to expect from Rush—and Peart. It's very telling that Peart demonstrated these multidimensional aspects of his playing as early as the mid-1970s.

*Fly by Night* was significant in other ways. Most fans know that Rush operated through a division of labor: Lee and Lifeson wrote the music (largely), and Peart penned the lyrics. Because Rush was still feeling around in the dark and mapping the psychogeometry of the band, it gave way to true democratization of songwriting. Lee is credited with having written "Best I Can," and Peart teams with Lifeson for the turbocharged, punk-like energy of "Beneath, Between & Behind" as well as the Tolkien-inspired (largely) acoustic piece "Rivendell." Peart and Lee are credited with writing "Fly by Night," and all three members worked on "Making Memories," "Anthem," and the record's centerpiece, "By-Tor and the Snow Dog."

The final song, "In the End," which most closely resembles the material found on the band's debut, was written by Lee and Lifeson, foretelling what was to come for this writing team in the future.

*Fly by Night* is a gargantuan step forward for Rush and one that would lead to greater artistic and commercial success. But before we move on, let's return to one song: the extended track "By-Tor and the Snow Dog."

Nineteenth- and early twentieth-century composer Jean Sibelius, inspired by the collection of Norse tales known as the *Kalevala*, worked to instill a sense of national pride in his Finnish countrymen in an attempt to reclaim their identity in the face of Russian oppression. Interestingly, the fantasy novelist J. R. R. Tolkien was also motivated by these same sagas to create an English mythology, or fantasy world, of Middle-earth.

Rush, being influenced by Tolkien and thus indirectly impacted by Nordic tales, invented a Canadian-style musical mythos to serve as a blueprint for progressive hard rockers in North America and, really, everywhere via "By-Tor and the Snow Dog."

As author Humphrey Carpenter points out in *Tolkien: The Authorized Biography*, Tolkien's works *The Silmarillion* and *The Lord of the Rings* were set in an imagined land in the Earth's mythical past. The action wasn't taking place on a distant planet. Rush and its fantasy excursions, including "By-Tor and the Snow Dog," operate very similarly.

Some might point to the Old English poem *Beowulf* as an antecedent for the entire shebang. Indeed. *Beowulf* captured the imagination of Tolkien, but the titular hero in that saga fights three monsters, not one. Likewise, the multisectional title track for Emerson, Lake & Palmer's *Tarkus* LP, from 1971, was based on an "armordillo" that destroys all in its wake and gears up for a final battle with fellow chimera, the Manticore.

There isn't a traditional "monster" in "By-Tor," or, even if there were to be, the roles are reversed. By song's end, the dark prince By-Tor retreats, and the Snow Dog reigns.

During the breakdown (4:35) in "Aftermath" in part III, "The Battle," Alex's distant volume-controlled sonic fog paints a picture: the sun burning through the clouds as snowy wisps waft over a desolate warscape. When Peart strikes the bell of the ride cymbal, it seems to indicate that the conflict is over; smoke and snow flurries drift across the battlefield. Snow Dog and his disciples survey the land, assessing existing threats. Lifeson's bluesy, emotionally charged solo in "Hymn of Triumph," might indicate a wounded but victorious Snow Dog.

The chilling chimes closing the song were etched into the pressing of the original LP as an endless runoff groove. They would ring in perpetuity, that is, if you did not lift the needle from the vinyl. The fable never ends.

Although the bandwidth of other songs on *Fly by Night* isn't as expansive as "By-Tor and the Snow Dog," the next-to-last song, "Rivendell," inspired by Tolkien, is a great early example of the band's need to express images through sound.

Unlike the barren landscape of "By-Tor and the Snow Dog," a warmth permeates the serenity of the pastoral, acoustic-electric "Rivendell." Ebbs and flows of the electric guitar swells perfectly capture the soft breezes, nourishing sun, meditative whoosh of a roaring river, and sweet libations freely flowing in this Elfin Avalon. Allowing yourself to be swept up in cyclical folky fare is half the fun of the tune. It's true transportive escapism, and Rush appeared to be demonstrating signs of writing competent and compelling visual tracks.

## CARESS OF STEEL

The band's next record, *Caress of Steel*, contains some of the very same elements that make *Fly by Night* memorable: acoustic passages, fantasy literature–inspired lyrics, points of reflection, extended tracks, and undeniable rockers.

"You're right," Geddy once told me. "In some ways there are some very accessible songs [on the album]."

By the same token, *Caress of Steel* benefits from an undeniable aura of the "other," an effect not weakened by the fact that the album was dedicated to *Twilight Zone* TV show creator and on-screen host Rod Serling, who had died a few months before the record hit the streets.

Listening to the entirety of *Caress of Steel*, specifically the twelve-minute-and-thirty-second "The Necromancer" and the side-long suite "The Fountain of Lamneth," the record's nightmarish, synesthetic, hallucinatory, and cinematic qualities are undeniable. The record's audio can be spoken of in terms of the color spectrum. Tracks range from dark blacks and light grays to ambers, gold, and clear light. They accentuate the illustration on the LP packaging, the first to feature the work of graphic artist and soon-to-be Rush art director Hugh Syme.

*Caress of Steel*: Underappreciated in its time, this 1975 record contains some of the band's most adventurous early material.

The story goes that the original design for the wraparound cover called for dark or black borders with silver lettering. A printing error changed the complexion of *Caress of Steel* entirely. Graphic lettering is seemingly composed of oxidized copper, and these golden and greenish hues do little for the vinyl format's aesthetic appeal. They do, however, strangely coincide with the post-psychedelic and progressive hard rock mood of the music it packages if not the general malaise of this period of the band's life.

More about this in a moment.

The band had been writing on tour and was not at a loss for material when they arrived at Terry Brown's Toronto Sound studios in July 1975. Rush was prepared for action, practically a prerequisite for any young band wanting to conquer the world at the time. The album took the better part of two weeks to complete.

Opening with "Bastille Day," *Caress of Steel* feels revolutionary, even slightly subversive. Alex is firing both barrels at us. The effect of multitracking guitars really gave him a kind of "wall of sound" yet contains a certain level of nuance. There's sophistication but also a level of rage here.

"Well, it's anger from the perspective of the audience, from which Rush themselves came," says Fred Barchetta's Eric Barnett. "It is perhaps an intellectual revolution, if not a physical one, 'Anthem' and '2112' being influenced by Ayn Rand, who didn't argue for revolution in the streets but almost a more organic revolution arising from what she saw as the inevitable decay of society through socialism and forced equality. . . . . So I feel like it was about making the listener think, rather than something so direct as a 'battle cry,' or call to action."

The second song, the raucous bluesy banger titled "I Think I'm Going Bald," was supposedly a takeoff of "I Think I'm Going Blind," a song by Kiss, whom the band had supported on the road in 1974 and 1975. Whether inspired by Kiss or not, the title was said to be informed by Lifeson, who was in an absolute state of terror when he envisioned a time when he lacked the ability to naturally produce folic growth spurts. In the main, an idea such as this is preposterous for someone so young to be thinking about, but it did provide, at least partially, the basis for the song—and a bit of comic relief, intended or not. Despite (or perhaps because of) its sizzling guitar tones and hint of funk, the song can be viewed as a piece of absurdist rock, a rarity in the Rush world.

Track 3, "Lakeside Park," is another early example of the cinematic qualities Rush was developing throughout the 1970s. Certainly, the sights, sounds, and aroma (it *was* the mid-1970s) place us in the setting Peart describes in his lyrics, perhaps similar to the way Chicago's "Saturday in the Park" does for the ethnic or hyphenated (and every other kind of) American.

Unlike Robert Lamm's snapshots of summer afternoons in Central Park, New York, however, we are plopped inside a lovely day at an open-air event in Canada and detect a slight chill in the late-spring air. It's not quite summer, which makes the late-season atmosphere unpredictable, adding to the song's reflective qualities.

Although the tendency is to equate the Canadian holiday Victoria Day with the American holiday Independence Day, July 4, it might be closer in spirit to America's Memorial Day both in calendar date and as an unofficial observance of the start of summer. Obviously, for the lyricist, ritual shrouds the national celebration in an aura of mysticism: the day, time, and location course with meaning. Yet Peart tells us that the magic of the annual day of observance is losing its allure or mojo.

Peart, even at this early stage as a lyricist, does more than just present a vision: He leaves us with an important message. New York poet Walt Whitman referred to his native Long Island as Paumanok, a phrase he took from the Native Americans and recognized by the author as having been imbued with an aura of mysticism. It might not be as exotic, but "Lakeside Park" functions similarly. It isn't site specific.

The song's real power derives from the Lakeside Park, not the actual place but Lakeside Park of our collective memories. There's a Lakeside Park in every town, every hamlet, and every state or province in North America. In essence, the universality of "Lakeside Park" erases the Canadian aspect of the song from our memories, whether the details of the holiday have been etched into Peart's psyche or not. As much as Peart describes a historically Canadian experience, maybe the point of the song is how it alleviates itself from its perceived geographical shackles. "Lakeside Park" isn't just a place; it's a state of mind.

Peart also takes something of a contrarian's stance in constructing the song. He not only is involved in the general thrust of action but also remains an outsider, shirking off the rose-colored glasses and infusing his saccharine memories with a subtle dose of poisonous reality.

"Lakeside Park" is both nostalgic and a slab of realism. It's the same two-tiered, enigmatic effect Peart would sharpen to a fine point for "The Camera Eye" from *Moving Pictures*.

Peart pulls from his own experiences in a number of Rush songs, although this type of memory-based lyrical expression willfully eluded him, it seems, at various times through his career. Peart's disdain (and to a degree Lee's) for the band's earlier material, particularly from *Caress of Steel*, could hardly be contained. The growing pains were apparently excruciating, and this may explain why the drummer veered away from realism and piloted a lyrical spacecraft into escapism for much of Rush's major works of the 1970s.

But the song is certainly not without its charms from beginning to end. Chiming harmonics ring at the close of the tune (E–F#–D), like a clock alerting us to the time, enhancing the song's theme.

More charms existed.

Nothing said escapism like the closing track of side 1 of the original vinyl release, "The Necromancer." It is a musical microcosm of the entire record, falling somewhere between the blues/hard rock of Led Zeppelin and the psychedelic end of the progressive rock spectrum, close to the blues/folk/prog of Jethro Tull at roughly the same time.

Goblins, pointy wizard hats, witchcraft, divine spells, and magical objects had emerged as stereotypes of the European and North American strains of progressive rock. Typical of most stereotypes, these concepts bore a grain of truth—mixed with loads of bullshit from those who were only casual observers of the genre.

Many of the artists who referenced Tolkien or the Arthurian legends and had emitted the slightest whiff of sci-fi or fantasy escapism in their lyrics were dismissed by the music press as either lacking depth or just downright silly. And Rush, for better or worse, exhibited what were perceived as the genre's boilerplate conceptual tendencies.

Customary or not, "The Necromancer" did hold some undeniable delights. This trippy tryptic sword-and-sorcery musical adventure is a multisensorial flight of fancy, rife with mindless captive drones and mesmerizing sorcery, zombified victims, and subtextual issues of dominance and submission.

It's been theorized that the "three travelers"—"the men from Willowdale" mentioned in the lyrics—are actually the band members mythologized for the song. The "dark and forbidden" regions of the title's namesake translate as the treacherous terrain Rush traveled, metaphorically and quite literally, for the music industry machine. In its own way, "The Necromancer," at heart a song about fighting physical and mental oppression, is a precursor to "2112," the first major cannon blast in Rush's fight to reject the soft tyranny imposed by the recording industry.

Rush's nods to Europe's chivalrous past is what author and scholar Chris McDonald called "romanticized medievalism" in his book *Rush, Rock Music and the Middle Class: Dreaming in Middletown.*

The psychedelic movement of the 1960s glorified the past too with the application of different and sometimes arcane and archaic musical styles. This fluidity of time periods is indicative of the psychedelic drug experience if not a hallmark of the entire counterculture in its approach to art, music, and fashion. Past, present, and future flowed into one another—reflecting the timeless dimension of the soul and mind.

Prog rock, of course, germinated and coalesced in the crucible of 1960s psychedelia, and by extension so did Rush's "The Necromancer," which seems to occupy a
time and space devoid of historical epoch.

The clouds of aromatic delights circulated in the studio during the creative and
recording process for *Caress of Steel* and can't help but collect around this track. Like
the mild hallucinogen that the band had repeatedly inhaled while toiling away in the
final stages of creation, the music carries the vague scent of psychedelic rock. If anything, "The Necromancer" is an inner journey, reflecting on the darkness (aka evil)
we each harbor, a theme Rush would explore later with greater clarity and a lot more
drama in "Witch Hunt."

The visual ingredients baked into this prog/psyche musical cake are intoxicating. Labyrinths, often symbolizing the soul or the self, make for evocative imagery. Prisoners literally emerge from a labyrinthine underground and find themselves
liberated, recalling (if only slightly) the theme running through "The Fountain of
Lamneth," which dominates the entire second side of the original LP.

Backward audio at the song's opening helps set the song's eerie mood. A forward
chorusy/reverby guitar track appearing in the stereo image is answered by a reverse
audio squall, then disintegrates into the ether like sonic wraiths. These guitar wisps
may have been recorded on a loop and set in reverse for effect.

This sound source provides a nice foil for Lifeson's relatively placid arpeggios
and half-strummed chordal ideas. Couple this with Peart's intentionally distorted
voice-over, and it may be the most shadowy track Rush recorded in the 1970s.
The musical elements are clear enough in the mix, yet a patina seems to distance
itself from the listener. It's filmic, but we're also aware we're watching a film. Then,
again, Hollywood scripts have been developed from far sparser and less convincing
imagery.

The song is intended to transport as much as entertain. For one thing, there
aren't really choruses in "The Necromancer." Narrative refrains appear, yes, experimental sounds roll "into frame," filling the would-be screen, but the song-film travels
along a linear path. And with the advent of each new stanza, we detect a progression
in the inflection of Geddy's voice. For instance, early on, the vocals are almost soulful
(as in soul music), capturing the earthiness, chasteness, and literal wholesomeness of
the three men of Willowdale.

This sits in sharp contrast to the second movement, in which we encounter the
vampiric presence of the wizard with the hypnotic prism eyes. Immediately, Geddy's

voice switches to a raspy scream carrying a twinge of vibrato. It's twisted, tormented, and tyrannical.

"I think *Caress of Steel* is so sadly unappreciated," says Fred Barchetta's Eric Barnett. "'The Necromancer' is an Alex Lifeson tour de force, as is much of that record. On the first Rush album, understandably given his young age, Alex's playing is a bit more monochromatic. A lot of blues bends, pentatonic licks, heavy Jimmy Page influence. *Fly by Night* expands on his playing but is still pretty rooted in the rock/blues oeuvre. But I think that *Caress of Steel* is where Rush really, first, became the Rush that propelled them to stardom and into our hearts, that ultimately led to *2112* and their breakthrough. So much of that is Alex, as he expanded his palette and ability to connect with the listener."

In the second, brooding section, "Under the Shadow," Lifeson goes for broke, displaying an array of textures and tones, complementing the lyrics. "He's just going for it," says Barnett, "while Neil plays Keith Moon–esque fills under him, the sound of battle. They kind of did this in 'By Tor' too, but 'The Necromancer' really advances the approach as their 'prog legs' develop."

In a surprise twist, By-Tor, the villain from "By-Tor and the Snow Dog," returns, switching from zero to hero for the final movement, "The Return of the Prince." Appropriately, Lifeson's placid chords breeze through the section, and his cathartic lead squeezes out a range of emotions.

"It's major-key happiness, the sound of triumph and victory, echoing the story line," says Barnett.

Anyone who listened to side 1 of the original LP knows that a wash of cymbals and a multitracked guitar riffs melt into one another and the fade—a cathartic if highly cinematic end to one of Rush's most adventurous tracks.

## "THE FOUNTAIN OF LAMNETH"

Occult or alchemical perfection of the soul, even the search for the magical elixir of life, provides the thematic undergirding for "The Fountain of Lamneth," the epic composition engulfing the entire second side of the original vinyl LP.

If "The Necromancer" was the appetizer, then "The Fountain of Lamneth" is the main course. Certainly, the band had looked to the major sprawling works of Yes, Emerson, Lake & Palmer, Genesis, and Pink Floyd for cues. Lifeson remarked that the band took time off from recording *Caress of Steel* to see Yes perform in Toronto in July 1975. Because of Yes's superior musicianship, there are reports that indicate that finishing the record (and indeed this epic track) became something of a disheartening experience, knowing they might not achieve a conceptual masterstroke on par with that of their heroes.

Supposedly, Peart had written the lyrics for the song or this multimovement, before the band had ever begun preproduction based on the assumption that the guys would flesh out this sonic pièce de résistance, spanning an entire side of a vinyl release.

The song might be about fulfillment and perfection of the soul, but Peart admitted in 1977 to Geoff Barton of *Sounds* magazine that the multisectional piece was initially inspired by a cruise on a mountainside road. He stopped on a cliff and viewed the glowing lights of the city below. "I got to thinking, 'What would life be like if you could only measure your position as a person by the level at which you lived up the side of a mountain?'" Peart posed.

It's difficult to avoid making comparisons to folklore here. The song cycle, a Tolkienesque reconnaissance mission for self-discovery, is composed of five distinct sections and a sixth ("The Fountain") that recalls the first movement ("In the Valley"). It draws parallels with traditional Grail stories in the West, and the mountain and the fountain, something that ultimately gives the narrator no real peace, have a constant presence in the narrator's life.

"The Fountain of Lamneth" is a step-by-step recitation of the phases of life told through vaguely fantastical imagery: birth ("In the Valley"), adolescence ("Didacts and Narpets"), being a young adult and going out into the big bad world ("No One at the Bridge"), finding love ("Panacea"), reaching one's winter and attempting to self-medicate ("Bacchus Plateau"), and eternal return and rebirth of the immortal soul ("The Fountain"). This multisectional piece was a counterpart, some observed, to Pink Floyd's 1973 iconic cradle-to-grave suite consuming the entire first side of *The Dark Side of the Moon*.

In the final section of the song, "The Fountain," Lee takes his vocals down a notch to coincide with the exhausted nature of our narrator. The music cycles back to the original hard rock and acoustic themes we had heard at the opening moments of the song.

During the second ending of the suite, the volume is raised gradually and then recedes. We hear backward cymbal swells—all of which is emblematic of the overall concept of eternal return, life-and-death cycles, and a never-ending, or Grail, quest. Interestingly, Pink Floyd's *The Dark Side of the Moon* is similarly thematically and sonically cyclical: that record opens and concludes with looped audio of a thumping heartbeat.

When Rush finished *Caress of Steel*, they thought they'd had a winner on their hands. The record showed signs of the band improving their compositional skills, a high degree of musical interplay, and even a certain amount of lyrical depth. They were a bit shocked at the reaction they received from nearly the get-go.

"Everybody hated the record," Geddy Lee told me. "The record company hated the record."

Serious negativity germinated and permeated nearly everything in the band's universe. It spread like an infectious disease among Rush's inner circle, advisers, and even those in the industry.

"The thing is, that all rubbed off on the audience too," coproducer Terry Brown told me. "It was the general feeling about that record that it wasn't quite . . . there."

When I once spoke with Lee, he'd conceded that the music often goes places that Rush had rarely traveled on its first two releases. "So much of the record is dark and a little cerebral," Lee told me. "It got taken in a weird way."

Brown expressed regret for the reception *Caress of Steel* received on its release, calling it a "shame because we were all very excited about it."

"When I look back at that stuff now," Peart told the *Boston Globe* in 1990, "I see the flaws very apparently, the disjointedness of a lot of it. . . . If your mother drags out your grade 2 crayon drawings, you're obviously not going to look at them as the pinnacle of your life."

Falling hundreds of thousands of dollars in debt, with a psyched-up progressive rock record to support, one Mercury poo-pooed virtually on delivery, was not the space Rush thought they'd be occupying in late 1975.

"That was more likely to break us up than anything," Lee told me.

Reading the music industry trades, you might be forgiven for thinking that anything was amiss behind the scenes. *Caress of Steel* broke the Top 200 Albums chart in *Billboard*, and a radio promo of the two most accessible songs on the record, "Lakeside Park" and "Bastille Day," was released as a single soon after.

The appearance of a review in *Billboard* was encouraging, but it admonished that Rush "will need a bit more of a distinctive sound if they are to progress much more."

Rush was reminiscent of "heavy metal groups from England," *Billboard* reported, such as Led Zeppelin, but were beginning "to build an identity of its own. Good FM fare."

In retrospect, despite some reservations, *Billboard* got it right, one thinks, and this review stands in stubborn defiance of the historical narrative quickly developing around the release of the band's third studio effort. Rush was in a death spiral: a nervous record company itching to drop them and a (likely) dwindling fan base that would certainly take up with one or more of the band's many competitors.

The tour to support *Caress of Steel* has, by now, passed from hardship to infamy and, finally, into the stuff of rock and roll lore. It's common knowledge that, with no small amount of black humor, the band dubbed their jaunt through North America the "Down the Tubes" tour.

In theory, the band's slightly raised profile, due to the minor successes achieved by *Fly by Night*, meant Rush was expecting to play to increasingly larger crowds with each new studio album. The story goes that this was not the case. Nearly depleted and defeated, Rush was relegated to supporting slots and performing in less populated regions of America, opening for the likes of Kiss, Nazareth, Lynyrd Skynyrd, and Ted Nugent.

That's the legend.

A quick look at the band's tour itinerary reveals that these shows were not in the local bar and grills in towns on the edge of the prairie. Granted, many of these dates, as indicated above, were as an opening act, but Rush did perform in cities from Atlanta and Boston to Montreal, Chicago, Detroit, Toronto, and St. Louis—great music cities, all, and with history. Nevertheless, the band's collective mind-set kept them locked inside crisis mode for the entire string of dates and dampened any instinct they'd had to spark a positive spin on recent turn of events. They were—or believed they were—passengers on a head-on collision course with catastrophe, even contemplating what they'd do once this music thing was over.

"In terms of creative and psychological survival," Geddy Lee told me, *Caress of Steel* "changed us."

The fact is that even the band members themselves believed that management wasn't fully in their corner. Comanager Ray Danniels didn't know what he was going to say to the label, but he had to come up with something. This was not the type of thing that just gets "smoothed over" or swept under the rug by a record label.

What was Rush's next move?

"There was pressure from SRO and from Mercury Records to produce a more marketable sound because, as far as they were concerned, a rock band was only good for two years at the very most," Peart said in 1978.

Danniels would have promised Mercury the moon. In reality, he practically had to in order for the boys to hang with the company. In actuality, he was crossing his fingers behind his back that the boys could come up with a straight-ahead rocker to please the company execs. Rush's next studio record needed to be something closer to the band's debut record rather than a metaphysical parable set to a tricky drumbeat.

Mercury agreed to Danniels's terms: Rush had one more record to do. Rush had survived, for the time being, but what's that quote about offering the illusion of freedom and independence? The label's support can be viewed only as dubious at best. How on earth could the label trust a band that was being prepped for the chopping block?

Was this all a cover by the label in an attempt to wring the most commercial value out of Rush possible—and break their independent streak? Was it merely a tax write-off? Did Mercury just hand Rush enough rope to hang themselves?

# CHAPTER 4

# THIS MACHINE KILLS FASCISTS

There wasn't much good news for Rush, but there was still some reason to allow themselves a little bit of hope.

Ever since Rush had been on the road to support (or publicly disown?) *Caress of Steel*, Geddy and Alex had been bouncing ideas for guitar parts off one another. Alex, in particular, was feverishly coming up with riffs, and band was jamming on concepts down at Brown's Toronto Sound studios.

"We had, in fact, gotten a bunch of ideas together while we were doing *Caress of Steel* that were carried through into *2112*," Brown told me. "When it came time [to record these ideas], there was a whole new renewed enthusiasm that leapt off the page, so to speak."

Shell-shocked, even feeling a little betrayed, the studio became a sanctuary. They were beginning to shut out the suggestions from management and the label. With Brown's support, Rush was even starting to believe in themselves and their music again, clinging tenaciously to a confidence that they could move forward as a hybrid progressive hard rock band.

Even if they didn't make it, even if they crashed and burned in the process of trying to become world-beaters, they were not going to turn in an album to Mercury that lacked conviction.

It just so happens that, at this point, the guys had another look at Ayn Rand's work and were discussing her 1938 novel *Anthem*.

The totalitarian society in *Anthem* has eradicated the concept of "I." In fact, the lead character, the narrator, of the novel refers to "themselves" in the plural and as a number—Equality 7-2521.

Strata of society were determined long ago, and each person plays "their" part. If society deemed you are to become a street sweeper, you must become a street sweeper. Refusal means punishment. Usually, for stepping outside the lines, society's corrective measures were similar to Roman floggings, followed by prison time. No dissent or individual freedom was allowed.

Rand's personal experience with totalitarianism and communism undoubtedly shaped the antiauthoritarian views she wove into the fabric of her works. Increasingly, the band equated what they perceived as heavy-handed tricks of a music industry with the collectivist evil Rand paints in *Anthem*. Peart, in particular, took the betrayal of the industry personally and was virtually indignant that he was being asked to compromise as an artist by a label that seemed to hold his career in the balance, one that expected rock bands to fold after two years' time.

Peart had been here before, however. Seventh Wave (not to be confused, to my knowledge, with the later prog rock synth/drums outfit from England) threw away the playbook and did not strategize about how to get on the cover of *Rolling Stone* magazine. They resisted the urge to achieve success on anything other than their own terms. Seventh Wave ultimately failed. Would Rush, the product of a more established organization, succeed when guided by a similar art-for-art's-sake credo?

Having identified so closely with Rand's story, it was clear what needed to happen: *Anthem* should serve as the blueprint for Rush's rebel yell—their science fiction rock opera set in the year 2112 in the fictional city of Megadon.

In *Anthem*, Equality 7-2521 discovers a cave and stumbles across historical artifacts: an abandoned power system built in the "Unmentionable Times," made of electrical wiring, light sockets, and bulbs. Eventually, Equality 7-2521 figures how the damn stuff works—through what they dub the "power of the sky"—and tries to bring light to the dreary world.

The World Council of Scholars is frightened by the protagonist's glowing filament box and immediately impugn their motives and condemn the details and very existence of this secret archaeological dig. The Scholars denounce Equality's supposed arrogance in presuming to have the authority to circumvent and rejigger society's infrastructure, such as it is, to power these light boxes.

The piece that became "2112" follows a similar trajectory. As the preamble to the album's printed lyrics state, all aspects of life and leisure of a compliant society are controlled and programmed via massive banks of computers. Art and culture are sanctioned by the largely unchallenged ruling-class priests from deep inside the wells of their gray-walled temples. Few personal liberties and dissentions (read: none) are permitted in the surveillance state. In its own way, "2112" possesses all the characteristics of the technological dystopia feared by the hippies, one we talked about earlier in this book.

In "2112," the protagonist finds an ancient relic, an electric guitar, in a cave and wonders at its purpose. This discovery of a heretofore unknown technology prompts catastrophic consequences. In the same instant our protagonist finds an ancient guitar, he also taps into a cavernous well of creativity, a foreign concept in this fictional world. Our narrator descends into the depths of the earth—a cave—to formulate a fresh view of a more optimistic life and future.

On rediscovering this ancient relic, Guitar Man decides to alert the priests. What happened next to our Guitar Man would simply make Rush history.

"2112" was a blast. The fact that the band had recorded some of the record live in the studio, altogether, at once, may have contributed to the immediacy and power of the music, not to mention the energy of the performances. The record was cut in about a week at Brown's Toronto Sound.

"The Fountain of Lamneth" was several songs strung together, but "2112," despite pauses in between movements, offers more cohesion. The narrative is much stronger than any of the band's previous attempts at long songs. It's what Rush does with dynamics, musical motifs, and guitar tone that paints a coherent, lasting image.

Created by graphic designer Hugh Syme on synthesizer, the sonic flares opening of the record are actually several tracks edited together in pastiche form.

The first two sections of "2112" exemplify the rest of the piece. In the "Overture," Rush uses nineteenth-century classical music references within the context of electric guitar–driven hard rock. This is followed by the brain-rattling vocals and turbo-charged electrified rock atmosphere of "The Temples of Syrinx," which concludes with a gentle classic acoustic passage played by Lifeson.

The variety of feels in "The Fountain of Lamneth" was impressive, but the seven-part "2112" was much more successful in contrasting shadow and light, heavy and soft, through sections such as the bombastic, classically influenced "Overture," the bone-crushing "The Temples of Syrinx," the jazzy-lilting "Discovery," and the dynamic "Oracle: The Dream."

The brashness of the "Overture" and "The Temples of Syrinx" seem self-explanatory: the opening grabs us with its hard rock volume and driving, rippling, rhythmic majesty and the slightly menacing, thunderous drum performance by Peart, not to mention Lifeson's biting guitar tones.

Geddy assumes a kind of character role, as he did for *Caress of Steel*. Throughout "2112," the hero's voice is represented by a gentle, melodious tone, which contrasts with Geddy's stratospheric screams, meant to represent the general tenor and dismissiveness of the oppressive priests of the Temple of Syrinx.

"Discovery" follows our Guitar Man as he unearths an ancient musical instrument. Here, Lifeson does a bit of his own character acting: just as our Guitar Man struggles to find a melody on the relic, the stringed instrument, Lifeson cleverly tweaks his detuned guitar as tape rolled in the studio.

"Presentation," in which our hero unveils his guitar to the council of priests, runs a gamut of emotions. Lee's measured voice represents the Guitar Man, who beseeches the council to listen to his music and understand the ramifications of his discovery. Peart's restrained, sparkling playing and Lifeson's chord choices recall something jazzy, even rock/folk, à la Led Zeppelin.

The priests shout back that the society they maintain has no need of this rediscovered technological device—a plot point underscored by Geddy's harsh vocals and Peart's ferocious, if at moments halting, double kicks and tom fills.

"The Oracle: The Dream," like so much of "2112," expertly juxtaposes opposites, in this case the passionate with the reflective and the dreamy with the tumultuous. The Oracle hacks our hero's dreams and conjures for him visions of an ancient, freer world, one forged by the so-called Elder Race, prior to the priests' muscling in and instituting their iron-fisted rule. This Utopia had once existed and, it's understood, will come to pass again.

The reverberating-tunneling effect at the opening of the section evokes the widening portal of the subconscious as Guitar Man descends farther into the recesses of his mind. He fades away into the subconscious, then the collective conscious, making contact with some sort of Akashic-like dimension. Lifeson recalls and also slightly variates from some of the opening chords we heard in "Overture" (15:21), giving the sensation of floating in and out of the hero's world.

Through the magic of cinematic rock music, we (the listeners) journey with the Guitar Man to the infinite, to a society built by the Elder Race.

In "Soliloquy," with tinkling and rushing sounds of waterfalls saturating his cave sanctuary, our hero steels his resolve. Lifeson spins his chordal array, beginning in D, which moves through a series of melancholy minor chords.

After the main character sobers and rationalizes the ultimate (and fatal) decision, Geddy's voice cracks to a screech, an intonation that, up to now, the singer had reserved to depict the behavior of the totalitarian priests. Musical motifs have fused. We receive flashes of instincts commingling and at opposition with one another as our Guitar Man commits suicide to escape an oppressive world and astral travel toward the Dreamland showed to him by the Oracle.

Rush's dreamer, who might be the "Anonymous" listed on the liner notes (written in the year 2112), cannot live in the world created by the Solar Federation—one that outlaws creative impulses and free expression.

Overall sonic brashness signifies the narrator's physical surrender to the all-powerful State. His body can be said to be claimed by his oppressors, but his spirit would never be.

"Grand Finale" bookends the piece nicely, recalling some of "2112"'s earlier musical themes while also conveying all the cacophony, rhythmic rumbling, and seizure-inducing sonic charges one would expect from a multisectional song terminated by an intragalactic blitzkrieg.

"First and foremost, with '2112,' I think it's the music that connects," says Eric Barnett. "I mean, the first vocals aren't until 'The Temples of Syrinx,' four and a half minutes in, and 'Grand Finale' is basically an instrumental, too. But the story is timeless and arguably appropriate for modern-day society. Art and individualism and freedom, clashing with an authoritarian entity. If you read it from a more literal Randian perspective, it's really about oppression of a communist society and its perceived inevitable downfall, but from a less focused viewpoint, it's just the struggle against authority, to be able to be oneself, expression versus conformity. In that way, it's almost punk rock in its ethos, and it contains a universal theme, even if told through the lens of science fiction."

In escapist literature, there seems to be very little concern with differentiating between past, present, and future. One could say that this is also true of progressive rock.

The image of priests inside their high-tech temples conjures, ironically enough, the torch-lit and arid environs of ancient Egypt. Likewise, it's difficult to ignore that Megadon, the city that will soon be bombarded by cosmic debris from apocalyptic intragalactic combat, could easily be mistaken for the biblical location of the final battleground, Meggido or Armageddon, of the Book of Revelation. Ironically enough, Revelation is an ancient but, some believe, prophetic Middle Eastern text.

The very object that causes so much trouble for Guitar Man is ancient but technologically advanced. It's likely, when they are alone and speak amongst themselves, the priests know all too well that the guitar is a visionary mechanism, one that threatens to undermine society, a kind of catalyst for revolution.

Whether the narrator was conscious of it or not, his electric guitar could bring the whole house of cards down on itself. The priests know the true power of the rediscovered device. You could say that the appearance of the guitar is a futuristic slant on the iconic note scrawled on the face of Woody Guthrie's acoustic guitar: "This machine kills fascists."

Even some of the audio effects injected into the song were from another time. Literally. In "Grand Finale," Peart's manipulated voice, warning the Solar Federation of their imminent demise, was the by-product of experimentation during the *Caress of Steel* sessions. It's still a bit unclear, but the announcement, "Attention all planets of the Solar Federation . . ." may have been conceptualized, if not outright recorded, *during* the *Steel* sessions.

Finally, the idea of the tortured hero is not uncommon in English and German romantic literature of the nineteenth century. In addition, it's possible that the heroic figure of "2112" is modeled not only on Equality 7-2521 from *Anthem* but also on Rand's other iconic creation, Howard Roark (*The Fountainhead*).

We must resist the temptation to call our Guitar Man an antihero in light of Rand's own thoughts on this subject. In the essay "The Cult of Moral Grayness" in the book *The Virtue of Selfishness*, Rand points out that the rise of the antihero in modern media is marked by his lack of distinction: "no virtues, no values, no goals, no character." None of this describes the lead in "2112."

Our hero is reminiscent, however, of a famous overdosing opium abuser and emotional wreck suffering from unrequited love—the soul central to Berlioz's nineteenth-century programmatic musical piece *Symphonie Fantastique* with just a smidgen of Monteverdi's operatic underworld from *L'Orfeo*.

*Symphonie Fantastique*, a narrative-driven large-scale symphony with recurring musical themes, floats around us like the smoke rings of a psychedelic dream—or, more precisely, a nineteenth-century "bad trip." Its central story follows a tortured individual through the pang-filled throes of suicide. In his agonal state, the main character begins his descent into hell. It's not an exact match for "2112," but the Rush song does carry shades of the earlier classical work.

Tchaikovsky's music may have been directly referenced in the "Overture," foreshadowing victory, but the ghosts of Berlioz's masterwork (as well as perhaps orchestral musings by other, earlier composers) haunt the whole of "2112."

"2112" is Rush's first mind–body–soul music. The volume and aggressiveness hit one in the chest; at the same time, its mystical, even occult, aspects are undeniable.

Our hero experiences what can only be called precognition. He is, in very real terms, a seer with extrasensory perception. Guitar Man's visions, witnessed in a sub-conscious state, provide him the courage to make a real-world decision—even if that means snuffing out his own life.

The white noise rushing forth from a waterfall becomes a meditative aid in guid-ing Guitar Man's psychic energy into the Next Life. Shepherding one's soul through the next dimension via meditation or administering psychedelic drugs at the moment of physical death was a sign of the times. Popular interest in ancient texts, such as the Egyptian Book of the Dead, and alternative religion was on the rise in 1960s and 1970s.

As with many of Peart's lyrics, dreams—for the exceptional, misfit, bored, des-perate, and everyday warriors alike—offer escape from one type of reality. It may be literal in the case of "2112."

The concept of ego loss, consciousness slipping from the mortal coil, raises the specter of Judeo-Christian spiritual rebirth and the Eastern philosophic notion of eternal recurrence. Dreams, like souls, are forever and can transcend our physical bodies.

Then again, "2112" could be the stuff of dreams: after the opening section ram-pages along, the music settles down for a few seconds, and Geddy sings, "And the meek shall inherit the Earth."

Is Geddy assuming the role of the protagonist by singing this?

Whether he is or not, "2112" is a musical movie whose plot is being retold in flashbacks by a main character drawing his final breaths. Scenes from a memory. If not, then he's speaking from the timeless void (which means he really *did* access and escape to Dreamland).

In visual terms, the camera zooms in for an extreme close-up of the Guitar Man's pupil, a journey to the center of the iris, as light slowly fades from his eyes and we travel through this circular portal.

The second side of *2112* offers stranger and more aromatic sensations to the listener. "A Passage to Bangkok" unmistakably details a global search for the hottest spots with the best hallucinogens; we can't help feel woozy in "The Twilight Zone" amid Lifeson's swirling, repetitive, ascending and descending arpeggiated notes, invoking the vertigo-inducing spiral seen at the opening sequence of the classic *Twilight Zone* TV program.

The gradual build of the Mellotron in "Tears" evokes slow streaming pain and eventual emotional release—of drifting off into oblivion, like flower petals circling downstream.

Although the rawness of "Something for Nothing" doesn't conjure the same vivid images as other tracks on *2112* do, this closing track was inspired by a very visual catalyst to the band's creativity.

Glimpsing graffiti scrawled on a wall can psychologically scar or bolster the thoughts of creative minds. From Eric Clapton to Roger Waters, spray-painted epitaphs scrawled by street poets are like cosmic messages channeled through everyday folk. Supposedly, Peart had seen the phrase "freedom is not free" etched on a wall, cementing concepts already fomenting.

Complacency and freedom don't necessarily mix. The former is cheap, and the latter is rarely handed out freely. We cannot rely on other people, the authorities, or mysterious supernatural forces to do the heavy lifting for us. If "2112" is musically exciting, at times psychically damaging, then "Something for Nothing" is a pep talk, a populist message to continue to fight the good fight. It reminds listeners that the power is in their hands to make a change, a revolution of the mind.

Lee penned a song with a shock of immediacy that appealed and should continue to appeal to prog rock as well as hard rock listeners. The use of acoustic and electric guitar tracks is especially effective here. Minor-key arpeggios automatically color the track in a dark tone, but they do lend the composition unsettling grittiness befitting its admonishment of the struggle that awaits anyone who wants to be truly free.

The time signature of the drums, 4/4, is virtually straightforward (as much as Peart could have been circa 1976). It's a far cry from the "Overture" for "2112," which dips into 3s, 5s, 7s, and 9s but acts as its complement nonetheless.

"Something for Nothing" is a pure, driving tune, a cry for liberty reflected in Geddy's throat-burning yelps. On the whole, *2112* was Rush's rebel yell: a defiant act and the band's declaration of independence.

Back at Mercury's Chicago headquarters, execs were frozen in thousand-yard stares. Their eyes glazed over and could not hear past the lengthy first track. A budding artist clashing with authoritarianism against the backdrop of a surrealistic sci-fi setting was one of the least rock and roll concepts one could imagine.

On hearing the record, the label was further dumbfounded. *Where is the single? How can we sell this?*

Perhaps Rush was so far along into their art, grown so thick skinned through weeks of dark humor and dwindling career prospects to get too emotionally involved with the label's dismissive attitude. Then again, what scenarios could play out in real life that had not already been imagined in their minds?

*2112* was not just a dense record but a record on which "the first song was 20 minutes long," Lee told me. "Take that!"

Mercury had to. They were stuck with it.

"We fought back with *2112*," Geddy told me, "which was probably the most important record we ever made."

As most people know, *2112* became a rousing success, rising up the charts, set-tling within the top half of *Billboard*'s Top 200 Albums chart, and gaining a small army of supporters in the process. *2112* has since gone on to sell more than 3 million units in the United States alone. Simply put, without *2112*, *Moving Pictures* would not exist.

Few rock artists can claim to create art and also make cash registers ring. Granted. Rush was not agonizing over esoteric avant-garde chord structures, anti-rhythms, and experimental electronic music, attempting to unlock the secrets of the universe—and living in squalor while doing it. Nor were they mass-producing bubblegum pop. Rush had overcome the doldrums of the "Down the Tubes" fiasco and quelled nag-ging uncertainties to map a musical course they could follow for the next several years.

"The word I would use to describe for Peter Gabriel, David Bowie, and Rush is courage," says Toronto radio legend David Marsden. "They had the courage to do what they believed in, each and every time they made an album or stepped on the stage. They had a courage to say, 'I think I'm on the right path, here. Some president of a record label is not going to tell me what to do.' It's no different than when a program director handed me a playlist and I asked, 'What is a playlist?' Because of things like that, I left, and I didn't know what would happen the next day. The artists who have lasted the longest have done it through their courage and their ability to constantly be finding the new, exciting, and original."

"Genesis and Yes are two bands I have never listened to," says Pete Agnew of Nazareth. "It is great playing, but it is not rock and roll. I think Rush took it even further than that."

Everything came together for *2112*, almost like a Hollywood production, rife with plot twists, the thrilling hairpin turns of a wild car chase, tussles between heroes

*2112*: The unexpected success of Rush's 1976 studio album made *Moving Pictures* possible.

and villains, and a feel-good ending for our protagonists: The album was a cinematic experience with a great backstory setting up conflict of apocalyptic proportions— both in and out of the studio, on and off record.

Visual aspects of the album's packaging further sealed the deal. Photographer Yosh Inouye lensed some of the snapshots that appeared on the original vinyl LP album packaging, including the cover image; Gérard Gentil shot the band photos on the back cover and the gatefold of the original LP.

The mesmerizing front image recalled some of Hollywood's motion pictures tricks, like the "burning letters" beam effect via intense lighting fixtures or actual flame.

"The glowing star effects was achieved shooting through water," says Inouye. "The red star [of the cover] was painted with black on a white paper. I photographed it with a large-format view camera, 8 by 10 inches. The film I used was a high-contrast litho film. The processed film was placed underwater. The lighting was from under the film, backlit. The light I used was a speed light with a strong modeling light. I used various shutter speeds in order to achieve combination effects of sharpness and movements. The red color was from a filter on the camera."

The inner gatefold of *2112* features the now iconic image of the naked man interfacing the Red Star of the Solar Federation. Art director Hugh Syme viewed the naked (or pure) man as someone who is unencumbered by societal norms. The star was said to be Peart's idea, and it became a band logo for years.

However, at the time, some mistook the pentagram for a symbol of the Satanic. Only fringe opinions leaders put any stock in this today. Rush were not attempting to transmit subliminal messages through backmasking, and no one in the band (as far as I know) had any contact with "The Other Side" via séance.

"I photographed the naked man. He was Hugh Syme's friend, Bobby King," says Inouye. "I only took his back, no front. He refused to show his front view."

A strong recovery, a rapidly growing fan base, a cinematic album—what was Rush's next move?

Touring, of course. From fall 1976 into June 1977, Rush performed blocks of dates for which they supported or shared the bill with the likes of Kansas, Boston, Aerosmith, Styx, Blue Öyster Cult, Starcastle, Chilliwack, Wireless, Cheap Trick, Max Webster, and others.

Amid their travel joy and travails, Rush returned to their hometown and recorded a live double record, *All the World's a Stage*, at Toronto's Massey Hall over three nights in June 1976. Arguably no one, not even the band, could have foreseen this a year earlier when Rush was on the verge of getting bounced and possibly disbanding.

*All the World's a Stage* contributed to Rush's early success, but, in actuality, it could be viewed as catching a rising wave of a live double-LP craze so prevalent in the mid-1970s. Artists such as Peter Frampton (*Frampton Comes Alive*), Bob Seger and the Silver Bullet Band (*Live Bullet*), Kiss (*Alive!*), Paul McCartney and Wings (*Wings over America*), and Blue Öyster Cult (*On Your Feet or on Your Knees*) fired off double-barreled slabs of vinyl, many of which are now considered classics of the genre and have earned gold (or better) status in the United States.

It was management and label, this time, that had read the tea leaves correctly and urged Rush to compile a concert performance LP. In the United States, a single for the medley of "Fly by Night" and "In the Mood," extracted from *All the World's a Stage*, charted in the Top 100 singles in the United States. The album would eventually go platinum in America in 1981. More about this later.

Rush appeared to be traversing the downslope of the rock and roll hump, but it didn't mean the road was ever easy to navigate. Because of the tough slog through the U.S. South and the Midwest, rock bands bonded regardless of their points of origin. A free exchange of ideas occurred, and relationships and friendships developed. The commonalities of their experiences created an overall sense of community and continuity in the bewildering and often surreal world of rock touring.

In a way, backstage or offstage heart-to-heart conversations, extracurricular activities, and half-crazed shenanigans are the backdrop, the hidden or esoteric history, of rock. The details of those experiences constitute a coded language that musicians of a certain era speak to one another about a time long gone.

This "internal" communication between bands could also be of practical importance. A progressive rock band from Fort Wayne, Indiana, called Ethos (Ardour), sometimes referred to as just Ethos, had just signed with and recorded their self-titled debut album for Capitol Records in the United States and may have helped to influence Peart's percussive choices circa 1977.

"I grew up with Neil Graham of the Percussion Center, Fort Wayne, Indiana," Ethos (Ardour)'s then drummer, Mark Richards, once told me. "When we toured with Rush, I turned Neil Peart onto Neil Graham. He said, 'Where did you get this stuff?' I said, 'Well, I built this [drum] cage, but [Graham] is the one that I took my drum ideas to and built all of this stuff custom.' I directed Neil Peart to the Percussion Center, and that was who built Neil Peart's original racks and everything."

The camaraderie could not be matched. Many of these musicians, whether they are still in contact with one another or not, shared—and share—a unique bond.

"I have a Neil Peart story too," Steve Tassler, original drummer of Starcastle, told me. "We would play with Kansas a lot. We did a show with Rush and Kansas, and I was standing off to the side of the stage watching [drummer] Phil Ehart [of Kansas] with Neil. Neil turns to me and says, 'You know, gosh, this guy is so great, I hope I can be as good as that someday.' Neil was already Neil, you know? I looked at him and said, 'That is what I think about you.' He smiled and said, 'Thanks, man.'"

# CHAPTER 5

# PICTURES AT 11

When the band was mixing *All the World's a Stage* in 1976, Peart snuck away and began writing down lyrics for future songs. One of those to emerge was for the demonic tone poem "Xanadu."

"Xanadu" would become the centerpiece for the band's next recording project, *A Farewell to Kings*, a tip of the hat to the band's British heroes. *A Farewell to Kings* would be a change in musical direction, one that would reach back to the band's influences and even further than that to create what some might rightly label an anachronism in the time of punk.

*A Farewell to Kings* is the rightful continuation of *Caress of Steel*, perhaps more so than *2112*. Some of the same elements that the band was attempting to perfect with *Caress of Steel* and the earlier *Fly by Night* reached their apex with *A Farewell to Kings* and the follow-up, 1978's *Hemispheres*.

*A Farewell to Kings* is defined by its contrasts, cliffhangers, anachronisms, and counterparts: "Closer to the Heart" completes the logical arguments presented in the title track; "Cinderella Man" and the title track combine acoustic and electric guitars; "Madrigal" is a magical blending of traditional acoustic guitar and cutting-edge twentieth-century keyboard technology; and "Xanadu" and "Cygnus X-1" are each marked by a narrator's almost fatalistic determination and unsatiated curiosity.

As was the case with "2112" and "The Fountain of Lamneth," the narrator of both "Xanadu" and "Cygnus X-1" is spellbound, blinded by his lofty personal goal. By exploring the inner and outer cosmos, under the guise of gaining knowledge, the heroes of these musical tragedies receive more than they'd initially bargained for.

Originally scheduled to record in Canada, Rush scrapped their plans after Brown investigated options overseas. The coproducer and band agreed they'd decamp to Wales at Rockfield Studios.

Rockfield was on the edge of a small town, with very little activity and not much to do but track the record and play mind games with cows.

A trip abroad, back to his native England, was a breath of fresh air for Brown, too. He'd been splitting his time between Rush and studio group Klaatu.

"A friend of mine, who was Rush's producer, Terry Brown, came to me with a project," recording industry vet Frank Davies told me once. "He said, 'I am working with these guys. I let them come in at night and they are very creative. Tell me what you think.' That was Klaatu, of course. I signed them right away [to Daffodil Records], and they became a big focus for me for several years, both directly and indirectly, for a long time afterwards."

Whether through the grapevine, effective marketing campaigns, or public and radio programmer misconceptions, Klaatu, having signed with Capitol Records through a deal Davies made with the label, had been mistaken for a reformed Beatles, working under a new name. Some heard Klaatu's studio-designed, art-pop stylings as the sophisticated sounds of the Fab Four updated for the 1970s.

The guys in Klaatu had done little to dissuade people in the industry from this type of thinking.

Nevertheless, Klaatu was outed by Dwight Douglas, who had been working at WWDC radio in Washington, D.C. Due to Douglas's proximity to the Library of Congress, he hit on a eureka moment (actually, Douglas's secretary, Rosemarie Winter, did the legwork): Documents filed with the copyright office in the nation's capital revealed that Klaatu was not the Beatles in disguise. They were, in fact, a bunch of guys from Toronto, one of whom, John Woloschuk, had actually worked with Terry Brown at Toronto Sound and is credited in the liner notes to *Fly by Night* as a recording engineer.

"I was a little, not bothered, I was curious," Dwight Douglas once told me. "Like any of us who grew up with the Beatles on *Ed Sullivan*, anything about the Beatles was special. The Beatles getting back together under some secret cloud would be monumental."

When it was revealed who and what Klaatu actually was, the industry turned and the public with it. "In a weird sense, I felt badly for the band because in the next few weeks, they went [makes nosedive noise]," Douglas told me. "Interest went down very fast. I have to say we kept playing the music . . . and announced them: 'Here's Klaatu. They're not the Beatles.'"

The progressive pop band Klaatu procured a rich if brief history of studio experimentation, great hooks, sonic innuendo, and mystery. The irony of ironies? They were good enough, in the minds of many, to assume the role of the greatest pop band ever to walk the planet, but after the Great Reveal, all that Klaatu could muster by the late 1970s was a steady commercial decline.

"You could make the argument that people wanted, so much, the Beatles reunion, that they saw what they wanted to see," Douglas told me. "They were listening to something so close they wanted to be able to shape it into their desire."

Wonders of public psychology and the music business never cease. It's a magic trick, really, and Terry Brown himself was set to disappear from the Klaatu scene.

"When it came to do *Sir Army Suit*, Terry Brown was still in a prog-rock mode because of 'Calling Occupants of Interplanetary Craft,' 'Little Neutrino,' and the entirety of the *Hope* album," Klaatu's Terry Draper once told me. "Somewhere along the line, the songs were not as commercial or as pop-y as we wanted them to be, and they are not as sophisticated and progressive as Terry wanted them to be. We were caught in the middle of a maelstrom where they don't fit any category."

With Rush's newfound success and faced with this Klaatu conundrum, Brown begged off and decided it was time to dedicate himself full-time to the Canadian prog–hard rock trio.

"Terry had a studio to run that he owned and had a family and a mortgage etcetera etcetera," Draper said. "He had to put bread on the table. He was not just recording Rush, but he was producing them. So, Rush was a big deal. Not only that, but they were becoming very successful. The *Hope* album was made at Toronto Sound and Olympic Studios in England with the symphony at the same time Rush was making *2112*. *2112* earned Terry Brown a lot more money than *Hope* did. . . . Terry had to take care of business and paying customers came first."

To Draper's point, Rush was moving further and further into progressive rock territory with 1977's *A Farewell to Kings* and *Hemispheres* (1978) and further from the historically accepted view of the popular tastes of the era.

After recording in Toronto for the last several years, it was time to change the scenery, and since England was home to much of the music that had influenced Rush, tracking in Great Britain would inspire the band. Recording in Rockfield was the answer. Besides, Rockfield had already played host to such legendary acts as Hawkwind, Queen, and Van der Graaf Generator.

Never ones to let an opportunity go to waste, prior to hunkering down, the band played some gigs in Europe, with a concentration of dates in the United Kingdom, before they headed to the studio in the Welsh countryside.

Some sources, including the liner notes for the original release of the album, state that recording began in June 1977. Most of the recording activity took place in the early afternoon. But as the days wore on, the gang may have gravitated toward organizing their sessions in night shifts or an after-dinner schedule. Work typically ceased in the early hours of the morning.

With the assistance of Rockfield recording engineer Pat Moran, tracking for *A Farewell to Kings* lasted somewhere in the vicinity of three to four weeks. Most of the record was done with the trio exchanging ideas in the studio while tracking. This was a departure from later efforts, in which the band would divide their time and work in different shifts, depending, for instance, on who enjoyed tracking during the day or who might light up a joint at night to complete a track.

So Rush went about recording the album, wrapping themselves in the sights, sounds, and smells of the U.K. countryside, virtually cocooned and unaware of the unfolding world around them.

Rush didn't realize at the time what a den of vipers they had stepped into by recording *A Farewell to Kings* when they did. Historic narrative dictates that the mid- and late 1970s were times of transition in consumer tastes. As mainstream rock's potency diminished slightly, urban dance (or disco) and punk were becoming increasingly popular—a response to Watergate, the disastrous wrap to the Vietnam War, economic doldrums, and the general cynicism and distrust of the age.

"The antidote to such feelings was disco," wrote Jim Curtis in his book *Rock Eras: Interpretations of Music & Society 1954–1984*. "Artificiality—conscious artificiality—was the order of the day, not just in the music but also the setting in which one heard music."

With DJs offering feedback on and monitoring what motivated people to shake their asses on the dance floor, major-label promotion departments had a direct pipeline to the public tastes. Most of the guiding principles and infrastructure of the record industry were either unnecessary or simply vanished where disco was involved. It turned the industry model on its ear.

According to Curtis, disco "merged the performers and the audience; it decentralized music by obsolescing the star system."

This cut-to-the-bone populism was something that rock and, frankly, prog rock could not compete with. Disco was the doctor, prescribing the medicine, the fix, that Europeans and North Americans craved. The experience was hypnotic: Orgasmic moans from Donna Summer, pill-popping euphoria, a sense of community and

*A Farewell to Kings*, 1977: Rush's nod to their British rock heroes.

individual freedom as four-on-the-floor pulses permeated the dance hall, DJs cradled their headphones to "beatmatch" two sound sources for seamless transitions between pieces of music, and flashing lights mesmerizing dancers in an otherwise darkened discotheque.

For a few solid years, nothing could or would splinter this dynamic.

Punk, as has often been stated, is the other side of the populist coin. The 1970s was a sobering time but also one of hedonistic self-centeredness, excess, rising crime, and stagnant economies. It slowly fractured the collective psyche of the populace—on both sides of the Atlantic.

Fueled by the anger of working-class Brits and, to a lesser degree, Americans, the punk movement railed against the status quo and what was perceived as systemic disenfranchisement precluding the economically downtrodden from pursuing opportunities in the recording industry and daily life in general.

Naturally, by extension, the musicians who employed expensive equipment to perform ambitious material in major sports arenas on tours that raked in millions of dollars became targets. It was a world that most punk bands could not and would not, by and large, ever experience or even aspire to.

On the other hand, the working-poor milieu from which many of the punks sprang meant that bands such as Sex Pistols were very much *by* the people as *of* the people for whom they were performing. Many lived a shared existence of poverty, lack of positive self-image, and no future. Indeed. Johnny Rotten's teeth were rotting in decay due to a lack of a hygiene routine, helping him earn the nickname.

"The punks tended to obsolesce the distinction between performer and artist, just as disco did," wrote Jim Curtis.

Circa 1976–1977, Punk's blood-and-guts assault campaigns had not coagulated; the vibe had begun to spill out onto the streets on both sides of the Atlantic, threatening to infect the wider culture.

Sex Pistols, Iggy and the Stooges, Television, Rocket from the Tombs, the Damned, the Clash, and many others picked up the frequency of popular consciousness and blasted listeners with their music on a visceral and, in some cases, an intellectual level. (At the same time, Throbbing Gristle, largely responsible for what would become known as the industrial music movement that blossomed over the next two decades, formed in 1975.) Supercharged and anguished sounds, emanating from the London, New York, and the midwestern musical undergrounds of Detroit, Minneapolis, and Cleveland, provided the rocket fuel for an explosive cultural uprising just as it appeared (or so we were told) that progressive rock was running on fumes.

"When I was in London, I worked on *Brain Salad Surgery*," says Paul Northfield, who for well over a decade felt he had to conceal portions of his résumé from the public. "In England ELP used to be a great band. Later, punk and Sex Pistols came along and it was like, 'Don't mention that album.' [laughs] Everyone is talking about Sex Pistols, the Clash, Generation X."

When it comes to understanding the supposed decline of progressive rock, the onslaught of punk, and the alleged overnight sea change in public tastes, it was always a chicken-or-egg proposition. Had individual listeners really grown tired of progressive music and, en masse, decided to burn their art-rock vinyl for the latest punk platter? Was punk the natural or organic response to progressive rock? Can all of this be explained in cultural and societal terms?

Of course, the ironic legacy of the 1976–1978 time frame, punk's and disco's respective heyday, is one of important and beloved progressive rock records. Consider this: the debut album from supergroup U.K., Genesis's *Wind & Wuthering*, Steve Hillage's *L*, 801's *801 Live*, Gong's *Shamal*, FM's *Black Noise*, Van Der Graaf Generator's *Still Life*, and Jethro Tull's *Songs from the Wood* and *Heavy Horses*—all released in the second half of the 1970s.

No one could deny, however, that these bands were changing their musical direction, in some cases quite rapidly, either through sheer boredom, record industry pressure, or trepidation over the uncertainties of a new decade just over the horizon.

Rush's material had a slight advantage over some of their U.S. and European cousins, contemporaries, and competitors. The scope of their compositions and willingness to experiment with studio sounds and effects might have been hallmarks of progressive rock, but the Rush variant successfully and credibly introduced muso-pyrotechnics and hard rock thrash into an arty setting—and made it accessible.

"The death knell of hard rock music, which many non-believers predicted would be sounding by this time, is nowhere to be heard," *Record World* magazine reporter Mike Harris noted in a 1976 review of Rush's show at the Starwood in Los Angeles. "Rush (Mercury), a power trio from Canada, is among those who have kept the faith."

For Rush's prime audiences—largely male from the suburbs and rural areas—the revolutionary ideology of the so-called New Left became mobilized due to the unceremonious death of the Utopian dream and was formulated in response to middle-class complacency. But many of the ideals of the New Left not only were foreign concepts to this demographic but also largely unappealing. Rush fans and aspiring musicians held solidarity with their newfound musical heroes. Clearly, this demographic harbored a taste for something complex and guitar-driven that safely fell outside the Top 40.

"I used to be babysat by the older girl who lived across the street from me," says drummer Jason Bittner (Overkill and Shadows Fall), who grew up in upstate New York. "She had a twin brother, Terry, who played bass. One day when I was over at the house, being babysat until my mom got home from work, the twin brother invited a friend from down the street. This was in 1978, and this kid was a senior in high school, long hair. I was in middle school, maybe not even. Anyway, this friend from down the street and Terry were listening to *A Farewell to Kings*. I knew that this was not Chicago or Ohio Players. Terry was African American and listened to the jazz-rock stuff and played bass with the records. All I can remember at that point in time was, 'I don't know what this is. It's not bad, but I can't follow any of this.'"

It's clear: By 1977, cracks in the pop culture crust, the tectonic social, political, and economic shifts experienced by North America and Europe throughout the mid-1970s, wreaked havoc on a world already in disarray. The time line of the trajectory of Rush's popularity fits neatly, historically, within the decline of Euro prog rock and the seeming simultaneous rise of North American progressive rock bands and punk on both sides of the Atlantic.

Critics, perhaps a bit shell-shocked, jaded, and pissed off by what they viewed were long-winded musical themes or retreads of progressive rock warhorses, welcomed something new to cut through the static.

It was around this time that Rush was making noise on the charts and laid the groundwork for their status as a bankable concert draw. However, the stats about their growing fan base were met by the press with indifference if not disdain and outright hostility. Rush was just too much to handle: some in the press took issue with everything from their personal ambition to Ayn Rand–informed political commentary. Yes, Emerson, Lake & Palmer, Genesis, and others may have bored factions of the music press, but at least they were prototypes. What was Rush?

"I think in the early days we had the difficult task of existing at a time when the people who influenced us existed or still existed," Geddy Lee once told me. "We were obviously influenced by a lot of English progressive rock bands, as well as Cream and Led Zeppelin, and a lot of those bands were still going when we started. So, we paled by comparison to our prototypes. I can understand the criticism."

Some people "got it." A midwestern newspaper ran a syndicated column by Tom Von Malder in which he wrote a fascinating review of Led Zeppelin's *Physical Graffiti* and discussed Rush's *Fly by Night*. Although the acoustic, Tolkien-based "Rivendell" was called out as being a musical misstep, Von Malder predicted that "Rush someday could be as big as Led Zeppelin."

Bob Mersereau, in his book *The History of Canadian Rock 'N' Roll* (2015), theorizes that although Canadian artists didn't invent rock music, doo-wop, rhythm and blues, or jazz, in some instances they improved on what was already created.

One could argue that this describes Rush to a tee: They did not conceive of blues rock, hard rock, progressive rock, jazz rock, or any of the hybridized rock strains, but they tweaked these subgenres to the point of putting together what would become the perfect progressive hard rock album.

And so what might seem at first blush to have been counterintuitive in retrospect is a perfect fit. Hard rock neutralized punk to a degree, and Rush's diluted progressive *thingie* distanced them from their British counterparts. Perhaps the timing of *A Farewell to Kings* couldn't have been better planned if it were scripted; no band was better positioned to record it than if they had been selected to do so by central casting.

In the immediate wake of *A Farewell to Kings*, Yes and Emerson, Lake & Palmer were increasingly demystified: They were losing their mojo. Emerson, Lake & Palmer toured briefly with a sixty-piece symphony orchestra to support the double album *Works, Volume One* until it became too cost prohibitive. What followed was a scaled-back tour, the compilation *Works, Volume Two*, and 1978's *Love Beach*, often cited as a compromised, post-punk effort. Some believe *Love Beach* to be not only the band's last gasp for air but *the* moment British progressive rock genre's balloon deflated.

Rush had an edge, however. Beholden still to some form of blues-rock guitar tradition and still seduced by volume, Rush injected hard rock into a genre that put sonic experimentation, even keyboard passages, above guitar riffs in the musical pecking order. As much as they were fans of these bands, Rush had to acknowledge that the progressive rock moment had come and gone.

Having said this, for one hot minute prior to recording *A Farewell to Kings*, Rush itself experienced a mini-crisis of identity. They'd pondered whether they should recruit a fourth member to play keyboards—an anachronistic urge, for sure, but we suppose that's the point of *A Farewell to Kings*.

Enlisting in a caped keyboard wizard to handle synths would certainly expand Rush's sound and possibly bring about a livelier interplay among the players, allowing Rush's music to grow dynamically. At least, that was the thinking. Ultimately, the idea was rejected, and the boys simply pulled double and triple duty in the studio and onstage. The idea was for the band to share some of the responsibilities, with most of them being handled by Geddy.

With the introduction of Minimoog synth and Taurus synth pedals, Geddy and, to a degree, Alex had the ability to create a soundscape that was prior to *A Farewell to Kings* not an option for the band. Synthesizers changed much of the functionality and dynamics within the band. Although Alex used synth pedals, Geddy's preoccupation with them meant the guitarist could concentrate on melodic lead lines while Geddy was painting with broad sonic brushes and holding down the bottom end.

*A Farewell to Kings* also tapped into one of progressive rock's great paradoxes: a combination of opposites. For instance, innovative musical equipment was used for the recording, yet Rush's material conjures music of past centuries. Lyrics were inspired by nineteenth-century literature; even the calligraphic font used for band's logo, as seen on the album cover, was reminiscent of writing inked on a medieval illuminated manuscript.

Despite the traditional feel of some of the songs, the music is undeniably modern and cinematic. For instance, "Cinderella Man" is Geddy Lee's lyrical homage to the 1936 Gary Cooper movie *Mr. Deeds Goes to Town.* And the first creative glimmers of "Xanadu" were sparked by the legendary Orson Welles vehicle *Citizen Kane.* This is to say nothing about the visuals the music itself conjures. The cinematic aspects of the record are enhanced by Geddy's interpretive skills and the characteristics of the singer's voice. Our body flinches when Geddy's voice becomes so intense that we *feel* the physical stress that the pilot of "Cygnus X-1" undergoes as he's being ripped to shreds entering a collapsing star.

As they'd done on the previous three studio albums, Peart would write partial lyrics, and Geddy and Alex would peruse and begin the process of matching lyrics with music. By the same token, if there was an idea Alex and Geddy wanted to play for Neil, they'd jam on the idea.

Immersion was the rule of the day. Rush intended to steep themselves in every aspect of the U.K. experience. Convinced that the reflective quality of Rockfield studio's courtyard would provide a natural echo chamber and add sonic richness to the recording, coproducer Terry Brown and his team of recording engineers took advantage of the surroundings to slip out of the studio and gain access to the outside world—when the intermittent Welsh showers would allow, that is.

For the opening instrumental section of the title track, Alex was joined in the courtyard by Geddy on Minimoog and Peart on percussion, who is using mallets on orchestra bells. (Neil would also record, in the warm June air, his temple-block knocking at the opening of "Xanadu.") A stereo microphone array was set up to capture the band and pick up bird chirps and other sounds of nature. This anachronistic track feels like a modern field recording of an Elizabethan-era music troupe.

This leadoff song acts as an overture in part because it hints at many of the record's thematic and musical high notes. The use of keyboard technology helps bolster the track to great harmonic and melodic effect. Peart navigates a chicanery of odd and common time signatures—mainly 3/4 juxtaposed with 4/4. The bass line and drum pattern (beginning approximately 3:12) bops underneath Alex's guitar solo, foreshadowing the odd-time groove of "Cygnus X-1," the album's closer.

The post-Watergate lyrics not only indict our so-called political leaders but also warn us that they are deliberately sowing division. Our once-trusted institutions are corrupted, those who populate it corruptible—and we are partly to blame due to our gross complacency. Having relinquished our individual voices, we have forfeited the precious moral high ground. We can no longer believe in leaders (much less ourselves), and we lack the mental fortitude to dismantle an unjust political and judicial power structure established to serve the people.

It's fitting that the last line Geddy sings (i.e., "closer to the heart") not only references the leadoff song of what was the original side 2 but also asks if we are capable of getting ourselves out of this spiritual and societal downward spiral. This sobering message was anathema to the disco ethos and, ironically, in line with punk's antiestablishment attitude toward the status quo.

Side 1 concludes with the epic "Xanadu," arguably the one song clearly delineated with and patterned on the pomposity and musical grandeur perpetrated by the British progressive rock movement. It was inspired, as indicated, by *Citizen Kane* but in larger part by the mystical early nineteenth-century poem "Kubla Khan," penned by Samuel Taylor Coleridge—something he pieced together from a half-remembered opium-induced nightmare.

Coleridge's poem, itself inspired by the work of travel writer Samuel Parchas, was one installment of a "daemonic group" that also encompassed *The Rime of the Ancient Mariner* and "Christabel," or so wrote editors Harold Bloom and Lionel Trilling in their anthology *Romantic Poetry and Prose*.

The English romantic era expanded on the instinct to explore the wilds of the human psyche and natural surroundings, fusing both the inner and the outer cosmos—something a few of the British progressive rockers were fascinated with as well.

The mythical mountaintop paradise, the rugged land of Shangri-La or Xanadu, holds the magical elixir of life—immortality. The speaker in "Kubla Khan" is intoxicated by the prospect of eternity and descends into a kind of divine madness—an "Apollo rebirth," Bloom and Trilling reason.

Intriguingly, the 1941 Orson Welles vehicle *Citizen Kane* references the Coleridge poem in the "News on the March" scene of the film, depicting a newsreel announcing the death of Charles Foster Kane—Kubla Kane, Landlord of Xanadu.

Peart himself admitted to *The Guardian* in 2011 that he had not expected the phantasmagorical Coleridge poem to steer the song; he thought *Citizen Kane* would be his guide. It was, indirectly. In *Citizen Kane*, the hushed whispers of Shangri-La are expressed through the loss of innocence, represented by a sled dubbed "Rosebud." Its loss haunts Kane to the very end.

Is "Xanadu" about a snow sled? Not quite.

The concept of paradise is both horrifying and irresistible. Coleridge's description of a demon lover, deep chasms, and mighty fountains cry out for Freudian psychoanalysis. Whereas Coleridge seems to wallow in his inhibitions with, frankly, a crazed lust for life, Peart's words work primarily as a puritanical cautionary tale that never seems to shake its purgatorial tone.

Arguably, "Xanadu" is a natural extension of Eastern influence that captivated not only the Beatles but also the Byrds, the Yardbirds, the Rolling Stones, and others. Many pop acts in the 1960s (and later the progressive and fusion bands of the 1970s) hybridized Eastern and Western musical styles, and Rush distilled these desires. Rush's use of Moog Taurus pedals provided the requisite Eastern music-like drone, and this sitarish whine complemented Lifeson's volume-controlled single-note runs up and down the neck, courtesy of his Morley volume pedal. Wind chimes abound; tubular bells reverberate like Tibetan temple bells or meditative singing bowls and bring forth the perfumed winds of Shangri-La.

After the ambient introduction resolves itself, the song transitions into a rather restless 7/8 time. The guitar riff fades in, and, as if we were witnessing a slow zoom-in via camera lens, the summit of Xanadu comes into "view."

When the first verse kicks in (approximately 5:01), the zappy flares of synth are reminiscent of an Eastern instrument, a stringed percussion, such as a dulcimer. Lee's voice coolly ripples like river currents.

The lead melody, played by Lee on keys, coupled with Lifeson's arpeggioed riff, presents an interesting psychological study: The synth line is virtually the same throughout the song, but the sound carries with it a different meaning as the music unfolds. For one cycle, the synth mutates into a siren song, whereas in an earlier appearance, it seems chipper and much brighter and comports with the notion of Xanadu as a shining Utopian society.

It's quite interesting also that Peart chooses to play xylophone underneath Lee's siren melody. Although not stringed like the dulcimer of Coleridge's original poem, the xylophone is a struck pitched percussion instrument and seems to if not bolster then certainly complement the song's Eastern aspects.

When the music breaks down, it separates the narrator's initial optimism from the realities of immortality. This appears to be the beginning of the narrator's long descent into depression. Eventually, the narrator's status devolves from welcomed guest to eternal prisoner. Our seeker is stuck in "paradise," a black hole one could say, where he presumably is to live forever.

Again, musical ideas that once seemed benevolent now take on a sinister quality. In the chorus, when the narrator speaks about his anticipation of paradise, Peart's fill is relatively tame. But as the narrator becomes trapped, the chorus is reframed as a negative, and Peart's flurry of furious septuplets captures the intensity of the speaker's anger and growing madness.

Lifeson's barking final guitar solo evokes the narrator's longing and utter disgust. Beginning with guttural sounds, Lifeson dips into David Gilmour territory with screaming string bends and finger vibrato. Lifeson wades through murky water but then turns into a digits-flying speed demon. The passage soars to vast heights and dredges the depths of emotion—perhaps Lifeson's greatest solo of the 1970s.

Peart plays a march as the main character is resigned to accept an inevitable conclusion. A mass of sonic clouds—a heavy metallic rumble—reflects the narrator's tremendous inner turmoil. The final funerary pattern signals a finality to mortal life, a solemn march into infinite *undeath*.

In the final notes of the song, it's understood that the door to the narrator's fate has been irrevocably slammed shut. Peart plays essentially two flam triplets on the snare preceded and followed by a single quarter-note beat, suggesting order emerging from the fog of chaos, perhaps the narrator accepting his fate. Lifeson's riff echoes against, presumably, the walls of the caves of ice—reverberating forever.

Side 2 arrives as something of a relief: the thought of new life.

"Closer to the Heart" could be Rush's greatest acoustic—or best known—acoustic songs but also one of the band's most enduring tracks. As the song's lyrics suggest, "Closer to the Heart" is about finding the one thing in your life that means something. If everyone in society understands this and heeds their calling, it would lead to a harmonious existence for everyone.

The music seems to mirror this concept. The difficulty level or simplicity of each member's performance is irrelevant. It's how all the moving parts fit together. This is never more evident than with the live version that appears on *Exit . . . Stage Left*, which may be superior to the original recording, and underscores a heightened state of synchronicity existing among the bandmates.

"Closer to the Heart" responds to the existential angst of "A Farewell to Kings" and offers a compassionate solution to the division among the populace.

Peart teamed with band friend and Pacific Northwest poet Peter Talbot for the lyrics. It was a successful collaboration, but something never sat well about it. Peart did not work with Talbot, at least officially, again. One has to wonder why the creative dialogue ceased when the drummer himself admitted that Talbot forked over plenty of raw material for other Rush songs.

Peart would sporadically receive input from Pye Dubois in the 1980s (and the 1990s), as we will see, but the Talbot episode seems like a chapter cut too short—a red herring in movie terms.

If there had been another "Closer to the Heart" lurking among Talbot's ideas, how different would Rush's catalog—and musical direction—in the late 1970s and throughout the 1980s be? For that matter, had work with Talbot continued, would there have been a creative need to enlist Dubois?

"Closer to the Heart" was a minor hit for the band, primed for FM radio play in North America: It's a 4/4 tune with multiple verses, an anthemic refrain, and an elegant structure that allows Lifeson to dip into suspended chord phrasings for a hot second. (The song seems rooted largely around A major.)

Although it fell outside the Top 40 in the United States, "Closer to the Heart" was likely the only Rush song American listeners heard on rock radio circa 1977–1978 with the possible exception of "Fly by Night."

For the next track, "Cinderella Man," Lee took his cues from the aforementioned classic film *Mr. Deeds Goes to Town*. A tuba-playing poet Longfellow Deeds (portrayed by Gary Cooper) inherits a fortune and travels from his hometown of Mandrake Falls to the Big City, where slick lawyers, the predatory press, and high-society types prey on his philanthropic nature. When the papers dub Deeds the "Cinderella Man," he becomes a target of derision for the Big Apple's upper-crust cultural elite.

Although there's nothing musical, in particular, that connects the song to the film, Lifeson's (largely) major-chord strumming evokes traditional folk (maybe even Richie Havens's hard-slashing, revolutionary style) and the romantic image of traveling bards. And in typical Rush and *A Farewell to Kings* style, the song contains several time-signature changes with lots of bars in 3/4 and 5/4.

Tracks such as "Closer to the Heart" and its follow-up "Cinderella Man" often eat up the most oxygen when discussing side 2 of *A Farewell to Kings*, but "Madrigal" is as overlooked as it is enchanting.

Centuries ago, a poem set to music was referred to as a madrigal. But, for that matter, complex choral arrangements circa AD 1600 were also. Having said this, there's something about the instrumentation—the acoustic guitars and, ironically, the electronic aspects of the song, almost fife- or flute-like in timbre—that invokes European folk, chamber music, and the pre-operatic orchestral tradition. By titling this entry "Madrigal," Rush instantaneously provokes a subliminal response in its audience and evokes a time distant from our own, perhaps as far back as the Age of Exploration.

By its end, the song slowly dissolves into aural mist. A chirping synth melody and polite rumble of drums guide us through fade-out. Like the later "Witch Hunt" from *Moving Pictures*, this was a so-called production number, a song that pulled the stops in the studio and was never meant to be played onstage.

*A Farewell to Kings* concludes with the second-longest track on the record, the nearly ten-and-a-half-minute "Cygnus X-1, Book I: The Voyage." If "Xanadu" speaks to immortality, then, in its own way, so too does "Cygnus X-1"—even if audiences (and perhaps the band) weren't aware of this fact back in 1977.

"Cygnus X-1" begins with the ringing of "cosmic bells," followed by the voice of God (i.e., Terry Brown's glitchy, staticky voice issuing a divine transmission).

In the Rush biography *Visions*, Brown mentions that in order to create the space sounds necessary for the cinematic track, Alex experimented with guitar pedals, processing effects were used, and tape-delay loops were made, enhanced by feedback and panning techniques to create this immersive sci-fi atmosphere. Some of the wind sounds and the faint dink of tubular bells may be tape loops, repurposed from Peart's performance in "Xanadu." If so, then it's a subtle way of recalling bits we've heard earlier in the album's song cycle, creating cohesion and marking the journey from side 1 to very nearly the end of side 2.

The tubular bells also work nicely within the context of the song: they have spatial dimension and send images of strings of rippling dark matter resonating in the chasm of deep space.

The bass, beginning at 1:24, is the first real rock riff introduced in the track. Arguably, Geddy's riff represents the spacecraft, the *Rocinante*, that burns through cosmic debris and comes into view on its way to flying toward the center of the black hole—the star system of Cygnus X-1.

Geddy's bass bounces with a funky groove that wouldn't be out of place on an rhythm and blues/funk/soul LP of the era.

Lee's words "to soar" repeat and ascend in pitch, mirroring the pilot's hopes. There's a clear mood change as a major-key chord sequence following this vocal section lifts the spirits: the pilot is spurred on by his need to explore the unknown of space. But as the *Rocinante* flies through a cosmic wormhole, the music shifts again, this time to minor keys. Notes ascend as the pilot nears the edge of the black hole; the music accelerates at a moderate pace, heightening the intensity of the action and mimicking the speed by which the pilot is slowly drawn into the center—like a tractor beam clutching onto the hull of the *Rocinante*.

After a staccato rhythmic interlude (7:53) with the pilot at the cusp of the dual star system, the band bounces around in 11/8—a jiggery-pokery shuffle on the precipice of chaos, like a whirling, warbling dervish that never tips over.

By their own admission, much of Rush's education on odd time signatures had come from listening to some of the British progressives, including Genesis's twenty-plus-minute revelatory epic "Supper's Ready" and specifically the section titled "Apocalypse in 9/8." ("Cygnus X-1" does one, or in this case two, better than this.) Later, their ears became sensitive to the metric madness of jazz-rock fusion bands of the 1970s.

This math-rock funkiness certainly captures the spinning motion of the spacecraft as it spirals through the denseness of the Cygnus X-1 star system. Lee's shouting voice evokes the agony of the hapless star sailor who had embarked on this fatal voyage as he's ripped apart by the intensity of the collapsing star and, supposedly, crushed by a celestial vice. The narrator in "Xanadu" was spiritually crushed by white caves of ice and here is gripped by a massive "hole" of seeming nothingness.

Some critics skewer Rush's sci-fi rants as hopelessly dated by irrelevant subject matter, bordering on amateurish. But as the pilot of the *Rocinante* meets an untimely end gliding into a collapsing star, critical darlings Parliament or Parliament-Funkadelic introduced the people of Earth to their Mothership stage production prop, which descended on the public in the fall of 1976 and lifted off in 1977, touching down with a live album that spring.

Critics may not have gotten it, nor may they ever. But as we'll see, "Cygnus X-1" was integral to the band's next recording endeavor. The idea of rebirth is important to the two-part story and is as integral (if not more so) than it was to "2112." Like any original cinematic sequel, most observers could not have guessed or predicted what the next installment of the story would be. It's been said that even Neil himself had only a sketchy outline of the direction of the story.

The piece closes as a heartbeat softly pounds under Lifeson's stream of languid E-minor chords, leading us into the unknown. The lyric sheet simply reads, "To be continued."

This was a prog rock version of "Pictures at 11," or "Film at 11," an old marketing teaser designed to draw a TV audience for the late evening news. Just as important, *A Farewell to Kings* as a whole as well as its successor, *Hemispheres*, act as a warm-up act for *Moving Pictures*.

Durrell Bowman references Stanley Kubrick's and Arthur C. Clarke's sci-fi film *2001: A Space Odyssey* in his essay on this song, which appeared in the book *Progressive Rock Reconsidered*. It is indeed difficult to shake the space-age comparisons we detect between the pilot of the *Rocinante* and astronaut Bowman (not the author) entering the vortex of Saturn (and beyond) in the 1968 film.

Just as filmgoers often reported being spiritually transformed by Bowman's on-screen metamorphosis in *2001*, Rush similarly invites us to move through the astral door to another plane of existence.

What's on the other side?

In August, near the release of *A Farewell to Kings* in September, Rush performed dates in their native Canada and then embarked on what was colloquially known as the "Drive Till You Die" tour in September 1977, an almost nonstop trek through North America and Europe, through the end of 1977. Tallies indicated that Rush had played to nearly 1 million people in 1977 alone. Pockets of support seemed to pockmark the United States. A market that has been strong for the band since the 1970s and 1980s has been Texas.

From San Antonio to Dallas and Abilene to Austin, from Heyoka to current King Crimson member Pat Mastelotto and former Crim Trey Gunn, the Lone Star State has a track record of supporting and nurturing progressive rock. Rush's outlier status and independent spirit may have been something with which Texans identified. If for no other reason than Rush's unwavering commitment to the road, a large portion of the center of the United States, from north to south, seemed to respond to Rush in the 1970s.

The press in Britain, particularly *Sounds* magazine, dubbed Rush "heavy metal kings," and a newspaper review of Rush's show with UFO at the Memorial Coliseum in Corpus Christi, Texas, in October 1977 claimed the same. Rush was a driving force in the "rejuvenation" of hard rock (the newspaper actually used the phrase "heavy metal").

"My first exposure to Rush was *A Farewell to Kings*, which is still one of my favorite albums," says drummer Rick Colaluca, drummer for thrash band WatchTower, formed in Austin, Texas. "*Hemispheres* came right after, and I think that album was glued to my turntable for about a year."

Being buoyed by support soothes the troubled mind, but rock bands can easily fall prey to excesses abundantly available on tour. Combine this with attempting to play demanding music every night and being caught in a daily grind.

Just to give a taste of how grueling tours were in the late 1970s, Rush played nearly every day, except for five, in October 1977 alone, with many back-to-back-to-back gigs and single-night engagements largely in America's western, southwestern, and southern states.

Hard work, for sure, but Rush was sowing the seeds of future success. Rush earned a Juno Award and saw the release of the triple-album anthology *Archives* containing the band's first three albums, soon to be supported by a tour.

Cynics may have poo-pooed the three-platter extravaganza *Archives*, but the rerelease of the band's early material did serve its purpose in introducing records, such as *Caress of Steel*, to newer fans and offering Rush a pathway to repackage an entry they'd believed never received a fair hearing the first time around.

Rush was correct, one thinks, in issuing it. Just listening to the albums one after another, the combined impact created an escapist experience that recalled some of the auditory triumphs associated with the British progressive rockers' greatest achievements.

But the droning flatness of daily life on tour, visiting Anytown North America, took its toll. As 1977 turned into 1978, the band was still on road. Nevertheless, having endured a physically exhausting and possibly psychologically damaging endless strings of shows, Rush was quickly approaching critical mass. Sooner or later, the fog of war either needed to lift or would utterly consume them.

"We're only now beginning to make money on tour," Geddy told the *Montreal Gazette* in 1978. "Physically it's demanding; you can't keep it up forever."

Would their burning ambition, threatening to go supernova, disintegrate this shroud of monotony? Could Rush slip the noose around their collective necks and escape myriad dangers of the rock profession?

Rush largely rejected the hive mind mentality and collectivism in general and was honest about their earnest belief in hard work—two values they'd retained as middle-class guys.

By 1978, Rush's desire to exalt the idea of personal liberty catalyzed some in the music press against the band. Allegations of "fascism" have long been hurled at progressive rock by some in the press. "Fascists" or not, if nothing else, from the media's perspective, Rush had injected far too many sci-fi and libertarian tropes to ever be considered cool or politically correct for the intelligentsia. As soon as the press caught wind of Rand's influence on Rush and given Rand's preferences for unbridled capitalism over communism, Rush was an abomination. Rand was anathema to the political leanings of cultural gatekeepers, who saw themselves as the arbiters of taste and artistic impact.

The feeling had become mutual, however. Rand had despised the counterculture and its hedonistic tendencies, believing the communal aspects of the hippie Utopia ran in opposition to true human progress. A notable series of essays written by Rand and fellow objectivist Nathaniel Branden were compiled in a book titled *The Virtue of Selfishness*, in which the ethical code of human survival, or "rational self-interest," is discussed.

Barry Miles's noted interview with Rush in *New Music Express* in March 1978 was a flashpoint. Miles was well known in the London art scene, having run Indica Books and befriended Yoko Ono and Paul McCartney. He'd documented moments of invention during the creative height of the London underground music scene and birth of British psychedelia. So he was immersed in English subcultures of music and literary innovativeness but was on some level also familiar with the general gist of Rand's work. This isn't to say that he agreed with Rand's points of view. It's a circumstance that certainly set up conflict before the first interview question was ever asked.

Sparks did fly.

It wasn't so much that the journalist disagreed with Rush and their stance on free markets, individualism, Rand, the reasons for Great Britain's economic collapse in the mid-1970s, and so on as it was the asides shunted into the piece that were a bit jolting to the band.

In attempting to connect Rush's lyrics with Rand and fascism in general, the article compares Peart's words with signs hung above the Auschwitz concentration camp. When raising a question about the band's commentary on politics and economics, the article suggests that the band's positions ring in sympathy with "the 1000 Year Reich."

As has been noted, Lee's parents were Holocaust survivors. It's doubtful Miles knew this. Even if he had, some cynics might declare it irrelevant anyway. Still, had this point been brought up or explored, an open dialogue may have given way to a deeper understanding and a truce reached.

This was all happening against the backdrop of a populist revolt, mainly punk music in the United Kingdom and urban dance music in the United States. Perhaps on some level, the critics simply thought Rush *stunk*. Sensationalizing, even demonizing, a divergence of opinion may have been one method of dispensing with a band they believed wasn't worthy of much attention anyway.

Still, Miles wasn't alone. Other critics took Rush to the woodshed. The *Cincinnati Enquirer* was relentless in its attack, especially in a review of Rush's May 1978 show at the Riverfront Coliseum. Rush was known for its flash bombs, dry-ice stage fog, and pyrotechnics, and after such visually obfuscating and explosive displays, audience members lobbed fireworks toward the direction of the stage during "Lakeside Park" and "By-Tor and the Snow Dog."

Lee attempted to calm down some of the attendees, beseeching them to cease and desist to no avail.

"It's too bad Lee's request was ignored," read the *Enquirer*. "It was the only thing Rush did all evening that was worth listening to."

Did these critics really mean what they said?

I'd be lying if I said I didn't imagine an exchange with J. Kordosh, an author and journalist I wanted to contact for this book project. Kordosh penned the now infamous feature article/interview with Rush for *Creem* magazine, published in 1981, the same year *Moving Pictures* was released.

I thought it would be a lively discussion had we disagreed about Rush's art. But I wondered, with the distance of some decades, whether he had changed his mind at all about the band and its music. The first thing that sprung to mind before attempting to track him down was my salvo and the exchanges we'd have at the opening of our conversation. I'd describe my book project to him, and his biting humor might have coughed up the line, "My condolences. I feel sorry for you."

It would have been a great opportunity and may have even strengthened the case for Rush, depending on what Kordosh related to me. Unfortunately, I was informed by his son, also a writer, that Kordosh had passed away a few years ago.

Regardless of what Kordosh might have said, Rush seemed to operate by some Newtonian law of countervailing balance. With greater frequency, it appeared Rush was impervious to press attacks, perhaps even gaining strength and support for "fighting the good fight" in the face of such public ridicule, following the path blazed by embattled British progressive rock giants Yes, Emerson, Lake & Palmer, King Crimson, Jethro Tull, and Pink Floyd.

If the critics didn't hate Rush before 1978, they certainly would before year's end.

What was it that poet Robert Browning wrote: Man's reach should exceed his grasp?

If *A Farewell to Kings* was in no small part homage, then *Hemispheres* attempted to break new ground despite being indelibly tied to its predecessor. The next phase of the band's career commenced with the sequel to the cliffhanger record *A Farewell to Kings*.

After announcing that fans could expect more to the story, it became clear that adding a "Book II" to "Cygnus X-1" was not going to please everyone. This was a post-*2112*, *Star Wars*–era record after all, so it's perfectly understandable how many observers thought the continuation of the story would involve conflict on a planetary scale.

As late as the spring of 1978, Peart was still working out the details but had developed a concept based on a Dionysus/Apollo dichotomy—a battle between passion and intellect—that existed prior to the recording of *A Farewell to Kings*.

Peart had been reading financial markets writer Adam Smith's 1975 book *Powers of Mind*, which explores Transcendental Meditation, searches for links between intuitive knowledge and scientific observation, immerses itself in a sensory deprivation tank experiment, and investigates all manner of psychical anomalies and supposed breakthroughs of "astronauts of inner space."

The book also contains an extensive chapter titled "Hemispheres."

Inspiration didn't stop there. Peart reached back further into history to philosopher Friedrich Nietzsche, who identified two opposing forces that controlled ancient Greek life and mythology: Apollonianism and Dionysianism.

Educator, author, and Rand historian Chris Matthew Sciabarra pointed out in an issue of the *Journal of Ayn Rand Studies* that Rand rejected Nietzsche's concept that "reason and emotion are necessarily in conflict."

However, Rand didn't dismiss Nietzsche's philosophy completely, and she even applied some of his reasoning to the dichotomy of cultural surges shaping the 1960s (i.e., the "scientific triumph" of the Apollo moon landing and the "emotionalism" of the Woodstock festival, which occurred just weeks apart).

By the time Rush was ready to record *Hemispheres*, Peart made no distinction between NASA's golden moment and the event that virtually defined the hippie counterculture; he was "excited" by both impulses, he said.

Some critics maintain that winding down a space-age exploration saga with the deities of the Greek afterlife was less wormhole than rabbit hole. But the initial germ of the idea for "Cygnus X-1, Book II: Hemispheres"—individual human souls serving as battlegrounds for two opposing Greek deities who eventually come into balance—became a logical framework for continuing the story.

As we've seen with *A Farewell to Kings*, Rush's progressive rock instincts seem to sit at a crossroads. An academic narrative dictates that circa 1970, when the psychedelic music movement fractured, two distinct splinter groups emerged: heavy metal and progressive rock.

Author Edward Macan writes in *Rocking the Classics: English Progressive Rock and the Counterculture* that progressive rock represented "the Apollonian side of the counterculture: the emphasis on the spiritual quest, the critiques of contemporary society, the fascination with sophisticated narratives."

Macan described heavy metal, which we could extrapolate as encompassing all of "hard rock," as representing the Dionysian aspect of the divide—the sex and drugs and rock and roll of the equation.

This is a helpful guide, but we wish to add to this picture.

Intriguingly, modern neuroscientific research suggests that the brain is much more complex than tidy lateral specialization theories propose. Data and findings released by the Dana Foundation, a private organization that describes itself as supporting "brain research through grants and provides brain information to the public" (https://www.dana.org), goes so far as to claim that cranial functions aren't as compartmentalized as was once believed.

Other recent studies seem to indicate that the processes involved in cognition and speech and our ability to analyze speech require both of the brain's hemispheres to work in cooperation, not in isolation.

This cross functionality has a musical corollary in the amalgamated sound of Rush of this era, which, typically, cannot be identified as one style or another. Rush began recording in the post-hippie era, complicating our acceptance of the theory of the Utopian dream fracturing into two distinct urges.

Interestingly enough, Macan himself, in *Rocking the Classics*, references the eminent music scholar Gunther Schuller when discussing progressive rock as a "third stream" music.

What did he mean by this? "[M]usic that fused elements of two formerly distinct traditions to form a new style."

Macan also talked about how British progressive rock, at its pinnacle, "brings forth a new tonality, never before heard in either rock or classical music." In Rush's case, the two styles could boil down to hard rock and prog with classical flourishes.

Rush's art is a "third stream" music; it ultimately was about commingling and balance. To wit, this is further evidence that the insistence on separating the Apollonian and Dionysian is an outmoded notion.

"Rush, in a way, were like *Star Trek*," says Eric Barnett of Fred Barchetta. "There's even a Facebook group called Cygnus X-1 that combines the two. Progressive, intellectual, never 'cool,' but with a mystique that initially appealed to nerds and outsiders and self-described outcasts, especially teenage boys—a category I certainly would put my teenage self in. But unlike Yes and Genesis, Rush were hard rock, power and precision and volume and more unabashedly rock and roll, stemming from their roots as evidenced in their debut album—really, one could argue, the singular intersection of the power of Led Zeppelin and the more traditional progressive bands like Yes and Genesis. But even at their most progressive, they never lost their power, their hard rock roots, and this differentiated them in a way that I'm not sure any band before or after ever accomplished."

*Hemispheres* cemented the firmament, the conceptual foundation that made *Moving Pictures* musically, thematically, esthetically, and, dare we say, philosophically possible, not to mention inevitable.

To help bring to life what was the weightiest concept Rush ever imagined to date, Rush believed the best way to proceed was by scheduling a return trip to Rockfield— the groves of the British rock gods. They'd initially believed it would take only six weeks to complete the album top to bottom.

In a farmhouse not far from Rockfield, over a three- to four-week period, Lifeson and Lee coughed up new ideas and improvised a bit. They whittled down these musical parts and began to shape them into formalized songs. Nearby, Peart wrote lyrics, and Geddy scooped them up to see where and how these words worked within the context of nascent songs. Unlike previous records, Rush had very little written prior to entering their preproduction stage.

*Hemispheres*, 1978: Dense, intense, and ferocious. Rush at its most impenetrable---and cheeky.

Things appeared to be bright at the outset, but they disintegrated quickly. Geddy had an Oberheim synth built for him, but by the time it reached Rockfield, the delicate piece of machinery had malfunctioned—a harbinger of the sessions ahead.

In addition, the process of writing and getting the material production ready was becoming increasingly more difficult in direct proportion to the number of movements the band had added to the conclusion of "Cygnus X-1." Instead of wrapping in a month and a half in Rockfield as expected, *Hemispheres* was barely half finished in this time. Rush needed an extra four weeks to close the project.

Terry Brown admitted to me once that the recording process "didn't happen as easily as we had expected. There was a little more care getting the guitars, and the approach Alex took was harder to record. [It was] harder to nail performances."

According to a conversation I had with Brown, the studio time was quickly evaporating until the band was working in its final hour. They'd been watching the clock and fretting, and as the moments whittled down, it became apparent that the vocals wouldn't be tracked in Wales. With precious little time left, Brown and the band agreed to say, "Forget it." They were lucky to get out with their lives—and maybe one vocal performance.

"Ged was fit to be tied," Brown said.

The production shuffled off to Advision in London. Here, they thought, they'd wrap up the vocals and all the rest. Easily. But as the band was laying down tracks and ghosting vocals, it become apparent that something was wrong.

"We said, 'Is this possible?' The keys were all . . . ," Brown trailed off. "Ged was [trying to sing] about a semitone over his range on that particular record, and when we were doing preproduction, the vocals hadn't really been written at that point."

It was an oversight and not something that could be swept under the rug or "fixed in the mix" as they say.

It was never a question of performance: The boys were on a mission that anything they played in the studio could and would be reproduced accurately and faithfully onstage. Most of the album, at least the bed tracks, were done live, even a track like the instrumental "La Villa Strangiato," albeit in sections. Accounts differ, but it appears that the nine-and-a-half-minute track was broken up into at least two pieces when tracking.

The point is that the band never checked to see if Geddy could actually sustain his voice—raise it high enough—to accommodate the songs.

Geddy knew what *needed to get done* but couldn't seem to do it immediately. He'd falter, become angry, and lose patience. He and Brown were, at times, at odds. They traded verbal barbs. They disagreed. Both he and Brown had no choice but to stick with it and persevere—for the good of the record. Getting Geddy's vocal strained the team's intellectual problem-solving resources as well as their physical ones.

"He sang it," Brown told me. "Bear in mind: You didn't have [digital software] tools available. Now I could go in, cut the track a semitone lower, and make it sound amazing by the flip of a switch."

Lee had talked about how *Hemispheres* had chipped away bits of the band's soul. Parts of Rush were left in Wales, and recovering them would prove to be too painful.

"We had to fight for that one," Brown said.

For critics of Rush's previous albums, Lee's singing voice was grating and tanta-mount to shrieking. Here, however, few would deny there was a certain strength and confidence in the vocals, even if his vocal range could escalate at times well into the upper stratosphere. Maybe the need to just maintain control while tracking vocals curbed any wild adventures in exploring heliocentric pitch. With a little (read: a lot of) hard work, self-flagellation, arguing, and cajoling, the recording was done.

Initially, Rush and Brown had planned on mixing at Advision, but the time they'd carved out for the mixing process was being spent largely recording vocals. "We then had to book another session to mix," Brown said. "We flew home and then came back [to England] and got stuck with two more weeks of mixing . . . at Trident."

Brown admitted that while the recording was a "protracted situation," *Hemispheres* ultimately "ended up being a great sounding record. I think [the hard work] was a factor in giving the record its poignancy."

The first track, the eighteen-minute, multisectional "Cygnus X-1, Book II: Hemispheres" might be the band's most ambitious piece of music. There's good rea-son for this: Any song that traipses through the mythology associated with an ancient civilization's beliefs in the afterlife, is organized in accordance with Nietzschean phi-losophy, attempts to answer some of the mysteries at the center of black holes, and offers a front-row seat to the birth of a Greek god might just require more than a three-chord melody to makes its points.

"Hemispheres" opens with Lifeson strumming a suspended F-sharp chord. Lifeson forms the chord by adding an open B string and high E to the F-sharp chord, and voilà. Interestingly enough, Lifeson picks the notes of a related chord in the early goings of "Red Barchetta" from 1981's *Moving Pictures*. More about this later.

Although Jimmy Page had used similar chords for Led Zeppelin, particularly on "The Song Remains the Same," the F-sharp chord is known to the classical guitar world as well. Its usage became a kind of hallmark of Lifeson's style.

The eerie, unresolved quality of Lifeson's chord reflects an air of uncertainty. The flange effect applied to the guitar tracks creates swirls of sonic swishing in 12/8 time, evoking the circling winds of the cataclysmic battle raging just above the clouds in the mighty heavens.

"Prelude," the first of six movements, acts as a classical overture, introducing most of the musical themes we'll be hearing throughout the piece, either directly as stated or recapitulated with some slight variation.

A bass line and the introduction of synth ratchets up the tension. It's unsettling, and it funnels into a kind of military march, beginning at 0:30. (a Pentti Glan influence again?) Around the 1:00 mark, the band crushes it with a hard rock groove: the bass is booming and harmonizing, the guitar tone Lifeson achieves is horn-like in timbre, and Peart's beat is driving, underpinned by a rhythmic pattern involving snare drum and open hi-hat accents.

Guitar harmonics enter around the 2:00 mark, as Peart plays a triplet-based pattern on the triangle. This triangle pattern is transferred to the hi-hat and performed with big-band swing aplomb.

The use of harmonics and dramatic pauses, even the recapitulation of concepts, makes "Hemispheres" one of the most complex and busy Rush tunes to date but also quite impossibly one of the smoothest. Vocals are introduced at nearly three minutes (approximately 2:58–2:59), and Rush glides through times signatures 7/8, 9/8, and 12/8, recalling the opening tempo of the song.

The second verse of the opening section flips back and forth between 3/4 and 4/4, and this juxtaposition creates a cyclical effect mirroring the tension and conflict between Greek deities.

"Prelude" ends in bombast and with cymbal blasts as we enter the second movement, "Apollo (Bringer of Wisdom")." The fading audio and (near) silence do not detract from the coherency of the piece of music as a whole. Rush injected a pause in "2112" as we enter "The Temples of Syrinx," but the receding audio here is much more effective.

"Apollo (Bringer of Wisdom")" begins with the entire band performing in simultaneity, hammering away on the same heart-pounding riff first introduced earlier in the tune (just after the one-minute mark). At 5:22 the airy, heavily chorused F-sharp chord reappears.

In the third movement, "Dionysus (Bringer of Love")," we are introduced to a new character as gentle arpeggiated notes are juxtaposed with harsh electrified chords.

Interestingly, the sonics of these sections are very similar despite these characters being polar opposites. Rush *could have* created more points of divergence here to represent the yin and yang of Apollo and Dionysus, but developing more pronounced musical motifs to differentiate between the two deities might have been a form of overwrought caricaturizing.

By the fourth movement, "Armageddon (The Battle of Heart and Mind")," Rush uses minor and major chords to signify war. Then, at the moment when the conflict between Apollo and Dionysus rages, a surprising turn of events occurs. Our old friend, the pilot of the *Rocinante* from "Cygnus X-1," reappears, a circumstance announced by the reprisal of musical passages from the recorded performance of "Cygnus X-1" (at 11:49).

The fifth movement, "Cygnus (Bringer of Balance)," sees a shift in mood courtesy of minor-chord sonic textures. Minor keys transition into majors as our pilot, now pure spirit, moves from one plane of existence to another. Here, Geddy proves himself an effective interpreter, being cast in a (nearly) incredulous role of psychic energy. Lee is an effective communicator, however, not allowing the music to slip into schlock and utter absurdity.

Audio snippets lifted from "Cygnus X-1" drift across the stereo image. This squashed audio skates into our frame of focus, having been panned from side to side of the sonic spectrum. Its transistor-speaker quality projects a sense of time and distance, recalling the *Rocinante*'s harrowing journey into and apparently out of a cosmic wormhole.

The *Rocinante* pilot may have been eviscerated by a black hole, but here he is, an immortal soul, in this new dimension—the land of the eternals. He floats above the clouds, basking in the warm, amber glow of Olympus, like a scene ripped from Maxfield Parrish's vivid imagination. As he further surveys the heavens, he sees the ethereal plane and its inhabitants divided; he's horrified by the sight of war and emotes what is described as a "silent scream."

The deific squabbling ceases immediately.

The captain of the *Rocinante* proceeds to tell Apollo and Dionysus his story of daring. In conference, Apollo and Dionysus realize the error of their ways—or perhaps the futility of continuing to battle one another over possession of human souls. They agree to stop the violence, but a realignment is in order: they dub the mysterious stranger, the pilot of the *Rocinante*, "Cygnus, the God of Balance."

As the rumble of timpani and gong dissipates circa the seventeen-minute mark, an acoustic guitar emerges in the calming key of D. We've arrived at the sixth movement, "The Sphere (A Kind of Dream)." Lee's plaintive vocals stress the melodic core of this movement.

"Hemispheres" concludes on a D chord, giving the movement and, by extension, the entire epic a kind of "roundness."

Peart's lyrical summation of societal cooperation, pursuit of individual freedoms, and dream of attaining a practical balance between our passions and intellect, is a rational and humanistic end to an otherwise fantastical epic. Intriguingly, Peart seems to indicate that out of a chaos comes order.

The printed words of "The Sphere (A Kind of Dream)" do not appear in italics on the original lyric sheet. Previously, italicized words had indicated that the captain of the *Rocinante* was speaking. But for this final movement, these statements do not appear in a different font. They, quite literally, rest outside the Greek Gods story line while ironically acting as the song's Greek chorus.

Is Peart speaking directly to his audience here? By offsetting this final section both lyrically and musically, is Rush suggesting that a true balance of passion and intellect might be just out of our grasp?

By subtitling this song fragment "A Dream," we have to wonder if this entire episode was just that. Or maybe Peart is illustrating how the two sides of our personality, or two spheres of our brains, must intermingle to ensure the success of the species—which, actually, is in keeping with later scientific research into brain activity.

Flipping the original vinyl over to second side of *Hemispheres* and dropping the needle is like a kick in the teeth. We immediately hear the crunchy guitar riff and cymbal crash announcing "Circumstances."

For a song that is not even four minutes in duration, a lot has been packed into it. Jagged and deceptive in its flow, with time-signature change after time-signature change, "Circumstances" seems to work despite itself.

As the band had done for "A Farewell to Kings," the acoustic guitar passage for the next song, "The Trees," was tracked outside in the courtyard of Rockfield Studios. Lifeson picked up a nylon-stringed Epiphone, Neil used his woodblocks, and Geddy pressed the keys on a synth. The electric guitars were, of course, cut inside Rockfield with a Gibson 355 and a couple different amps—inside at a later time as overdubs.

Second only to "Cygnus X-1, Book II: Hemispheres" in its filmic qualities, "The Trees" lends itself to visual interpretation. An allegory about civil rights, using talking trees as its main characters, the song borders on comedic but manages to drive its point home. The Maples claim they are "oppressed" by the Oaks, who absorb most of the sunlight beamed down into the forest. The Maples undertake a campaign to appeal to the tree council to level accusations of fundamental unfairness.

After a wash of cymbals and chimes (1:45), Lifeson's arpeggios drift out like leaves being blown off branches. Lee's sleepy, evocative synth line carries us away to the lofty realms of the forest canopy. Peart strikes temple blocks—the pitch rising with each pair of sixteenth-note beats he lands. He slides down the sonic ladder, creating a kind of percussive conversation and evoking the sound of hollow wooden trunks being battered by a striking implement. It's a tiny forest-percussion symphony.

A portion of the middle instrumental section slips into 5/4, marked by Geddy's synth bursts and Peart's cymbal blasts. The piece sends chills up the spine as Peart plays steady quarter notes on the ride cymbal, offsetting them with surgical strikes on his crash.

Lifeson's almost bullhornish tone sets the tenor of the debate between two different classes of trees. The band glides over an odd-time section until the music pours out into pure minimalistic joy: Most of the bottom end of the ensemble drops out as Lifeson enters into a conversation with Peart, who pivots over to his rack of cowbells to play a descending sonic pattern, matching Lifeson's downward run. As Lifeson plays ascending notes and the bass drops out again, Peart matches these runs with patterns on his cowbells (beginning at 3:32), accenting these percussive patterns with his splash cymbal stabs.

The exciting exchange becomes more idiosyncratic with each round of call-and-response, as if these back-and-forth musical interludes were meant to represent the trees' open debate. Finally, in the last round of this call-and-response, Lifeson mutes his strings and reduces his riffs to single-note plucks; Peart responds with a series of pithy eighth-note beats on cowbells of descending pitch. It's bordering on cartoonish, harking back to the song's inspiration.

The final track on *Hemispheres*, "La Villa Strangiato (An Exercise in Self-Indulgence)," a multisectional instrumental recorded in different segments, has its roots in the subconscious visions of Alex Lifeson: his dreams.

Dreams often unfold without (seeming) rhyme or reason. So too, the sequence of the sections of this instrumental may not make logical sense to some observers since, by design, there was no overarching concept organizing the song.

One precursor to "La Villa Strangiato" is King Crimson's "Larks' Tongues in Aspic, Part Two," a similar hard-driving instrumental by an innovative progressive rock band.

If Crimson patterned the harsh rhythmic stabs of "Larks' Tongues" on Stravinsky's *The Rite of Spring*, then Rush's "La Villa Strangiato" and, to a degree, the later instrumental "YYZ" from *Moving Pictures* are *Street-vinsky*, inspired by the sounds of the world around (and within) Rush—from funk, hard rock, blues rock, and some might even say a bit of country thrown in for good measure. Other adornments are present, such as Spanish classical guitar, which synthesizes rhythmically incessant patterns and pulverizing displays of the band's technical dexterity.

To wit, the first movement, "Buenos Nochas, Mein Froinds," opens with, appropriately enough, flamenco-esque classical guitar, the residue of classical guitar lessons Lifeson had taken for a year in the early 1970s. The second movement, "To Sleep Perchance to Dream . . . ," floats into our ears as Lifeson picks arpeggios on electric guitar (in what sounds like some configuration of an individually picked C chord); glockenspiel (or orchestra bells) ring, and Moog Taurus pedals zap along to the atmospheric feel.

The music transitions into the key of A in the third movement, titled "Strangiato Theme" (approximately 1:59 into the track). Peart introduces accented sixteenth-note beats on the hi-hat in the previous section, but here he seems to lay into it. Open hi-hat beats mimic the rhythm played by guitar and bass. The crunchy main "Strangiato Theme" is stated on guitar, the fast attack of the main riff supported by bass and Moog foot pedals.

The piece begins to breathe a bit more in the fourth movement, "A Lerxst in Wonderland" (just before the 3:16 mark), with a shift to an F chord. This transitions into A only to return to F again as the music is bolstered by foot pedal synth notes (and possibly the addition of multiple guitar tracks). Lifeson injects A minor into the musical proceedings, lending the section its slightly sinister quality.

The wordplay of the title perfectly captures the hazy atmosphere of the music while reiterating Lerxst's important role in the song's creation. It sends us through a Lewis Carroll–like psychedelic rabbit hole, adding to the movement's mysterious aura.

Peart continues his sixteenth-note beat assault on hi-hats in 7/8 as the guitar wails an almost daemonic bluesy howl in 7/4. As the section further breaks down, Peart collapses the beat and essentially alternates kick note beats and eighth notes on his hi-hat. His right hand steadies a pattern up top (on the hats), and kick notes weave around these, clicking into one another like pieces of a puzzle. The accents and punctuation of all this seems odd (Rush *is* working in 7), and the patterns seem to threaten to burst into some kind of polyrhythmic alternate reality reinforced by Peart's feel. The fabric of the song almost seems to break down.

Lifeson's solo is stoked from the embers of a simmering instrumental, hinting at the flamenco style we heard at the top of the song. Before long, Lifeson's guitar whines like indigent cats wailing in a dark alley (3:45).

Lifeson admitted to *Guitar World* that his middle-section solo was overdubbed, but his initial scratch take was not completely eradicated: it can still be faintly detected in the final track.

"One of the things I think that sometimes gets overlooked with Rush is how much fun they had, how much they loved what they were doing, and their sense of humor," says Eric Barnett of Fred Barchetta. "I think Rush all along was doing what inspired them musically and lyrically, to the dismay of their record labels at time. I don't know that 'pursuing' is the right word—I don't feel like they ever had that kind of 'intention,' like, 'The next album needs to be more progressive.' It's just what happened when they came together, and it's that authentic nature of creation that I think is part of what the audiences resonated with, at each distinct period in their evolution."

"I think Rush were sincere in everything they pursued," says Kevin Aiello, drummer for Fred Barchetta. "Yes, they composed material to highlight their still developing chops, and they could get a bit overzealous at times—and they would admit it. Example: 'La Villa Strangiato,' an exercise in self-indulgence. I remember reading something where Neil said they were playing way over their heads on that one. As the years went by, the compositions didn't require that kind of playing anymore. They still had the chops, but the focus shifted to writing songs, which they became quite good at."

*Hemispheres* was released in October 1978, and by November, radio stations across America were adding cuts to their play lists. Portions of the record were being heard up and down the East Coast, from Hartford, Rochester, and Philadelphia to Tampa and Fort Lauderdale, and out to Detroit and perennial cheerleader Cleveland (WMMS), San Diego in Southern California, and Seattle and Eugene in the Pacific Northwest.

Within weeks of its release, *Hemispheres* went platinum (in Canada) and was well on its way to becoming gold in America when Anthem pressed the title onto red vinyl for the Canadian market, a trend popularized by Styx and Devo. In addition, at a run of 50,000 units, a picture disk of *Hemispheres*, the band's first in this format, would arrive on December 15.

By then, Rush had already embarked on a North American tour, rolling through major cities, that would last from the fall of 1978 into the winter of 1979, when the album had just missed *Billboard*'s Top 40, climbing within the Top 50.

Pleasing fans was becoming a bit easier. The challenge was convincing critics of the value of their work. Rush was still getting horrendous music and concert critiques. The review of the show at the Music Hall in Boston in January 1979 by the *Boston Globe* eviscerates the band for daring to introduce classical literature and mythology into hard rock and being "incompetent at it." Called "flash without substance," Rush was accused of, among other headscratchers, "legalized assault."

For one of the band's shows at the Palladium in mid-January 1979 in Manhattan, the *New York Times* proclaimed the band as being of the technically proficient but musically vapid "souped-up, neo-King Crimson" ilk. The writer did acknowledge, however, that fans came out in droves to see the band.

In the spring, essentially the first half of April and all of May into early June, Rush rampaged their way through the United Kingdom, Belgium, Sweden, Norway, Germany, Switzerland, and the Netherlands as headliners.

Throughout the North American and European legs of the tour, Rush received support from the likes of Cheap Trick, Head East, Molly Hatchet, Max Webster, and Ambrosia. Another band, Wireless, also on the bill, had evolved from the Australian group Autumn, a pop-rock band with flavor notes of jazz, folk, and soul. Guitarists Steve McMurray and Allan Marshall and drummer Glenn Beatson had relocated first to England before flying across the Atlantic to Canada.

After releasing their self-titled debut on Atlantic, Wireless was picked up by Anthem and SRO in Toronto. Manager Ray Danniels, after re-signing Rush to Mercury in 1977, negotiated a deal for Wireless for the American market.

"Wireless had been signed to a record deal before I had arrived," explains former Wireless drummer Marty Morin (Heat Exchange and Classic Albums Live), who effectively replaced Beatson. "When I joined, we signed a publishing deal with SRO, our management company. This was all under the Rush umbrella, so it was like a big happy family. Ray Danniels, the manager of Rush, just started putting together packages, with Wireless, Rush, Max Webster, and we would do a lot of shows together. Since we had a record deal in the States, it meant we could really start working there. I had been playing in clubs and stuff in the Ontario area, but when I got into Wireless, we opened for other acts in stadiums and arenas. Suddenly the production grew, and it became big business. Rush taught us so much about that and the responsibility of that. When they told you that you were supposed to be on at 8:30, you had to be on at 8:30."

The so-called Tour of the Hemispheres dates concluded on June 4, 1979, at the Pinkpop festival in Geleen, the Netherlands.

The run-up to the show was inauspicious to say the least: keyboard tech/programmer Tony Geranios (Jack Secret) broke both feet in a freak accident the day of the show, and Lifeson had bruised his finger the night before in a now infamous "bedroom" incident.

Yet if there ever was a moment that crystalized Rush's commitment to changing musical directions, it was the bill at Pinkpop. In short, it was a watershed.

They'd shared the stage with Elvis Costello, the Police, Dire Straits, Peter Tosh, and Average White Band. It appeared that they had glimpsed not only the artists who would shape the next decade but also many of the musical styles that would inspire their next moves. Rush saw bands with a different center of gravity playing modern music and being successful at it.

Rush's set, full of syncopated limbs and bruised fingers flying, included the likes of "La Villa Strangiato," "A Passage to Bangkok," "Xanadu," portions of "2112," and "The Trees." Even in 1979, it seemed a bit out of step with the fashions. What these bands were doing was a million miles away from Rush's twenty-minute "concept" pieces involving battling Greek deities.

We're reminded of the Ralph Waldo Emerson quote on conformity from his essay *Self-Reliance*: "Consistency is the hobgoblin of little minds."

To wit, continuing to write (rewrite?) major long-form compositions was the expected and safe decision and nowhere near the band's creative zone circa 1979–1980.

Punk's becoming more palatable had many effects, including giving way to a more refined and synthesized sound. The co-opted term "New Wave" now described techno rock from Britain, which inevitably led to a sea change in attitude toward this new sound.

"At the time I lived with Rhonda Ross, who worked at SRO and Anthem, and I became friends with Geddy and Alex," says Rodney Bowes, a graphic artist who worked on packaging for Anthem artists Aerial, Max Webster, Boys Brigade, and, later, the *Moving Pictures*–era Rush. "I was into punk rock, and Geddy and I would go to movies and hang out. We had a lot in common, and we both loved the Ramones, Blondie, Talking Heads, Richard Hell. A lot of that stuff. That was what we would talk about. Alex and I would joke around about the fact that I was not really into prog rock and more into punk."

Acutely aware of the populist message embodied by the New Wave movement, the Anthem label knew what time it was. In 1979, Anthem signed B. B. Gabor, a Hungarian-born vocalist who unleashed his Terry Brown–produced debut in 1980 on Anthem, riding the final tremors of punk's first devastating wave of cultural upheaval.

Prior to this, Anthem inked a deal with a Beatles cover band called Liverpool who had been signed to Danniels's label, Taurus. After their time on Taurus, Liverpool morphed into the band known as Aerial and released *In the Middle of Night* in 1978. Vic Wilson looked after them.

"Vic was a little older than us and could be a bit firm," says former Aerial/ Liverpool bassist and vocalist Brian Miessner. "Then, on the other hand, he could be one of the boys. Ray was harder to pin down. He didn't show as much of himself as Vic did."

Anthem label bands Wireless, Aerial, and, to a degree, Max Webster seemed to represent the future: a combination of New Wave with a symphonic or progressive rock edge. It's something Rush would come to perfect.

"I was a huge progressive rock fan," says Miessner. "I saw Yes live in Toronto, and I was listening to this stuff as it came out. It turned my crank. We had a keyboardist in the band [Malcolm Buchanan], and he liked the stuff too. I started writing this material with movements in them, musical movements. I wrote the bulk of the material, and then we had Gary O'Connor, more pop oriented, and he wrote 'Easy Love,' which was determined to be the single."

Hybridization may also help explain why hard-core Canadian progressive band Nightwinds, led by keyboardist Gerald O'Brien, never inked a deal with SRO—this despite talk circulating of the possibility of signing the Genesis-esque band with SRO.

"Rush were starting to take off at that point," says Miessner. "[SRO] were putting all their efforts behind Rush."

"Ray had a great team," says Mike Tilka, formerly the bassist for Max Webster and a one-time SRO employee. "Pegi [Cecconi], who took care of publishing, Tom [Berry] who took care of the label, Val [Azzoli] who helped with a little bit of everything, me on the management side. . . . We had an in-house lawyer, even. We had a great team. SRO managed Larry Gowan: he was, in Canada, huge. He wasn't on Anthem but CBS. SRO/Anthem was a really well-put-together, well-thought-out company. Having a huge band like Rush helps, too."

But how well prepared were Rush and their management for the coming decade?

# CHAPTER 6

# ^ ^ ^ ^WAVELENGTH^ ^ ^ ^

By Geddy's own admission, Rush had already passed through three stages of their development, claiming an identity (which they did with *2112*), reinforcing it (what the subsequent albums did), and accelerating their art to a third, symphonic/gadgetry phase in which they'd introduced more "machines and toys," Lee said.

Fancy equipment was still tethered to them, but we can extrapolate and determine that Rush had entered what we can in retrospect term their "fourth" phase: a streamlining of their ideas, which had been only implied in Lee's conversation with reporters at the time.

It was a pivotal point in the band's career, a struggle for survival to attain the proper headspace to accept musical changes at the dawn of the 1980s. Even if they threw off the shackles of progressive rock and pursued New Wave to the hilt, would the result be as artistically and commercially successful?

With renewed sense of purpose, recuperating from another grueling tour, Rush regrouped in mid-July and drifted up to Lakewoods Farm in Windermere in the Muskokas Mountains of Ontario to rehearse new material in an old farmhouse.

Lee and Lifeson swapped ideas in the house's main living area, laying down their nascent creations on a cassette recorder; Peart scratched out words in a nearby cottage, trying to piece together coherent stanzas. Whenever Peart was confident enough to show the band his lyrics, he'd walk the quarter mile or so to the cottage to personally hand deliver Lee and Lifeson his organized thoughts. These two creative factions exchanged ideas and began looking for commonalities, ways to fuse music and words.

In the basement of the old farmhouse, packed with gear, the three band members jammed on musical ideas. After an exhaustive initial run at the material and by the end of the first day, a patchwork piece was dubbed "Uncle Tounouse."

Over the course of the first few days, some of Rush's most beloved material, "The Spirit of Radio," "Freewill," and "Jacob's Ladder," took shape. Within a week, nearly the entire first side of the original LP and part of side 2 were in the works or near complete.

Producer Terry Brown found his way to Windermere and stayed only a few days, occasionally dropping in to check on the trio's progress. When I spoke with Brown, he indicated that he remembered brainstorming with the band and everyone offering suggestions for how a specific song should sound.

The material for the record came together quickly, but there was a false start or two. Peart had been working on lyrics inspired by an Arthurian tale from the 1300s, "Sir Gawain and the Green Knight," written by an anonymous author, supposedly from the English Midlands.

In the story, Pagan and Christian traditions intermingle, and the author stresses nature as something wild and eternal. The four-act romance fired the imagination of none other than J. R. R. Tolkien, largely due to the legendary fantasy author's fascination with Middle English. Rush had previously exhibited a deep Tolkien obsession, but at the dawn of the 1980s, reggae and skinny ties, not Hobbits, were hip. Clearly, the subject matter of this would-be epic was out of step with the band's Pinkpop revelation.

It was promptly dropped.

With the Gawain piece chopped, nothing existed to fill the void left by its omission. Peart was fresh out of lyrical concepts but holed up in the guesthouse, whittling away. He struggled for two days and then on the third, fragments of themes swimming in his brain for years, surfaced in the guise of "Natural Science."

In the Rush tour program for *Permanent Waves*, Peart had indicated that "Natural Science" contained bits of the doomed "Sir Gawain." It should be noted, however, that most sources do credit pieces of the abandoned multipart "Uncle Tounouse" with being the foundation of the track. "Natural Science" could include kernels of lyrical fragments from Gawain, while bits of "Uncle Tounouse" were repurposed.

Within two weeks, the writing was virtually complete, and the entire record was ready for demoing at Toronto's Sound Kitchen. Simultaneous with recording their demos, Rush prepped for a string of dates in August and scattered engagements in September in the United States, Canada, and the United Kingdom. Rush would perform older material and introduce "The Spirit of Radio" and "Freewill" to audiences. Road testing new material was something the band was slowly becoming accustomed to. They had, after all, performed "Xanadu" before the release of *A Farewell to Kings* to work out the kinks and gauge audience reaction.

On the road, there was discussion about where to record their next album. They'd flown overseas to England for the last two records, and being that *Hemispheres* was a nightmare to finish, they'd decided to stick closer to home. They needed a hideaway, a getaway, a place to focus—someplace comfortable.

But where?

If you've ever seen the 1993 movie *The Fugitive* with Harrison Ford, you know that the city of Chicago—or what passed for Chicago and the outskirts of the Windy City—became a kind of character of the film. In the story of Rush, *The Fugitive*'s musical corollary would be Le Studio for the making of Rush's *Moving Pictures* and the earlier *Permanent Waves*.

Tucked inside the Laurentian Mountains, sixty miles outside Montreal, Le Studio had opened its doors for business in 1972. Le Studio's remote location meant that Rush could get away from the madness, distractions, and noise of the city and concentrate on recording—and little else. When Le Studio owners and life partners André Perry and Yaël Brandeis fostered an atmosphere for the adventurous to retrieve their innermost visions, word got around.

"[Le Studio] had a different philosophy, and it was less about being a business," says Perry.

Bee Gees decamped at Le Studio for a portion of the *Children of the World* record and the *Saturday Night Fever* sound track, and by the late 1970s, a host of other artists had either recorded or mixed there: Ian Hunter, Cat Stevens, Chicago, Nazareth, Crack the Sky, Wilson Pickett, Starcastle (with Queen producer Roy Thomas Baker), and the Ramones, among others.

"Rush were always looking for a home, you know," says Perry, "a home like what the Beatles had with Abbey Road. By that time, by the time they came for the first time, we already had a reputation."

Le Studio was meant to function as another instrument. A musician and producer, in theory, could generate any sound he or she dreamed and not be hampered by men in white lab coats holding clipboards policing the recording policies of the studio.

"I couldn't accept the fact that we might be associated with a kind of 'sound,'" says Perry. "In those days, journalists would call us all the time and ask us about gear and how we achieve sounds. I would tell them, 'We use our "under the lake" echo.' It was just goofing off, you know? People started to call here and request the 'underwater' echo."

It seemed counterintuitive to downplay technical aspects, but Perry followed his instincts. Even the name Le Studio, nondescript as it was, signified a place in which artists and producers came to press the record button, let the tapes roll, and got down to business. Le Studio forged ahead with its innovative, nay, progressive attitude— one that complemented Rush's ever-evolving musical direction.

Having said this, the Bavarian-like wooded environs, the picturesque residential lake, and its vaguely French Canadian moniker lent an air of exoticism to the place. Le Studio had something intangible that was greater than the sum of its parts. And as Perry and Brandeis welcomed recording artists, Chef Andre Moreau of La Barratte restaurant prepared food for visitors.

During downtime, the band and/or members of the recording crew would paddle across the lake or play on the makeshift volleyball court set up just outside the cottage house—the band's living quarters for the duration of the recording. Most of these matches took place at night, so a temporary lighting configuration enabled players to spot the ball against the dark Canadian sky.

At the time, Perry had converted a barn into a video production suite equipped with cameras, and one of the band's techs, Tony Geranios (aka Jack Secret), hosted a mock late-night talk show type of program titled the *Jack Secret Show*. Secret would interview the cast and crew that made *Permanent Waves*. Some of the skits featured fictional scenarios involving historical figures.

"We once had Oscar Peterson's son playing the president of the United States," says Perry with a laugh.

Le Studio was insulated from the outside world in other ways. Despite a new-found focus on Canadian rock artists in the early 1980s, there was a dip in activity at the studios in the Great White North. The business was agonizing over an industry-wide recession, one that impacted not only recording studios but also record labels and retail outlets, leading to a decline in sales of LPs and cassettes in Canada. In addition, in the United States, the economic slowdown in the late 1970s spilled over into 1980. The value of manufacturer shipments increased even if the number of units shipped declined. In essence, the average retail price of LPs was slightly higher, but there was less supply, and fewer LPs were being released relative to years past.

Studios in Canada had experienced a dip in activity prior to 1979–1980, and some shuttered their doors permanently. Montreal had once been the site of the famous RCA/Victor recording studio, where one of Neil's early heroes, London

(Ontario) drummer Graham Lear of Natural Gas, all of twenty years old, recorded an influential drum solo in the song "Rameses I" live to an eight-track machine. But this facility closed in the late 1970s, signaling wasteland for the city but also opportunity for nearby Le Studio.

Le Studio seemed unaffected by these changes. Then, again, Perry never did the expected, even prior to establishing Le Studio.

Perry had been a musician himself and gradually developed his production and engineering skills through his travels in North America and Europe. Perry had also recorded 1969's "Give Peace a Chance" for John Lennon and Yoko Ono during the newlyweds' "bed-in" in Montreal in March 1969. The original audio recording from Room 1742 of the hotel Le Reine Elizabeth, Perry told me, was "absolutely terrible" prior to his production enhancements. "Everybody was screaming and banging on ashtrays. It was ridiculous."

Thinking it was time to have a more permanent and better-equipped physical base of operations, Perry set up shop in a converted church in Montreal, a sizable space that could accommodate a large orchestra if necessary. "I later sold that studio in Montreal and took a sabbatical for a year," says Perry. "I went around the world, worked in different places, in New York and Europe and England and went to Air [London] and did some productions there. Every time I saw something and it was great, I thought, 'I can do better than that.'"

After returning to Montreal, Perry's dream of owning a brick-and-mortar recording space had come to fruition. This was not going to be a basement studio. Nor would it be a facility that scrutinized every microphone placement by in-house engineers cloaked in white lab coats. Unlike some of the clockwork studios Perry had observed, he did not demand that the crew or visiting recording artist act in accordance with house rules or a tradition. Transparency was key.

Indeed. Perry took this idea to the extreme, one thinks, by defying conventional wisdom and installing large plate-glass windows in main recording area—something that was considered a no-no by studio designers. The windows overlooked the lake and the beauty of the Canadian wilderness—ricochet reflections be damned.

"You'd mentioned about the glass in the studio," says Paul Northfield, one of Le Studio's in-house engineers and lead recording engineer on *Permanent Waves* and *Moving Pictures*. "It is interesting because nobody has ever brought that up. It wasn't a particularly beneficial thing, other than being inspirational, because it was such a beautiful room to work in. Glass, generally, is not a great acoustic material in the studio because it is brittle and harsh for the cymbals. But the studio was big enough that [the effect of the glass windows] didn't overwhelm [the sound]."

Peart's drums would typically be positioned in front of this glass windows, offering a scenic view of the lake and woods just over the drummer's shoulder.

"Advision was one of the deadest studios I worked in, and it was also one of the first I ever worked in," says Northfield. "The philosophy of the '60s and '70s was control. As multitracking came along, you recorded everything independently, and then you add reverb to give you the most control. Great recording rooms were almost accidental.

"Morin-Heights was a beautiful studio with a reasonably live room," Northfield continues. "But not really that helpful for Neil's kit. Not earlier on, anyway, particularly his snare drum because he had it tuned very high, and he hit it very hard, and sonically it didn't really speak until you stood back from it. If you put a close mike on it, what you got from Neil's kit was [makes faint clunking noises]."

In a new studio environment, stressing a fresh perspective for their music, Rush knew this record was going to be different from the outset. *Permanent Waves* was a bridge, a necessary one for the band's long-term survival, connecting Rush's progressive leanings and synth-rock ambitions. Rush had made a conscious effort to shift gears out of the conceptual song phase and into something a bit more palatable to the casual listener and radio station programmers—all without throwing away the heaviness, detail, and complexity that made Rush music special.

Having successfully survived punk rock's onslaught through a combination of unflinching devotion to its hard rock roots and concrete support from a loyal fan base, Rush, as far back as 1979, had the blueprint for longevity. The title *Permanent Waves* was as much an indictment of popular thinking as a statement on the band's perception of its own music. Although Rush was quite taken with trends, they had decided that they would not be set adrift or swayed by them but rather would make music to last.

The band was condensing its creative approach but retaining some progressive elements from the mid- and late 1970s. They were honing their songwriting craft and tapping technology to facilitate more streamlined performances. Taurus pedals, for instance, could now control Geddy's polyphonic synth not only in the studio but certainly onstage.

"Rush used bass pedals and a thin string synthesizer that would gloss over the top and give them this slightly orchestral feel," says Paul Northfield. "If Geddy had departed from low-end rhythm section bass with the kick drum and started to do riff-ing with Alex, for something like 'Natural Science,' that kind of thing where Geddy is playing up the octave and doubling with Alex, at that point you have no low end. That is why they had bass pedals, so you could play the root note and hold down the bottom end so it didn't disappear."

With relative quickness, the band recorded the basic tracks for "The Spirit of Radio," "Freewill," "Entre Nous," and "Jacob's Ladder," which had been pieced together at sound checks during the late summer/early fall dates of the 1979 tour.

"Different Strings" was a chance for the band to embellish—a studio track that would be enhanced by overdubbing, including Hugh Syme on piano.

Although "Natural Science" is over nine and a half minutes long and "Jacob's Ladder" seven and a half, there were no long-form twenty-minute epics à la *Hemispheres*.

The first song to ever be recorded by Rush at Le Studio was "The Spirit of Radio," a homage to the Toronto radio station CFNY, the first to use the titular term as a kind of marketing slogan to separate itself from other radio stations in a media business becoming increasingly corporatized and conglomerated. David Marsden, who'd moved from CHUM-FM to CFNY, had thought up the phrase, "The spirit of radio."

"CFNY was a heavy alternative radio station," says Marsden. "I didn't have the best signal in the city and I felt I had to do something that was different, otherwise why would anybody tune us in? I needed a slogan, something that would sound cool. I was driving around one day and, I don't know, maybe a voice from some other place spoke to me and said, 'Spirit of radio.' I do not know where it came from. It just popped in my brain. I understand that Neil was listening to the radio and heard the phrase."

Demonstrating a world that could be, Rush shows how radio could reject corpo-rate interference and homogenized play lists and keep its integrity while broadcasting music of substance. The song's subtext contained some harsh truths about Rush. They had received very little airplay beyond "Fly by Night" and "Closer to the Heart."

"Even a station like CHEZ 106 in Canada, which I was able to get from upstate New York, they didn't play a ton of Rush material," says drummer Jason Sutter (Cher, P!nk, Chris Cornell, and Marilyn Mason). "At the roller rink, around the U.S./Canada border, you'd hear 'Fly by Night,' and it got played in Canada and a little bit in the States, but it was not enough to put them on the map."

It's ironic, then, that "The Spirit of Radio," issued as a single backed with (b/w) "Circumstances," did get into rotation on stations across Canada and the United States, just missing Top 50 on the *Billboard* Top 100 singles chart.

Juxtaposing different styles of music in one song, Rush used "The Spirit of Radio" as a vehicle to re-create the sensation of a listener scanning the radio dial—or finding one station courageous enough to spin records of different genres.

Somehow it all works: progressive rock flourishes, a section in faux reggae, programmed percussive/flutey synth patterns, rock and roll–style piano thumpin', Peart's groovin' performance interspincing propulsive Latin-esque ride cymbal patterns, timbales adding further "ethnic" seasoning, orchestral keyboard percussion lines, out-and-out hard rock bashing, a juggling act of numerous odd times, and halting jazz-rock fusion rhythmic staccato stomps.

A flanged guitar riff opening "The Spirit of Radio" carries a bit of distortion. Lifeson pulls off from the strings, creating the rapid-fire notes that charge the riff with absolute electricity. The famous stuttering rhythmic pattern opening the song is a good example of what Rush had referred to as a "flying brick"—a term employed to identify a lockstep rhythmic pattern the band plays in simultaneity. It was so dubbed because even the band admitted to not always knowing exactly where the beats were going to land.

The guitar is in 4/4, but the syncopated fills, rife with sixteenth-note triplets, move through several time signatures, including 5/4. Those who heard Rush for the first time with "The Spirit of Radio" were changed forever by perfectly timed yet (what seemed to be) randomly placed notes. The rapid-fire series of bass notes and flams and triplets that Peart uses were a revelation for some.

Intriguingly, Paul Northfield indicated that when recording the vocals for the chorus of the song, the idea went up to put a flanger on the entire track. Apparently, there was some sort of technical malfunction regarding the flanger unit, and as a result, a barely perceptible trail of distortion chases Geddy's vocals for a section, adding a brittleness to the sound. The audio artifact imitates the sound of music emanating from a handheld transistor radio.

Guitars were wall to wall. There were as many as three guitar tracks per channel—left and right—making a total of six guitar tracks on a single song. This recording approach was true for both *Permanent Waves* and the later *Moving Pictures*. More about this later.

Rush keeps up the intensity level with the second track, "Freewill." It's cerebral, yes, but also quite kick-ass. The odd times, sizzling and scintillating riffs, the philosophical take on individual freedom, and Geddy's high-octane (and just plain high) vocals made "Freewill" foreign from everything else on the airwaves at the time.

But what is it about? Victimhood for starters. Peart seems to indicate that personal choice is a key in escaping an overwhelming feeling of helplessness. We are perhaps not fated to be—anything. We ought not shrug our shoulders and hand power over our lives to superstition or some misguided belief in fate.

The independent spirit professed in the lyrics matches the variety of fierce sonic textures. Much like their British progressive rock heroes, Rush balances a level of collective interplay with individual expression. After the opening riff, Lifeson plays arpeggios and, during the verses, mixes arpeggios and strummed chords. Lifeson cranks it up again (1:32), transitioning from picked chords to full-on strumming, following in the footsteps of Pete Townshend, who had practically perfected what could be classed as "lead strumming," powered by his windmill arm calisthenics.

Geddy's bass solo highlights how well Peart and Lee communicate as musicians. If progressive hard rock ever had a groove, it's this. Synth overlays on top as Geddy's bass foreshadows the upcoming vocal lines.

During Lifeson's rippin' guitar solo, chords mix with single notes until the transition into the last verse, which leads, once again, to arpeggios. Alex's frenetic picking in 6/8 gives Peart safe passage to let loose with something resembling early funk metal—a performance not a million miles away from what Billy Cobham had been doing with Mahavishnu Orchestra. Neil is all over the kit, accenting with crash cymbals, opening and closing the hi-hat while striking the top cymbal, and bashing away at the China.

Side A concludes with "Jacob's Ladder," which, on paper, would seem a disjointed nightmare to perform. Let's discuss the lyrics first. Peart fuses some of his favorite themes: the elevation of the human spirit and the power of natural phenomena. The deceptive title has some thinking that it's biblical, but this is untrue. Peart was fascinated by weather patterns, and it was Geddy who offered the name Jacob. Anyone who has seen light beams projected through a billowing cloud onto the ground floor below can attest to the fact that it seems—and feels—otherworldly. The weather system hovers just above us, so close you can touch it. Yet it seems to float in the heavens. So, in a way, there's a certain level of divinity in "Jacob's Ladder," just not in the way we might believe.

Peart echoes the musings of nineteenth-century traveler, nature writer, and avid tree climber John Muir. A self-professed "poetico-trampo-geologist-botanist and ornithologist-naturalist," Muir, among his other passions, listened to the "Aeolian music" of storm winds whipping through the Sierra wilderness, harmonizing with the play of sunlight in the forest. Peart too documented the rare alignment of natural phenomena and perhaps, like Muir, believed that "nature conveyed to him sacred revelations," wrote Fred D. White in the introduction to a compilation titled *Essential Muir*.

"I love to go hiking in the woods and dream of being a forest ranger," Peart told Steve Morse of the *Boston Globe* in 1982. His position as both a nature observer and a nature enthusiast is also one that Peart maintains in "Natural Science," the closing track of *Permanent Waves*, but also extends to *Moving Pictures* in his lyrics for "The Camera Eye."

The final image of columns of light cutting through dark clouds convey an episode (or episodes) of mental clarity—brief moments of enlightenment and spiritual transcendence.

Musically, the boys beautifully capture the ethereal setting through a veritable symphony of light and sound: atmospheric distant rumbles meet a thunderous, dirge-like rhythm of orchestral percussion. As light breaks through the dark clouds, shimmering synth tones and Geddy's celestial voice echo as if emanating from the skies above. The toll of tubular bells and twinkling keyboard percussion signal an unveiling; the low tones of Moog Taurus pedals evoke the ominous qualities and awesome power of a developing storm system.

"Jacob's Ladder" takes a simplistic idea but infuses it with the complexity of nature and its grand designs—designs, yes, but sleek in their operation and function. Cyclical patterns, typical of African or other so-called world or Eastern music, abound as Rush tiptoes ever so slightly into contemporary classical genre, or minimalism, popularized by the works of Philip Glass, Terry Riley, LaMonte Young, and Steve Reich. Musical passages birth fractals, replicating and reflecting nature's mathematical beauty.

At the opening of "Jacob's Ladder," Lifeson frets and then picks a C–A♭–F–G–A♭–E chord progression, as the notes flick back and forth between alternating bars of 5/4 and 6/4. Lifeson's arpeggios are met with Peart's faux march containing just a faint hint of a rudiment-based, New Orleans syncopated second-line snare drum feel.

When vocals are introduced, bars of 4/4 do arise, but the meters change frequently and furiously during the extended instrumental section. A measure of 6/8 is followed by one in 7/8. Mirroring the rhythmic repetition, Lifeson's chords (or the notes he picks in those chords) modulate between repeated measures in D and F# (until an E chord makes an appearance). The music then moves from D to E to F# (for two measures) and then to D, E, and F# again for the grand finale: the rapid-fire "flying brick" section.

"The end part of 'Jacob's Ladder,' where Neil kicks back in grooving to Alex's single note odd rhythm part . . . I think it's 6/8-7/8, or some might count it as 13/8," says Brian Tichy. "That's some of Neil's craziest playing because he barely gives you a sense of where '1' is and just plays around the riff with no true 'backbeat' for most of it. He avoids the '1' entirely on the kick here and there as well until he settles into a simpler rock beat. But he's also giving us part of his trademark ride pattern as chord changes come in."

The liminal nature of this rhythmo-muso experience loops us into some other headspace, precipitating metamorphosis. Not some elaborate psychical trick or sleight of hand based on mathematical pulses, this section is a catalyst to opening doors of perception.

Peart once pointed to Peter Gabriel's "Solsbury Hill" as a great example of smoothing out odd-time feels." ["Solsbury Hill" is] in a long seven pattern, but all the casual listener feels is the quarter note pulse," Peart told *Rhythm* magazine in August 1988. "Odd time is not truly 'odd'; it has a lilt to it, a flow, a human cadence."

"I love odd times," says Rick Colaluca, "especially ones that involve some sort of polyrhythmic aspect and juxtaposed with 4/4 gives it a hypnotic feel. Rush was there in the beginning to help us gain an appreciation and feel for odd times."

The only drawbacks about the instrumental section of the track are that Rush didn't feel compelled to introduce it earlier in the song and that it was not extended beyond its current length, thus (slightly) truncating the hypnotic effect it induces in the listener.

Side B is like the dawning of a new day. The windows are wide open, a gentle breeze puffs through, and sunlight floods the room. Largely a major-key statement on the complexities, synchronicities, and fragilities of relationships, "Entre Nous" is the sunlight dispersing the billowing strati and cumuli that blanket "Jacob's Ladder."

Either through conditioning or cultivation, we remain largely isolated and/or mysterious to one another, or so say the lyrics. When we do make connections, they are like rare occurrences of celestial alignment. We retain, even if tenuous, gravitation pulls on our significant other but must leave space for personal growth. We are a part and, yet, apart from one another.

Lifeson's magnetic storm of chordal tones brilliantly electrifies the sonic foreground and coincides with the phrase "brief eclipse" (circa 1:00). Both acoustic twelve-string and electric guitars provide a cushiony foundation for Geddy's vocals.

Initially intended to be titled "Between Us," the English-language translation of the French phrase "Entre Nous," the entry was released as a single in the United States and Canada b/w "Different Strings." A May 1980 edition of *Billboard* magazine had bestowed it the honor of a recommendation, but the single never made much of a dent in the charts, never breaking into the Top 100. It's best remembered now as a slightly overlooked album track.

The flip side of the single and the following song on *Permanent Waves*, "Different Strings," is a typical Rush production number on par with "Madrigal" and "Tears" before it.

Considering that the song is a kind of dance between the listener and creator (infrequent Rush lyricist Lee), it seems wholly appropriate that it opens in 3/4 time, a traditional tempo for a waltz. Using fantasy elements as metaphors as a reflection of the distance that the music maker has traveled whence he came, the song also measures the space between artist and audience.

Lee seems to be talking directly to fans who have played Rush records as a sound track of their life for the last five or so years and have remained loyal, even in the face of critical ridicule. Rush was signaling that their music has gone through stylistic changes. Will the audience come with them on this next phase of their careers?

Hugh Syme's understated contribution on grand piano can't be understated. Reminiscent of Dire Straits from the same period—1980's *Making Movies* and *Love over Gold* (1982)—Syme's jazziness adds a layer of iciness that helps chill this song.

The half-time feel propels the music forward almost in slow motion, and the mood Lifeson conjures with sustain, which becomes audible approximately at 1:34, is like a psychedelic ray gun, a slice of progressive hard rock on an alternative plane—one from which "The Necromancer" had sprung. Even though this song was never intended to be reproduced live, we can't escape the visual it paints: a trio in a dimly lit nightclub, a silvery spotlight cutting through the darkness and highlighting the guitarist. It's simultaneously intoxicating and sobering.

At one point, Brown had suggested the band speed up the pace, but this was rejected, most overtly by Peart. This surely would have destroyed the sonic smokiness of the track. However, Neil accommodates the request on one level by nicely accompanying the half-time bars found in the music with cracking snare and spindly sixteenth-note hi-hat beats, seemingly paddling against the rhythmic current of the track.

By the time Alex's slow-burn guitar solo hits peak, the guitarist embarks on a barking, bruised, rabid, reverberating, and raw metallic tear (beginning at 3:09), sending the composition into another realm, practically devoid of time.

We arrive at the final track a bit woozy.

"Natural Science" is a nine-plus-minute track composed of three movements: "Tide Pools," "Hyperspace," and "Permanent Waves."

This tri-panel musical kaleidoscope, marked by bursts of dynamic shifts as well as changes in mood, feel, and arrhythmic audiovisual content, complements the brevity, diversity, and immediacy of "The Spirit of Radio." Assisted by the studio techniques, enriched by found recordings, the song roams from atmospheric art folk to progressive hard rock and even, dare we say, electronic experimentation.

Lifeson's twelve-string acoustic guitar passage opening the song is drenched in reverb, as if echoing off distant rocky cliffs along a shoreline. Lots of suspended chords here, and Lifeson even drops an occasional minor, invoking a sense of longing—we are lost in both the lush and the languid. This ebb and flow, major/minor, soft and rugged, come at us like waves rolling toward a distant horizon we never quite reach.

The repetitive, hypnotic seven-note guitar riff (in 7/8) at the opening of the second movement, "Hyperspace," reflects the currents of time and cycles of life and death, picking up on the visuals present in Peart's lyrics.

Neil kicks in with the drums in a kind of pre-echo of the funky 7/8 pattern he'd play one record later for the synth section of "Tom Sawyer." The accents are not the same, but Peart plays single-handed sixteenth-note beats on his hi-hat, giving the pattern a similar feel. The pace of the "Hyperspace" section and "Tom Sawyer" is in the average vicinity of 160 beats per minute.

The famous swirling "time warp" vortex, opening at 2:19, can be interpreted as humans entering a new technological age—teleporting through a wondrous cosmic window foretelling the technological future or dragging us into an inescapable spiritual quagmire of our own creation. Interestingly, the electronically manipulated sonic "vortex" prefigures the cyclonic noise opening "Tom Sawyer."

Peart warns us that invention and the application cuts in both beneficial and sometimes detrimental ways. It is not our disciplines—art, science, and so on—that need to be tempered but rather our own nature as human beings. Interlacing and overlaying concepts of nature, conservation, and scientific (if not human) progress, Rush manages to spin a multiverse of musical and lyrical concepts.

The "most endangered species," what Peart calls the honest man, can help himself and the world through a reverence of nature, art, and science as well as his vigilance toward its wayward ways.

Much of this boils down to balance, a crucial concept tied to the success of the band's next record, *Moving Pictures*. The very title of the track, "Natural Science," seems an attempt at fostering a harmonious coexistence of human beings and their systems of observation and nature.

As the song closes, the sounds of the tide rolling in (and out) speaks to the cyclical nature of life. It evokes the earthworks/art piece *Spiral Jetty*, conceived by Robert Smithson and completed in 1970 in Utah. "The Jetty already suggests and anticipates its own ruin," wrote author and philosopher Gary Shapiro. "Clearly, Smithson intended the work to embody a number of themes and topics concerning entropy."

Creation, erosion, destruction, and rebirth, nature reclaiming what was once its own, a permanent wave.


## TAPEHEADS AND ERASERHEADS

With recording completed in November 1979, Rush flew to Trident studios for two weeks of mixing, where the finishing touches had been done for *Hemispheres* a year earlier.

Adam Moseley, one of the assistant mixing engineers on the album who had also worked on *Hemispheres* (uncredited), remembers the sessions: "*Permanent Waves* was the first time I got to sit with the grown-ups at the big table. I sat at the console, on the left, and had the first ten faders, with my hands on them, and Terry Brown was next to me. Then on the right side of center was Geddy and then Alex. Shoulder to shoulder. You could barely get three chairs across [the console]. I had not understood what mixing involved up to that point. I was mystified."

Knowing when to act and when not to was an art in and of itself. "We sat at the console and mixed 'The Spirit of Radio' in sections, getting the second part of the intro, the main rhythm or rocking rhythm, when it drops in, and we might spend four or five or six hours, the four of us, organically performing on the faders trying to capture something on the faders—or not capture something," Moseley says. "I was, of course, as an assistant, scared shitless of screwing things up. For each [playback], everyone was exploring their faders and their 'sends' and . . . trying to find a different moment or different spatial or magic balance between the components that had been recorded, just to bring this whole new level of purpose out of the notes."

At the time, the late 1970s and early 1980s, Trident was well equipped to bring spatial dimension to the projects recorded there.

"At the original Trident, in Soho, where the Rush and U.K., the Bruford solo albums, the Kiss albums by producer Mike Stone were done, the first floor was one floor above street level," says Moseley. "That's where the mix room was, and the floor above that, the second floor, had been gutted. The building had an amphitheater and some offices. They gutted the floor and were going to build more offices or production rooms, but it was never done. The second floor of the building, the whole length of it, was an empty shell. So, what we used to do was re-amp drums. We had a pair of huge JBL speakers on one end and position them slightly facing away from one another, just like a rack of toms.

"When it came time to mix," Moseley continues, "we would put the speakers up in the floor above us, the empty shell, pump the drums from the mixing desk through to the speakers above—we did this on the Rush records as well—and then have a pair of 67s or 87s that we would move closer to the speakers or further away to create a tighter ambiance or big reverberated kind of sound."

No one at Trident could have guessed, however, that by setting up a microphone array in an empty chamber, they'd capture sounds both natural and, perhaps, even supernatural.

"We had speakers and two mikes open up there, and even though no one was up there we could hear someone or something moving around," says Moseley. "The minute you heard the handle turn and thought you would catch someone up there, the noise would stop. On some records they even thank the Trident Ghost—TG—for letting the album going without any weird unexplained technical problems."

Having said this, engineers of the time had to acquire an almost supernatural knowledge of the music being recorded—sometimes having to recall it in real time.

"As an assistant, doing all the punch-ins, you had to learn the solos as the solos were being constructed," Moseley says. "This went across the board: if Alex was playing a solo . . . and played a lick, it might have a note that overhangs and goes over to the next backbeat and hits a harmonic, you had to learn what had been played in the moment. It would be, 'Back [the tape] up. After this note, drop in. I have something else I want to try.'

"You had to anticipate your punch-ins and anticipate your punch-outs and not clip anything," Moseley continues. "You had to memorize what had been played only a few seconds before and know the tape machine. You pretty much knew every note that was [recorded] and why and the reasoning behind it and the alternatives that didn't work."

Rush had come under the spell of the David Lynch movie *Eraserhead* around this time, and the descriptions of some of the scenes haunt Moseley's psyche.

"They would not stop talking about it," says Moseley. "They were freaking me out about it, and every day they would talk about the character Henry in it. I also remember that Alex used to like to cook. I got into Trident as a chef, and they knew that. During mix sessions, if Terry and Geddy were working on something, Alex and I, we would go up to the kitchen on the fifth floor and cook a meal and compare recipes.

"On the two albums, one of the most fun things is there was a fantastic French restaurant in West London in Shepherd's Bush, and at the end *Hemispheres* and *Permanent Waves*, we went out to dinner," Moseley continues. "It was always mellow and focused . . . and drinking forty-pound red wine, and then they would bring the brandy out, the Otar brandy."

Moseley recalls that when Rush blew off steam, it might have been the cleanest fun he'd witnessed in the rock world.

"They were staying at a hotel, a private hotel called the Montcalm, and after some red wine and Brandys, when the dining room was open, they had a food fight with some finger food, and it was the politest food fight I had ever seen," says Moseley. "It lasted, maybe, three minutes before they realized that they were being a little out of control. That's compared to working with Rod Stewart, which was the most out-of-control record I've ever been on."

*Permanent Waves* was very nearly ready for prime time. The title of the album was intended to be "Wavelength," the cover for which was to feature graphic images

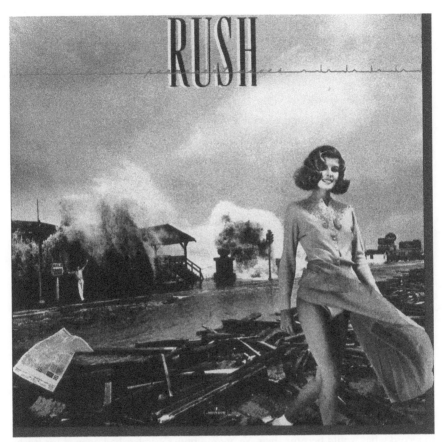

*Permanent Waves*, 1980: Rush made music to stand the test of time.

of electrocardiogram readings for each member of the band while exerting themselves recording in the studio.

The cover image is a montage in the Hipgnosis tradition, created by art director Hugh Syme and photographer Deborah Samuel, using the Galveston Seawall during Hurricane Carla in 1961 as a backdrop. Model Paula Turnbull, with windblown skirt and Donna Reed perm, is spotless despite the carnage literally raining and flowing all around her.

"I started shooting photographs of bands when I was in college," says Deborah Samuel. "A friend of mine who was at the same college needed shots done for his band called WhistleKing, and because I was a photography student, he asked me to do it. They got an album deal, changed their name to the Kings, and needed an album cover. That was kind of how it started for me.

"I was a huge Hipgnosis fan, both Hugh and I were," continues Samuel. "I would stare at 10cc covers for days, you know, figuring out all the nuance. Fin Costello was a photographer in London, and I think he came over to shoot the guys. Then Fin went back to London, and Hugh said, 'I need you to style this girl that's going to be on the cover of *Permanent Waves*.' I used to do fashion as well, so I fashioned the girl on *Permanent Waves*. Then Hugh asked me, 'Can you help me put this cover together?'"

*Permanent Waves* was complete, but Rush had little time to pontificate about this. Moving forward was the only way to progress.

"I received a phone call from Ray Danniels one afternoon, and he said, 'Our new album is coming out tomorrow,'" David Marsden says. "I said, 'That's great. You want to give me an advance copy?' He said, 'No. I just want to tell you that we're going to call one of the songs on the album, 'The Spirit of Radio,' and I know that's your phrase. Do you have any problems with that?' I said, 'I'll take three points on the album.' No, I didn't say that, but I wish I had. If you ever get hold of a vinyl copy of Permanent Waves, you should look at the run-off groove. The catalog number for the Anthem label version of the album, which is 1021, was etched on there. CFNY's frequency was 102.1. The band brought up a copy of the album and we discussed the fact that we can't tell people that it's about a real radio station because other radio stations won't play the album. Come to think of it, I wish I would have asked for five points."

In December 1979, just before Christmas, the Anthem label band Wireless was set to record what would become their *No Static* album. Wireless had opened for Rush, most notably as reported by *RPM* magazine, for a sold-out performances on New Year's Eve 1976 and a few days later on January 3, 1977, at Maple Leaf Gardens' Concert Bowl in Toronto. (Chilliwack also appeared.)

"We went into Nimbus 9 in the Yorkville neighborhood in Toronto, famous because Peter Gabriel had been working there and Alice Cooper had done hits there," says one-time Wireless drummer Marty Morin. "We were assigned a producer by the name of John De Nottbeck. He had made some recordings with Max Webster. We knew right away it wasn't working. We spent about a week and had done a lot of bed tracks, and, again, we just weren't getting what we wanted out of it.

"At that point, we had done a number of shows opening up for Rush," Morin continues. "We had become pretty close to Geddy in particular because he and his wife Nancy lived in our neighborhood in Toronto. We decided that he would produce it and that we would go to Morin-Heights [Le Studio] with Terry Brown and

Geddy Lee and do this record. About two days before we were supposed to leave for Morin-Heights, December 10, suddenly there was a problem."

Brown had been looking for certain commitments from management, but apparently they were never met. "At the very last moment, Geddy decided to do it himself," says Morin. "We used Paul Northfield [recording engineer], who'd been working with Rush. We had done a lot of rehearsals before this, and we were ready when we went into the studio."

With Geddy, Wireless had a second crack at recording the album and refining their double-axed Aussie-styled American southern rock/funk/pop/prog style. "The whole recording of that album with Geddy was easy," Morin says. "There wasn't a lot of rearrangement when we came into the studio. We paid a lot of attention to the double guitar sounds.

"Geddy would put in long hours," Morin continues, "and Paul Northfield, who would wave the white flag, and say, 'OK, I give up. We have to stop.' We would go for hours."

"[Geddy] was always pushing everybody to do the best he can," former SRO employee and future co-CEO of Atlantic Records Val Azzoli once told me. "I used to executive produce for Rush [in the 1980s], and Geddy would say, 'Is that good? Is it great?' I would say, 'I don't know what great is.' So he would spend the next three days on the mix. You know what? It was better."

"When I heard about Geddy's parents, then it was all understandable," Morin says. "I thought, 'OK, that's where the drive comes from.' When we would have conversations sometimes, late at night, he would say his parents told him, 'We didn't go through all of this for you to screw around. There was a responsibility to become successful. This is why we are here.' That taught me a lot."

Witnessing Geddy work firsthand, Morin had a newfound respect for Rush and its band members.

"Neil Peart was proud of the fact that he never visited the band's office," says Morin, "but Geddy was the driving force that thought, 'OK, these are the tours we are going to do.' Whether or not you liked Rush, there was no denying that the machine Rush—the Rush machine—was incredible to witness."

If it wasn't obvious by late 1979, Rush was composed of three strong, often distinct personalities. Geddy, the organizer or face and literal voice of Rush; Neil, the perfectionist-conceptualist; and Alex, the impulsive Trickster. He can be lethal but also unpredictable; his spontaneity an inspiration to his bandmates.

"Geddy seemed to have two sides," Morin says. "I say this in a good way. There was one side hanging out with us in the studio. He was, and I say this in a nice way, 'a typical goof.' We could joke around. Nobody was into alcohol or drugs. We had beers and stuff, but there was no abuse. We were all working together, and it was loose and easy. But every once in a while, he would say, 'Look. I have to do an interview. Someone is coming to the studio,' and he would suddenly change. He had to become the spokesperson for Rush. He would become very serious. Methodical."

Morin had also received a front-row seat for some radical shifts in Geddy's life. "We were right in the middle of session, and suddenly his wife called," Morin says. "He had to take his call—this was before cell phones, and he had an odd look on his face. We said, 'Holy Christ. Everything OK?' He said, 'Nancy just told me that we are going to have a baby.' He freaked. But I told him that I had just had a baby. He was born in September [1979], so my son was about three or four months old at the time. I bought a pair of little baby booties and gave them to Geddy. He tied it to his belt loop, and he wore those booties for the rest of the session."

By the following summer, Geddy and Nancy would welcome Julian, and all three members of the band had become fathers.

"Those baby booties were always around, even if they were on the board, you know?" says Morin. "They reminded him they had a baby coming. As anyone is when they are about to have a kid, you are apprehensive. I said, 'You're going to love this.'"

The place? The Palladium, a music venue in New York City. The date? May 8, 1980. *Permanent Waves* had been released on January 1, and Rush had been on the road since mid-January, having made their way through the United States and eastern Canada watching the record go gold in the United States, platinum in Canada, and silver in the United Kingdom." "The Spirit of Radio" had hit the Top 40 in the United States, and *Record World* touted the song, as the album's "intricately arranged," a "prime cut."

At the Palladium for Rush's four-night stand, Cliff Burnstein, who had been so instrumental in the band's early success, was listening to the band's next plans.

Rush was feeling their oats: They became the first rock band to sell out, for a four-night stand, the 12,000-seat capacity International Amphitheatre in Chicago, and they were burning it up in the Northeast and the East Coast. They were confident in the strength of *Permanent Waves*, and now they wanted to cap off a great if tiring run with a live record issued, marking their evolution as a unit.

Maybe this was the time to let the tapes roll and sift through them at Le Studio and compile a live album before they sunk their teeth into the red meat of a new studio album.

"What do you think, Cliff?"

The response: "Are you guys nuts?"

*Why issue a live album, the province of the creatively depleted?*, Burnstein quipped (or something along these lines).

This likely wasn't the feedback Rush wanted to receive, even if they probably half expected to hear it. Rush had the resources, energy, ideas, and momentum; they were getting airplay like never before, and addiction and musical burnout weren't ripping through the ranks. *Why whittle away all that capital on material that has been already released in one other form or another?*

It's likely the band had already been thinking about recording a new album. Further, it was gut instinct that commanded them to see their next career move from a different perspective. The story goes that it was Peart who put the bug in the ear of the other guys. Maybe they should rearrange the plans they'd sketched out for the next two years?

"Something got into Neil about doing a studio album instead and the more he thought about it, the better the idea seemed," Lee told *Music Express* in 1981." He brought it to us, and Alex and I started getting excited about it."

In retrospect, could an industry insider, A&R man, radio personality, or manager ever truly tell Rush what to do? The fact is that Rush was working on new material already during sound checks on the *Permanent Waves* tour, and it did appear that serious consideration was given to recording this new music.

"We were all so fortunate that they did make this decision," says Paul Northfield. "It was the energy of the moment and fact that they got momentum after 'The Spirit of Radio,' and they wanted to try to capitalize on that. They already had the seeds of things, and they tended to go away and write together and . . . during sound checks a lot of ideas come together."

However, Rush still had weeks of touring to do. Helping ease the pain of the five-month-long mental and physical slog, the tour became a consistent sellout, including for headlining shows in which Rush had no opening act.

Mike Girard, lead singer of the Fools, formed in Ipswich, Massachusetts, what Girard calls the true birthplace of the American Revolution, remembers sharing the bill with Rush a few times in May 1980. In his book *Psycho Chicken & Other Foolish*

*Tales*, Girard points out that the revolution occurred in 1746, when Massachusetts coal miners demanded better working conditions. A certain amount of defiance in the Fools' approach carried on the legacy of the rebellious forefathers of America, especially considering that their song "Psycho Chicken," a spoof on "Psycho Killer" by the Talking Heads, was clucking about on radio and generating a buzz.

"When we played 'Psycho Chicken,' [Geddy] stood at the side of the stage, and my memory of it was that he laughed at the appropriate times," says Girard, who intimates that the Fools started their own label, Ouch!!!. "I did not ask if he enjoyed it, but it was rare for headliners, unless the openers were their friends, to be watching you from the side of the stage like that."

Rush had decided when they became headliners that they were not going to harass, hinder, or harangue opening acts on their way up the success ladder.

"Geddy was such a regular guy," Girard tells me. "They seemed like real people. I was stunned that they held the door until we finished our sound check. I thanked them for it after, and [Geddy] said, 'We went a little longer than we thought, and of course, you guys have to get a sound check.' I can't remember if we talked to Geddy or Neil, and my memory was that they were matter of fact about it: 'Of course, you do that.' It really speaks to the band being unaffected by the trappings and retaining their humanity through that."

Although they'd abandoned the idea of releasing a live record as their next title, the band did not cancel their scheduled recordings at venues in the United Kingdom. Rush toured Britain through June, playing nearly twenty dates, making stops at the Hammersmith Odeon in London as well as in Glasgow, Scotland, and Manchester and Newcastle, England.

The *Philadelphia Inquirer* quoted Geddy, who reported that ten dates on this tour were recorded. They'd get tucked away for later use. The band's June 4 through June 8 shows at Hammersmith were later made available with the fortieth-anniversary reissue edition of *Permanent Waves*. Only "Jacob's Ladder" was culled from a mid-February show in St. Louis, Missouri, at the Kiel Auditorium.

Finally, it was time to record in the studio. Rush had come off the road, had a few weeks to decompress, and near the end of July was back at Phase One Studios in Toronto to track original material.

The thing was that it wasn't their own. Instead, Rush was fulfilling a bargain that had been made years ago.

Max Webster had been kicking around the anthemic "Battle Scar" for years, and now they'd finally decided to include it on their upcoming record, *Universal Juveniles*, to be released on the Anthem imprint in Canada and on Mercury in the United States. Geddy had made it known to Max front man Kim Mitchell that if the band had ever decided to cut the track in a controlled environment, Rush wanted "in."

"That song was one of the first originals we ever did in Max Webster," says bassist Mike Tilka, who took a job working for Rush's management company after his exit from Max Webster. We played that live a few times, even before the first Max Webster album came out. It was a really old song. Max was touring with Rush, and Max would do it at sound checks because we used to jam on it during sound checks. The guys in Rush, mainly Geddy, really liked that tune."

While it is unclear if this specifically happened during "Battle Scar," when Max Webster opened for Rush on live dates, Peart would play along with drummer Gary McCracken from underneath the tarp covering his considerable drum set.

Now Peart got to do it when it counted, as the red light was on.

David Greene, already a Toronto recording scene vet by 1980, was the engineer for the session. Greene had extensive experience tracking music and sound in general in and out of the confines of the studio.

A native New Yorker, Greene began his career in the Big Apple but worked on the West Coast and in Canada, including on the session for the Guess Who's 1969 blue-eyed soul ballad "These Eyes"—RCA's first stereo 45-rpm single and a Top 10 hit in Canada and America, which was produced by future Max Webster producer Jack Richardson. Greene was gaining experience in leaps and bounds but always felt he was an "Eastern Time Zone kind of guy," he says.

As the malaise of the 1970s was just beginning to infect us, mind, body, and soul, Greene accepted an offer to work at Toronto's then new Manta Sound studios in the early 1970s.

Over the next decade, Greene moved from one extreme recording setting to the next, becoming one of the premier engineers in the city and in Canada.

Prior to the sessions for *Universal Juveniles*, Greene had recorded what many believe to be the first digital rock recording in Canada—progressive rock band True Myth's self-titled debut.

Earlier, Greene had worked with the Toronto-based band Heat Exchange at Manta Sound. For the heavily effected voices in the song "Four to Open the Door," Greene devised a plan. "It involved snaking the audio tape around the room at Manta Sound, creating a twenty-foot loop that eventually found its way back to the tape deck," says former Heat Exchange drummer Marty Morin (Wireless). "We were all holding the tape [loop] at different places to keep it tight. I loved the result of doing that."

Greene had also accompanied jazz/experimental artist Paul Horn for a three-night stint in Egypt for the 1977 release *Inside the Great Pyramid*. Horn, a Transcendental Meditation instructor, had released the popular 1968 LP *Inside* (recorded in the Taj Mahal). With Green in tow, Horn braved the unknown to capture sound wave frequencies interacting with the geometric structure of the pyramids—to great meditative effect.

"We had no idea what we were going to face," says Greene. "What we did know was that when you get into the King's Chamber in the Great Pyramid, you had to go up a crawlspace that was three feet high and four feet wide, and I can't remember how many feet long. We had to carry all the equipment through there. It took about twenty minutes just to get to the chamber.

"The pyramid was illuminated by fluorescent lights that buzzed," continues Greene. "Once we got in there, we had to have them turn the lights off. We actually bought a box of candles from the hotel, and they were similarly well made: they sputtered and made noises from time to time."

So setting up two different rock bands in a single studio and capturing them simultaneously wasn't exactly going to throw Greene—or producer Richardson for that matter—for a loop. Both had been there, done that.

"Rush is only three guys and Max is only three guys, but Max had Terry Wilkinson playing keyboards on that one song," says Greene. "I cannibalized the other studio at Phase One and dragged their twenty-four-track recorder into my studio, so Rush was on their own twenty-four-track. For Max, we were using the same twenty-four-track that we'd used for the whole project. We couldn't tear everything out and set up the studio in a different configuration for this one song.

"It was live with both drummers, Neil and Gary McCracken [Max Webster], and everybody playing together," Greene continues. "The vocals were only a guide at the time. You can't get that feel any other way, other than live."

Did Peart have his full kit?

"Neil never went anywhere without the whole nine yards," Greene confirms. "It is just part of what he did, whether he needed it or not. We did it to a click track, from what I remember, a digital metronome. We basically set aside one day to do this one track, and we did it in about five or six hours. We already had a pretty good setup and sound on Max Webster, and it was just a matter of getting Rush and the guys comfortable with the setup and making sure everybody can see, hear, and feel. That's the key to recording. If they can hear properly and feel properly, then it makes the engineer's job so easy. I learned this from my mentor Phil Ramone: give the players the space and what they need in order to play and then let them do the work for you. They will."

It was a smashing success on more than one level: Peart reported that the joyous noise and crash of percussion shook the studio walls of Phase One with "a Wagnerian tumult."

"I'm sure it had bits and pieces changed, and it pretty well got rejected by every producer we worked with," says Mike Tilka of the song he once performed. "I don't mean that in a negative sense. People like it because it is an anthem, Rush is on it. Try to listen to it and pretend it is not Rush or Max Webster or a big production with two drummers and the grooviness associated with the production value . . . and it's an okay little tune. Personal taste changes immensely because it's Geddy Lee singing, and there are two amazing drummers, and everybody is amazing on it."

Although "Battle Scar" became a cult favorite, it effectively became an appropriate swan song for a band on the verge of breakup. When Rush brought Max Webster on the road with them in 1981, guitarist/vocalist Mitchell had grown tired of being away from home and exited the tour, leaving his band members without a front man.

A report from the American South indicated Max were a no-show for that particular night's performance, and by mid-April 1981, a spokesperson for the band announced that Max was canceling the rest of its tour dates. Two weeks later, by the time Rush was winding through the South before traveling north through Ohio and the Northeast, it was a forgone conclusion: Max Webster's dissolution was inevitable.

Kim Mitchell would later appear on the Anthem label, but Max was a dead duck. Of all the bands Anthem signed, it's likely Max Webster was the most underrated. "All I have to say is that right after Kim won a Juno in 1983 for Most Promising Male Vocalist of the Year, Anthem dropped him," says drummer Paul DeLong (Kim Mitchell and FM). "Thank God that Tom Berry decided to start Alert Records."

Ironically, the session proved crucial to the development of Rush's forthcoming record, one that would catapult them to unprecedented heights.

Pye Dubois (aka Paul Phillip Woods), Max Webster's lyricist, was at Phase One to witness both bands banging away at "Battle Scar," partly there to witness spectacle and partly to pass along his lyrics to Alex, Geddy, and Neil.

It was a calculated risk. Max's Kim Mitchell said Dubois knew "virtually nothing about music," he told the *Ottawa Journal*. "He's saying turn left, here, and turn right there, and I'm thinking in terms of musical concepts."

As it turned out, Rush was fans of Dubois' poetic, psychologically deep, and experimental lyrics and intrigued by the prospect of collaborating. Dubois had kept notebook tablets full of his poetic scratching—the contents of an active mind spilled out across page after page—and handed Peart some of his lines. Specifically, there was a piece titled "Louis the Lawyer," which Peart later deemed a work in progress. Under development or not, Peart knew Dubois had something. Perhaps he couldn't put his finger on what exactly, but it had something. A certain swagger, mystery.

Peart kept the lyrics in the recesses of his mind—his psyche's back pocket, as it were, for possible use on Rush's upcoming studio album.

Audiofile's Delight: Original Master Recording release of *Moving Pictures*

**MUSICVISION** ™

# Rush

### Through The Camera Eye

**8 Great Songs including:**
Subdivisions
Distant Early Warning
Tom Sawyer
*Never Before Seen:* Afterimage

**RCA/Columbia Pictures Home Video**

**VHS** Hi-Fi Stereo

*Through the Camera Eye*: This 1985 VHS collection features videos of "Tom Sawyer" (live) and "Vital Signs," directed by Bruce Gowers, and filmed at Le Studio, Morin-Heights, Quebec.

Making Movies: Rush at Le Studio. *Photo by Yaël Brandeis Perry*

Geddy Lee with double-neck guitar—late '70s musical firepower grandeur. *AF Archive/Alamy*

Alex Lifeson (left) and Geddy Lee blasted concert attendees with both barrels during live renditions of their classic epic, "Xanadu." *Pictorial Press/Alamy*

Rush prided themselves on flawlessly recreating their studio records for live audiences. *Pictorial Press/Alamy*

A Rebel and a Drummer: Never much for crowds, Neil Peart nonetheless gave his all, every night. Seen here on stage, in Hamilton, Ontario, Canada, July 2013. *Zuma Press/Alamy*

Geddy Lee on the Time Machine tour, 2010. *Zuma Press/Alamy*

Alex Lifeson and Rush return to *Moving Pictures* for the Time Machine tour, 2011. *WENN/ Alamy*

On a Raft: Neil Peart on Lake Perry outside Le Studio, in Quebec, Canada circa 1982. *Photo by Yaël Brandeis Perry*

On the Cusp of Stardom: Rush, pictured here in Seattle in 1980 on the Permanent Waves tour, won many fans in the Pacific Northwest. Note the *Eraserhead* movie button Alex Lifeson (left) pinned to his lapel. (Alamy Seattle Center) *Alamy*

# CHAPTER 7

# COMING ATTRACTIONS

## THE CAMERA EYE, PART 3

He's a keyboardist, drummer, all-round musician . . . a musical genius, really. Let's call him Darrel, to protect the innocent and not-so innocent.

Darrel had listened to, played along with, and been weaned on a steady diet of the Beatles, the Who, Led Zeppelin, and a few dozen other rock bands from the early to mid-1970s. In short, he knew his shit and could reproduce this music rhythmically on a drum kit or melodically with a keyboard.

One afternoon, a few of us were sitting around listening to music when my brother put on two records: *Permanent Waves* and *Moving Pictures*.

Initially, as the needle dropped on the *Moving Pictures* vinyl, Darrel attempted to keep up with the rhythmic pattern Peart was playing. Within minutes, he was lost. It wasn't so much that he couldn't play what Peart was doing (eventually, as an older drummer, he certainly could) but rather that he had never heard anyone approach playing the way Peart had. It wasn't backbeat stuff. These patterns were built on concepts. They told a story.

This was earth-shattering: Darrel could do nearly everything with and knew nearly everything about rock music. And yet here was something else.

In those days, everything seemed fresh about music and Rush. Even the packaging seemed strange and wonderful. Those portraits of the band on the inside dustcover sleeve, the only images of the band featured on the entire *Moving Pictures* packaging, were somewhat reminiscent of the Jimmy Page rainbow wand–waving vignette in the concert film *The Song Remains the Same*. These portraits seemed to present photographic evidence of the band possessing certain superpowers—the guys bending or commanding space and time.

In retrospect, some observers might liken them to multiarmed deities of Eastern origin. Whatever your interpretation, the images are striking and unforgettable, and we can all agree that their holographic properties capture motion.

That's what it felt like back in the early 1980s: Things were moving fast, and this was the sound of something different, new, challenging, and even dangerous. For Darrel and many of us like him, the paradigm had radically shifted.

The Canadian rock scene in the 1960s and 1970s could be described as a network of connections, a kind of Six Degrees of Ronnie Hawkins. This includes Rush and coproducer Terry Brown. Let me explain.

The Arkansas transplant had shown great talent for seamlessly moving between rootsy Americana styles and was being groomed by Roulette Records as the next Elvis. Hawkins rebuffed these advances, left the American South, and instead settled in the Great White North, cutting his own path through the music world.

Backed by his band the Hawks, later known as The Band, featuring Robbie Robertson and Levon Helm, Hawkins became a seminal figure on the Toronto night-club circuit, having shaped the careers of numerous artists and the music scene along Toronto's Yonge Street in the 1960s.

"Ronnie Hawkins had a rockabilly style from the late 1950s and early 1960s," record industry vet Frank Davies once told me. "Ronnie was a great coraller of musicians. He just knew how to put players and bands together. The Band met Dylan and up and left for Woodstock, much to Ronnie's chagrin, because his incredible band had gone, and he then started putting together another group. It was really that group that was the focus of my coming to Canada the first time, March 1970. He said to me, 'Would you be interested in running a record label that we would co-own?' Being whatever I was, twenty-three at the time, and itching to make records and produce, I had already moved from EMI to Liberty Records in London but saw a long climb to be anywhere I wanted to be. A couple of months later, I came to Canada, and I started recording the album with his backup band, which was then called the King Biscuit Boy with Crowbar. I formed the Daffodil label around them, and they then split into two acts short thereafter when the King Biscuit Boy, Richard Newell, went solo. I made a deal with my alma mater, EMI, which was Capitol in Canada—the first label deal, to my knowledge, for a Canadian company of any sort in this country with a major. It was sort of groundbreaking, although I didn't think of it that way back then. A year or so in, I had bought out Ronnie because he had signed to Atlantic to have another solo career shot. Jerry Wexler signed Ronnie—it was going to be a big revival of his rockabilly past, and they made a record down in Muscle Shoals [Alabama] and in Florida. Ronnie had no time to help build a record label in Canada. Then he and Ritchie Yorke, an Australian journalist, had gotten involved in the John Lennon peace effort because Richie had developed a relationship with the Beatles and their office in London. Ritchie got to know Lennon pretty well earlier on. When Lennon came to Canada, Ronnie Hawkins put him up at his ranch house out in the country near Toronto. Basically, at that point, I became the sole owner of the company and continued on signing artists and putting out records."

Crowbar's 1970 debut record, titled *Official Music* and credited to King Biscuit Boy with Crowbar, was recorded at Toronto Sound and engineered by none other than Terry Brown. So it is no surprise that in August 1980, Rush descended on Ronnie Hawkins's very own Graceland—a compound at his Stony Lake farm.

Tales from the band's time at the Hawkins farm have passed into legend: Alex's remote-control plane dinging the top of Hawkins's truck and Terry Brown, with his model sputtering out of control, needing to let the motorized aerodynamic toy run out of gas before he could safely grab it after it came to rest.

"They were gluing model airplanes on the dining room table, and the caretaker, Terri, who was looking after the house, came along and said, 'Oh, my God,'" says Wanda Hawkins, Ronnie's widow.. "Paper had to be put down so they wouldn't destroy my table."

When they weren't spinning the blades on their whirlies, the band was making serious progress on the album, having hunkered down to write most of the components of what would become songs such as "The Camera Eye," "Tom Sawyer," "Red Barchetta," "YYZ," and "Limelight."

Sequestered, Peart would pen lyrics back at the farmhouse while Alex and Geddy hammered away at their ideas in the barn. Nightly, the trio reconstituted, applying Neil's new lyrics to the framework of the intended songs. Before *Permanent Waves* and *Moving Pictures*, this was virtually unheard of.

In the past, the band wrote sweeping, lyrical, steamroller hard rock, marked by jarring flare-ups of jagged odd-time tempos. This was a new decade, however, and Rush sensed something on the horizon. Time-signature shifts were still present in Rush's musical language, but the tracks had to evolve into something more centered on groove.

"In the past we've often used many time and tempo changes around a chord sequence we liked," Peart confirmed in the Rush Backstage Club newsletter in August 1982. "This time we wanted to resolve the note structure around a good, strong pulse. This made for some interesting developments in the style and substance of our writing."

"It always bothered us why we could enjoy listening to music with steady feels and few changes and yet couldn't write it for ourselves," Lee told *Music Express* in 1981. "I think in the process of attempting that, we learned it's not so easy to write something simple. It was a difficult adjustment for us."

The material seemed to be both expanding and contracting, rooted rhythmically and yet growing dynamically in different directions. Like cold air mixing with warmer air, a spinning tornado of creativity developed rapidly, and these supercells of musical energy could barely be contained. Each song had developed a whirlwind, ripping a path rarely traveled by the band but devastating in its own way. These spiraling juggernauts helped bolster a theme that the band had discussed in the past but had never made an organizing principle.

These shorter songs (on the whole) were quite deliberately cinematic, more so than Rush's previous material. *Moving Pictures* slipped the noose of sonics to ascend into the realm of the audiovisual, as if each track were composed as the musical equivalent of mini-movies.

Now, let's take a step back.

A link also exists between the band's present sound (circa 1980), psychedelia, and classical music's tradition of conveying images/colors with sound—a concept that dates back at least to the nineteenth-century romantic period of classical music.

Phil G. Goulding discusses "tone color" in his book *Classical Music: The 50 Greatest Composers and Their 1,000 Greatest Works*: "Romantic composers thrived on the relationship of music to painting, literature, and nature, which they sought to express in various ways in their works."

Fast-forward more than 100 years, and who would deny that psychedelic rock was the production of hallucinogenic experimentation as well as the reexamination of social mores? Whether it was the Beatles, the Beach Boys, the Rolling Stones, 13th Floor Elevators, Pink Floyd, Love, or Grateful Dead, psychedelic music, constructed via either hypnotic extended jams or textural experimentation, was not only a catalyst for escapism but also an opportunity for a kind of self-psychoanalysis.

The Jimi Hendrix Experience recorded *Axis: Bold as Love* and *Electric Ladyland*, which boasted Leslie speaker–inflected, wah-wah, and distortion-fueled cross-genre visuals. These Utopian or sci-fi images that Hendrix had envisioned through the aid of psychedelics were connected to the legendary guitarist's unifying concept of an electric church, an art that knew no musical or social boundaries.

What am I driving at? *Moving Pictures* sprouted from the same rich soil that nurtured the first wave of progressive rock: the classical or romantic classical tradition from which the Brits, in particular, drew inspiration as well as the cultural milieu that birthed the subgenre: the counterculture's explorations into psychedelic music, studio experimentation, layered orchestration, and Eastern modalities and instrumentation.

By turning each sonic ditty into a mini-movie, Rush bolstered an important pillar of the psychedelic and later progressive rock sound: the need to create spatial dimension in music by exploring inner space, or the psyche.

*Moving Pictures* worked the crease between technique, hypnotic beats, streamlined compositions, and what could be described as a synesthesia-inducing song cycle.

From here on in, during the production process, Rush's music was discussed in visual terms. Not fragile or completely incendiary, these songs had exceptionally high emotional quotients and provided an immersive experience for the listener, inviting him or her to enter the theater of the mind.

Instead of referencing or gathering inspiration from outside poems or paintings, a twentieth-century band like Rush created their own imaginary movie scripts for the songs on *Moving Pictures* and blocked the movement in each musical scene with the precision of a seasoned cinematographer, who perfectly frames each shot.

The German (Krautrock?) group Can composed and rehearsed music in an abandoned movie theater, dubbed Inner Space, which may explain the oddly audiovisual nature of their sonic experimentations from the band's beginnings. Can released a compilation in 1970, titled *Soundtracks*, containing stray tracks they'd recorded for film. You could say that Can had a head start in that direction. Perhaps Rush was not as lucky.

Aside from gazing at the grazing cows in Wales, Rush had very little visual fodder to fire their creativity prior to recording at the scenic residential retreat Le Studio. But even the lush Canadian wilderness, both at Le Studio and at Ronnie Hawkins's farm, can't explain the band's creative center of gravity. Whatever cinematic delights they hatched sprung from their imagination.

Having said this, Rush couldn't have handpicked a more appropriate setting and site to facilitate the progress of the upcoming album. Hawkins was no stranger to moving pictures, having appeared in Martin Scorsese's 1978 concert film *The Last Waltz* with his one-time support group the Band. And just months prior to Rush's stay at the farm, Ronnie was featured in Michael Cimino's period western *Heaven's Gate* from 1980. It was a role that, according to an interview I conducted with Hawkins's wife, Wanda, was originally meant to go to Ned Beatty (*Deliverance* and *Superman*).

After hammering out most of the material on the record, the next phase, which began in late August, saw Rush and coproducer Terry Brown return to Phase One in Toronto to record the demos for the upcoming *Moving Pictures*.

"Phase One was in an industrial area, but they had the latest gear, from what I can remember," says Brian Miessner of Aerial, who recorded the George Semkiw and Paul Gross–produced *In the Middle of the Night* for the Anthem label at Phase One.

Although the band had crystalized its approach to most of the record, one song, "Witch Hunt," the second track on side 2 of the original vinyl format edition, had eluded them. The band wasn't hearing it or, in the language of *Moving Pictures*, envisioning it. With each passing day, however, it was obvious that the song was destined to be one of Rush's fabled "production" numbers, never to be performed onstage before a live audience, similar to "Madrigal" and "Different Strings."

The appropriate mental calisthenics required to finish "Witch Hunt" would need to be conjured later; for the moment, the band's tour dates beckoned. Beginning on September 11, Geddy, Alex, and Neil finished their first show of what would become known as the extended, or pre-, *Moving Pictures* tour. From mid-September through early October, Rush traipsed through Virginia and the American South, then zigzagged across the Midwest, the Mid-Atlantic, and the Northeast.

Although the record had yet to be released let alone recorded, Rush auditioned "Tom Sawyer" and "Limelight" on the sixteen-date jaunt. Bootleg recordings of the early fall dates on the East Coast and in the South reveal that the band had a little tweaking to do before these songs were battle ready.

Alex's solo in "Limelight (1980)" erupts with a revengeful scream, making it dramatically different from the nuanced elasticity exhibited in its considerably supple and subtle finished version. In addition, "Tom Sawyer" operates at nearly warp speed relative to its studio cousin. It does, however, settle into a more controlled groove as the song progresses. Hearing Geddy's near–spoken-word delivery bouncing over Neil's faster clock dimly recalls shades of the Clash's *Sandinista!* and Blondie's "Rapture," both released in 1980.

Roots in modern history for this kind of speech-song can be found even earlier in the work of Kurt Weill, Bertolt Brecht, the beat poets, Bob Dylan, Jim Morrison, and Patti Smith. This might make some readers' brains twinge, but Rush's "Tom

Sawyer" ran parallel to a grand creative tradition (by some people's estimation) of speech-song, blending high and so-called low art.

Pye and Peart's words capture the pulse, heat, and beat of the street. Its attack seems subversive and psychological, probing our minds with such invasive cunning that we're hardly aware we're being "worked on" or transformed by the meter phrasing. You could say it's the lyrical equivalent of *Street-vinsky*.

Lee, Lifeson, Peart, and Dubois were not, in an attempt to grab artistic credibility, clueless and privileged rockers engaging in culture wars, effectively muscling in on the artistic turf claimed by poets at slam competitions or by composers, playwrights, and entertainers in theatrical productions.

Dare I say, with "Tom Sawyer," Rush created something fresher and harsher: they forged a work of sonic toughness in speech and music that defied genre boundaries.

"Somewhere I've realized that I didn't have to aim at being Thomas Hardy, anymore," Peart told the *Boston Globe* in 1982, "and that I could write five-word sentences like Hemingway."

There's an avant-garde, mystical, and headbanging chemistry inhabiting "Tom Sawyer" that few have been able to copy before or since, including Rush. It embodies the very idea it enshrines: individualism, not bowing to conformity, and cutting one's own path without concern for corruption or undue influence.

In its more polished version, on the final recording—the one everyone is familiar with—"Tom Sawyer" is not quite as punky but is funkier and groovier. This and Geddy's vocal pacing may explain why some hip-hop artists gravitated to it. Whereas "Limelight" would later breathe with the benefit of more space, the overall timing of the live 1980 "Tom Sawyer" was variable and would tighten once the boys completed their work at Le Studio.

## GOOD FRIDAY

Rush's rock and roll caravan ground to a halt, and the crew struck the entire stage production at the end of the final performance on October 1 in Portland, Maine, at the Civic Center.

When the tour was over, Rush decamped to Le Studio. The boys were well rehearsed, and recording the initial tracks for *Moving Pictures*—the drums—went relatively quickly.

"The time to make records progressed as they moved forward in their careers," Terry Brown told me. "We did *Fly by Night* in three weeks from start to finish. Frightening."

The Quebec winter had come early, and the band holed up in the studio with little else to occupy their time but concentrate on recording the album. It took only one evening, the night of Friday, October 3, to nail down the drums. "The drum sound was one of those magic drum sounds we got the Friday night we arrived there [in Le Studio]," Terry Brown told me. "We tweaked it, but we didn't do any major changes [to the setup or sound]."

Brown said they had a drum sound "that killed," and the following day, Peart cut the drums for "Tom Sawyer."

From mid-September, when the band was still feeling their way around the rhythmic pacing for the song "Tom Sawyer," until early October, a dramatic change occurred. Neil settled down, feeling the pulse of the song as being much slower. Once he had this epiphany, piecing together the feel—and the entire track—went much smoother than it could have.

Peart, along with coproducer Brown, lead engineer Paul Northfield, and assistant engineer Robbie Whelan, were ready to go. "You could feel it in the control room—there was magic going on," Brown told me. "You could feel the energy coming out of the studio and onto the tape."

Northfield intimated that miking changed on nearly every song, although it is difficult to spot because of the consistency in performances and sonic clarity. It's deceptive to the point that you'd believe the recording setup for the drums, for instance, was the same for each song.

"There were seventeen mikes on drums," says André Perry. "That was quite a challenge. A day or more, at least, to get the drum sound. Neil was a perfectionist, a rocker musician, but he was beyond that. Innovative, not only with his lyrics but his playing. Rush didn't spend that much time doing a record. We've had groups that are three, four months, and, in certain cases, six months. Asia took an awful long time to do [*Alpha*]. Basically, *Moving Pictures*, not only was the music extraordinary, but it was also an experimental album."

Peart, in a feature article he wrote for *Modern Drummer* magazine for the December 1982 issue, claimed that his smaller twelve- and thirteen-inch toms were closed (leaving both heads on the drums) and were tuned tighter than he had previously done, affording the drums a higher pitch and a ringing resonance.

Peart's kit is punchy, orchestral at moments, and even wide-screen; Brown and Northfield used the entire array of microphones at their disposal. Peart employs a variety of percussive colorations and flavors in his drum setup to create a diversity of timbres, and the magic of the studio helped to provide directional audio to expand the stereo image.

Because Peart was consistent in his critique of his drum sound (constantly dissatisfied), believing that Rush's albums failed to capture the timbre of the drums from his vantage point of sitting behind the set, Northfield suggested using a pressure zone microphone (PZM) and taping it to Neil's chest while he performed the drum tracks for "The Camera Eye" and "Vital Signs."

There's some contradictory information floating out there as to how much and if the PZM microphone was actually used in the final print. If it had been used, it did not make a big chunk of what we hear on *Moving Pictures*. In addition, there's some discussion regarding Neil tuning down his snare head, but this likely did not occur either. As far as this writer knows, Neil kept his snare drum head tight and ringing.

*Modern Drummer* magazine reported in January 1983 that Brown "more than once reverse[d] the phase on the bass drum mic," Peart noted. "This would somehow intensify the depth of the note, giving a round, 'cushiony' low end to the sound, allowing it to sort of sit below the rest of the track. There was an increase of presence, in effect, without increasing the level."

Peart's tastes notwithstanding, other aspects of the record seem to sparkle with a kind of clarity. Despite the number of guitar tracks Lifeson recorded, the record in general retains transparency that eludes some of the hard rock or heavy metal bands of the day.

Northfield said that Lifeson's tracks were wall to wall. There are as many as three guitar tracks per channel (left and right), making a total of sometimes six guitar tracks on a single song. This was true of both *Permanent Waves* and *Moving Pictures*.

"With *Moving Pictures*, the guitars were all multitracked to a high degree. Same thing on *Permanent Waves*," says Northfield. "Essentially, there were six guitars for all the power parts, not soloes. Not the clean guitar parts. It would have been triple tracked on each side of the speakers, so it is exactly the same sound. Usually, the first track recorded with a dominant performance, the best one, would be the dominant [track] in the triple [track], and you just kind of play along and copy what you did. . . . That over-the-top multitracking approach kind of comes a bit from the

Roy Thomas Baker/Queen school of recording. Nick Blagona, the other engineer at Morin-Heights, had worked quite a bit with Roy Thomas Baker at Morin-Heights."

This may be one reason why Lifeson's chords cut through. "If you play a full chord with a lot of notes through an amp which is on raging distortion, the sound becomes a mess," offers Northfield. "Alex plays a lot of suspended chords, which are open-sounding, broad chords, and he has open strings playing with fretted strings as well because he was covering so much ground. So that means he is playing quite wide chords with lots of notes on a full chord. That limits how much distortion you can crank up because it starts to trash out. I think that's why it works. The layering and multitracking means the guitars sound super full, but they are not crushed with distortion so that you can't hear the notes."

Perhaps subconsciously, Lifeson was still being guided by the spirit and actual sound of Led Zeppelin records. In the 1970s, Jimmy Page did something similar with his "Guitar Army"—his catchphrase for multitracking guitars on Led Zeppelin's productions—a sonic jigsaw puzzle, if not just a sonic jigsaw, of choreographed frequencies.

In many of the Rush songs on *Moving Pictures*, it seems that most of the harmonizing I am hearing is not necessarily occurring among Lifeson's recorded performances but rather with those multitracked guitars in relation to Geddy's synth, bass, or bass synth pedals.

Circa 1980, Lifeson had begun changing his method of recording. Not only had he transitioned from Gibsons to custom Fenders, but he was no longer satisfied with playing in the recording studio and capturing the signal from his amp via a microphone. Because in past projects he'd spent more and more time in the control room, listening to playback, he liberated himself: he entered the control room and recorded there.

Lee had a similar evolution in musical tools. He used his trusty Rickenbacker, just as one of his idols, Chris Squire, had with Yes, but also Fender Jazz basses. Lee's technique would evolve, too. Having tried a pick in his right hand, he largely dispensed with it and began using his fingers, specifically his forefinger. As the 1980s progressed, Lee explored more techniques, such as a multidigit, flamenco gallop. His left hand largely frets the note most of the time. Stability in his left while being active with his right helps to define Geddy's bass sound and approach.

We hear this being applied throughout *Moving Pictures*.

Throughout the process of recording, the guys went about everything quite methodically: with a click or a metronome as Peart's guide, the drum parts were laid down, with the other guys playing along with him in the studio. These scratch tracks would later be replaced by Alex and Geddy via overdubs. Once the drums were down, Geddy recorded the bass and then keyboards. Alex cut his guitar tracks, and finally Lee did his vocals.

# CHAPTER 8

# AUDIOVISUAL: THE PERFECT SIDE

## THE CAMERA EYE, PART 4

Alex Lifeson is a tricky one. I've seen him perform onstage many times, and he always appeared fired up, even prone to improvisation when the moment allows: the very picture of the excitable rock star.

Improvisation: That's a good word for what Lifeson does. When he is feeling the moment onstage before thousands, he can be unpredictable. Even when not "performing," Lifeson is an iconoclast. The rambling and strangely decipherable acceptance speech he gave at Rush's induction ceremony into the Rock and Roll Hall of Fame in 2013 was proof of this. Lifeson used no other words but "blah" to express his gratitude. It's the most nonverbal verbal communication you'll ever comprehend.

Seconds before he uttered these words (the word?), when Lifeson stepped up to the podium and the first blahs escaped his mouth, you can almost see the wheels turning in the guitarist's head: *Am I really going to do this?*

We all know the answer and perhaps could have guessed it before he did: Lifeson likes to play practical jokes. Big ones. He's good at them.

But judging from the times I've spoken with Lifeson, it isn't his arm acrobatics performed with the guitar before an audience or the endearing, good-natured, Tom Sawyer–ish tricks he manages to pull off, but what has impressed me is his ability to organize his thoughts, make his point, and take your inquiries seriously. When I have spoken with him, he has carried a subdued confidence and was respectful of my questions.

One of those times in 2007, Lifeson told me a story that seems relevant. He and his wife Charlene used to visit Greece, where they stayed with friends in Mykonos. Their hosts owned a bouzouki, and Lifeson quickly fell in love with the instrument, plucking its four sets of double strings.

Every morning, he'd strum or pick, sitting on a stone wall at the top of a cliff, sipping a cup of coffee, and overlooking the fishing boats as they'd pass by. The geography, scenic backdrop, and even the weather, just the way Lifeson described them, conjured cinematic images difficult to shake.

"I was getting up early in Mykonos . . . and Greek fishermen would hear me playing and they would . . . be saluting me," Lifeson told me. "If they only knew there was this middle-aged Canadian sitting on a stone wall just messing around with an instrument that is very important to the Greeks, important to their culture."

During the conversation, we referenced the acoustic instrumental "Hope" from *Snakes & Arrows* (2007), and to me, it sounded like Indian classical music channeled through Jimmy Page, and I told Alex so, to which he added, "Yeah, and played in Ireland. There is a Celtic quality about it, as well. There's a Middle Eastern quality."

This was, mind you, a song that was composed and recorded by a Canadian of Eastern European heritage, an instrumental that by its very nature needed no vocalizations to impact the listener. The kicker? Lifeson used a bouzouki on *Snakes & Arrows*, almost as if it were fated to happen this way.

"I love when stuff like that happens," Lifeson told me.

This mixture of genres is emblematic of Rush's music generally and represents one of the purest examples of music found on *Moving Pictures*: the instrumental "YYZ." "YYZ" is not jazz-rock fusion or a melodic instrumental but something in between. This melding of two elements—this alchemy—created a third, new musical identity.

Much of *Moving Pictures* exists due to this type of alchemy, and much of this can be attributed to Lifeson, Lee, and Peart moving outside their comfort zones.

Let's have a look at the music on *Moving Pictures*.

## "TOM SAWYER"

This Rush's entry point into adulthood as a band. Moments of *Permanent Waves* do carry similar vibes, but it's "Tom Sawyer" that captures Rush at their most gritty, slick, sly, catchy, and sophisticated.

With "Tom Sawyer," Rush, at least for one hot moment, shared a similar esthetic with Steely Dan's material from the 1970s. Certainly, "Tom Sawyer" is head and shoulders above the sci-fi lyrical and mystical musical creations the band had been spinning years prior.

The cyclonic whirlpool of synth textures opening "Tom Sawyer" is barely stabilized by its bass-tone undertow. It was derived from a musical idea Geddy played on synthesizer during Rush sound checks on the *Permanent Waves* tour.

Tucked away and forgotten, these jams were unearthed when the band reviewed their sound check tapes. On playback, the lightbulb went off. In piecing together the song, Rush had been searching for a game changer, something that would shift the texture and mood of the song, and there it was.

Lee shelved his trusty Rickenbacker and picked up a Fender Jazz for the track, a bass he'd owned but never used on a record. Lee went direct into the board as well as being plugged into a couple different power amps and some custom cabinets.

Just prior to the guitar solo, at 1:52, amid a churning swirl of synth and guitar, Lee virtually transfers the lead keyboard line to his bass. He modulates, of course, during the solo, which has the effect of grounding the music, but with all the rising and falling in sympathy with Lifeson's guitar lines, Geddy's performance becomes a bass showcase. It's collective soloing.

Northfield had given Lifeson a Gibson Howard Roberts electric guitar, a big-bodied six-string that some may say resembles the smaller Les Paul. It was this guitar that Alex used for the song. (Some sources say Lifeson called on his custom Fender for the solo.) The screeching, sonic squalls and primal emotions Lifeson squeezes out of his guitar took five passes to achieve the correct intonation and feel.

"Tom Sawyer" does not operate within a typical AABA framework. There's an opening verse, what could be considered a second verse, and then something resembling a bridge, followed by a chorus (i.e., "The world is . . ."). When the second cycle spins around ("Today's Tom Sawyer . . ."), the 7/8 instrumental synth section breaks up an already unorthodox composition. Lifeson's guitar solo and Peart's iconic drum breaks follow, and proceeding these, there's an extended instrumental passage that echoes a less decorated one from earlier in the track. The song continues on from a bridge, followed by another chorus.

"Tom Sawyer" concludes with a single stanza of a new verse, then an instrumental section fades out, during which Peart bashes away in 7/8, playing accents on his China crash and sixteenth-note triplets by engaging his snare and double kicks.

Got all that? We're breathless just having to recount it.

Weird? Perhaps, but wonderfully so. Being strange is no crime. It's unusual in that a hard-driving song can be full of such contrast. For one thing, Lifeson plays a kind of combination picked-notes/strummed-chords approach in the song's verses. It's powerful but also detailed.

Synths soar above and mortar the fragments to the structure of the tune. At the same time, at its opening, the synthesizer rips a hole in the space-time continuum. Peart performs groove-based patterns but also takes mini-solos near the song's conclusion, having a similar effect.

Whether we're discussing rock or big-band jazz, this solo within a song phenomenon can be traced back decades to drummers such as Gene Krupa, Buddy Rich, Sonny Paine, Chick Webb, and even John Bonham of Led Zeppelin with "Moby Dick."

Peart used this time-honored tradition to bolster his and Rush's profile. In so doing, Peart become instantly identifiable in ways that that other rock drummers were not—even some of the greats. Even those with a superior musicality and clear mastery of the kit had not played on such a monumentally and commercially successful song as "Tom Sawyer."

For instance, compare and contrast "Tom Sawyer" with Phil Collins's brilliant drum break from "In the Air Tonight," also from 1981, which nearly knocks the song off its axis.

Peart had seen Genesis perform live in 1974 and once described Phil's playing as "lyrical" and "melodic-sounding" in an article dedicated to Collins, published in the British magazine *Rhythm* in 2011. Yet the technical dexterity (or perceived dexterity) inherent to Peart's singular moment or series of mini-moments in "Tom Sawyer" was enough evidence for true believers and even some casual listeners of his superhuman drumming ability.

But Phil's break could be viewed as timbral more than performance based. Many drummers of Peart's ilk did not always necessarily conceive of memorable meat-and-potatoes drum riffs. Some did not have the same opportunities to do so.

"Tom Sawyer" and, indeed, Peart's playing is Jungian in the sense that their impact penetrated musos' collective consciousness (and, in turn, unconsciousness). By 1981, Peart was an archetypal figure, a condition that was accelerated toward its zenith with *Moving Pictures*.

"I think Phil Collins played mostly by sense of feel," says Jonathan Mover (Joe Satriani, Aretha Franklin, Alice Cooper, and ProgJect). "Meaning: what he was feeling at that moment he was playing. I don't get the feeling there was a lot of forethought, other than the basic road map: the beats, the patterns, and the ideas, they just came out of him. It worked because it was about the music and the spur of the moment, whereas Neil was premeditated and very well thought-out, which is a different approach and formula to playing, writing and recording, but absolutely works as well. Neil's parts are composed and his drum tracks are songs, in and of themselves. When you saw Rush play live, you knew they would play 99-percent of their parts the exact same way they played them on the record, unless they changed them for fun."

"This was back in 1983, 1984, and I was already aware of Rush, and I was start-ing to get into metal," says drummer Jason Bittner. "I was listening to Iron Maiden and Judas Priest and stuff like that. But a friend sat us down and made us listen to *2112* from beginning to end. That was the first time I had done that with a Rush album. At that point, my drumming heroes were Stewart Copeland and Terry Bozzio, who I'd first seen with Missing Persons. When I heard *2112*, I said, 'This guy [Peart] was playing drums like my heroes.' That's what caught my attention. I heard *Permanent Waves*, and when *Moving Pictures* got dropped on the record player, that was it for me. That was the 'aha' moment. 'Tom Sawyer' is probably still my favorite song of all time."

"*Moving Pictures* changed a lot for me because so much was happening at once by the mighty Professor," says Brian Tichy." There were a ton of well-thought-out and very catchy parts. There were odd times everywhere. There were involved arrange-ments. And it was all taking place inside songs I loved upon first listen, which took me on a journey. Neil plays a large kit with so many sound sources. He made it sound fun—technical yet possible to be learned."

Peart's paradox, the oxymoronic nature of his playing, was this: slamming his fourteen-piece rosewood-finish Tama kit tore up his hands and feet but was also immaculate conception—a kind of well-thought-out precision banging that suited Rush's material.

Neil himself admitted that after striking the drumheads so hard during the recording of "Tom Sawyer" in a session spanning two days, he collapsed. And playing "Tom Sawyer" every night on tour was a challenge, even after having performed it for decades.

Maybe it's the funky groove that transitions into an odd time, the symphony of cymbals he crashes in melodic succession, the rumbling of quads (two beats on toms followed by a beat each on the two kick drums), taking a swipe at a crash cymbal mid-fill, or microphone placement in front of kick drums that retained their heads. Of course, it likely is all of these—and more.

Keep digging, and the track gets even stranger. There was always a kind of limbs-frozen-in-ice feel as we enter the guitar solo—a slight hesitation. Unlike John Bonham's bold 4/4 patterns plowing through the 5/4 rhythm in "Black Dog," Neil accents and follows a tricky time-signature transition from 4/4 to 7/8 into rhythmic patterns that most normal or levelheaded musicians would sidestep.

"You could tell that Rush had analyzed everything, mapped it out, and then forgot about it," says Jason Sutter. "It was never methodical sounding. Other bands may have sounded mechanical when playing the odd times, whereas Rush always had a grease to it. Rush straddled that line between it being methodical and mechanical and being organic. I think that is how they were able to have massive hits where every bar wasn't in 4/4 at times."

"I have always been influenced by drummers who bring their personality to what they do percussively," says Dave Krusen (Candlebox, Pearl Jam, and Unified Theory). "Peart, Copeland, Bonham, Moon, Watts, all these guys made the music they were a part of, better than what might be considered 'more apropos' by a producer or band wanting a more traditional, anonymous approach. Peart changed drumming for the better and, in my opinion, is one of the greatest—a top ten drummer of all time."

As for Lee, it's interesting that his greatest contribution isn't necessarily on bass or vocals but synth. Although we've talked about the lead characteristics of Geddy's bass in "Tom Sawyer," it's Alex and Neil who take (what most people would deem) actual solos. What Lee does with synth is provide the mechanism for transportation.

On *Moving Pictures*, Lee continued to use Minimoog, Taurus pedals, and an Oberheim, as he did for *Permanent Waves* and *Hemispheres*. Arguably, Geddy's command of keyboard could categorized generally as a "punk" attitude in a progressive rock setting. The rebelliousness of the playing, a nod to New Wave, transformed "Tom Sawyer" into a hybrid creation of various forms of popular music of the day.

"With *Moving Pictures*, Rush had a polyphonic synthesizer," says Paul Northfield, lead recording engineer for the *Moving Pictures* sessions. "Geddy's big synthesizer, the Oberheim he had, was essentially tuned to one note, one sound, and was used to make a string sound—four Oberheim modules all tuned to a high octave that would be triggered from the bass pedals as well so you could hit a low note on the bass pedal

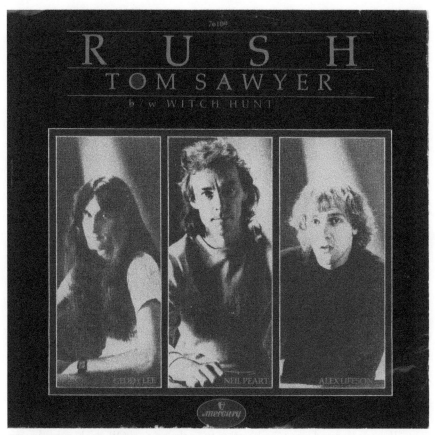

"Tom Sawyer": The definitive Rush song.

and then you get two or three octaves [notes emanating from the synth keyboard]. That would give them this wide-open, slightly orchestral quality and still could put the three-piece pounding through it."

Synthesizer guru and pioneer Bob Moog once said that everything has consciousness and that perhaps through the application of sound wave technology, we can tap into this psychical energy. The Moog, ARP, Buchla, Oberheim, and similar instruments helped foster a music revolution that was as much about generating vast soundscapes as about communing with the collective consciousness. Attempting to retrieve and interpret one's inner visions through technology, those a musician had witnessed or "sensed," became a form of musical gnosis.

The act of discovery of the inner self was never more apparent than on *Moving Pictures*. It was Peart, after all, who said he would be fine knowing that Rush began its life with *Moving Pictures*. One could argue, then, in very practical terms that with the advent of the growl emanating from the Oberheim OB-X, Rush found its identity, sonic signature, and characteristic voice.

So the widening sonic vortex spreading across the stereo image, commencing with "Tom Sawyer," works on at least two levels: it relays a visual image but manifests an idea that defines this period of Rush's life span while foretelling a synth-rock era looming on the horizon.

More than "The Spirit of Radio," "Closer to the Heart," or later tracks "Distant Early Warning," and "Time Stand Still," "Tom Sawyer" defined a moment in time. Given its ubiquity, I once asked about the inclusion of part of "Tom Sawyer" in various movies and TV shows, and for one instance, Lee offered, "All they wanted was the instrumental part. I think they just wanted the [synth] effect."

For many, the opening seconds of "Tom Sawyer" was life-changing and may have helped shape the course of their lives.

"The first synth bass note on 'Tom Sawyer' just set the scene for a magical ride," says bassist John DeServio (Black Label Society, Richie Kotzen, Derek Sherinian, Zakk Wylde, and Vinnie Moore).

Why? Perhaps it's not difficult to understand. "Tom Sawyer" was released as a single, b/w "Witch Hunt," and fell into heavy rotation in major radio markets across the United States and Canada. When those spiraling and low tones hit you right between the eyes and in the middle of your chest, its power was frightening.

"The actual sound was a stock setting from the original OB-X," Northfield says. "Geddy may have modified it, but it would have been very early days of him having an OB-X. There was a function called cross modulation. A synthesis would describe it as cross modulation with a 'sync' button. So the oscillators are being forced to synchronize when they are being simultaneously forced to be out of sync by what is called cross modulation. Cross modulation would produce wide, random pitch shifts because one oscillator is aggressively modulating another. But because you have a sync button, where the oscillators are locked, it basically gives you this twisted, spiky filtered sound. In the case of the Oberheim, it's also that the filters would have been driven by an envelope, which is the thing that makes it sweep."

The low end in particular has a sparkling yet enveloping sound. "Underneath it would have been Taurus pedals—and there are Taurus pedals all over the record on the super low end. That low end, the part of it I was involved with, I used a Loft flanger phaser, a 440," says Northfield. "I had it set up so I could feed off the bus architecture on the console, and I could feed anything into it, and it would blend into the mix and make the low end very wide but very clear. Low frequencies can get very cloudy. If you use something as simple as a stereo panner or a stereo chorus unit—and this [440 flanger] was essentially like a stereo chorus on the low bass pedals—it made [low frequencies] wide but super clear. That would have contributed along with the fact that the OB-X was a stereo output synth to give you this big, wide stereo filter sweep. The 440 was such a fundamental part of making that record, so much so that the guys kept telling me off for using it too much, especially on the low end. Sometimes I'd blend it on a bit of bass to give us a clarity in the low end. Part of the reason for that is it stops the buildup of resonant frequencies because it moves it around from one speaker to the other."

Would you believe that we have not yet passed the Rubicon of the song's lyrical eccentricity and eclecticism? The pièce de résistance is Pye Dubois' contributions to the mysticism of the track.

Paul Phillip Woods (aka Pye Dubois), reportedly a psychotherapist who practiced psychiatry at the Clarke Institute of Psychiatry in Toronto, knew what emotional and psychological buttons to push with his lyrics.

"I don't think I write strange stuff," Dubois told *RPM* magazine in 1976. "It may not be lyrics, but it's very poetic."

Peart made sure of that. This Louis the Lawyer character Dubois hatched wasn't quite the right fit for the direction Peart wanted to go. Peart substituted him for an American literary figure, a vortex fictional creation nurtured from the fertile mind of Missourian Mark Twain, one Peart was introduced to through comic books, namely, the *Classics Illustrated* series.

Fundamentally, the song asks, What does it mean to be independent? What kind of responsibility do we have to society as a whole? How do other people's perceptions of us shape our psyches?

"Tom Sawyer" dabbles in the twentieth-century literary tradition of turning convention on its head. This was far from the apple pie mischievousness of Twain's nineteenth-century imagination; it was a pale reflection, a fun house mirror image really, of the traditional independent spirit. Tom Sawyer is all grown up in Rush's song, maybe a bit cynical, and his actions follow on from his experiences with the world at large. While Rush's Tom Sawyer retains an unabashed love of life, he has become a little edgy, beholden to no one—possessing free will and thought, perhaps much like Sawyer's boyhood friend Huckleberry Finn.

Tom Sawyer is not presented as a composite criminal-hero, Robin Hood meets Jesse James, an outlaw type filtered through the recesses of the minds of Patti Smith and John Lee Hooker. There's murkiness and mystique lurking on the banks of the river, yes. But Peart's hero is an Ayn Rand–ian character beholden to no institution or system of thought.

The missive of "Tom Sawyer" isn't to menace; it doesn't celebrate creativity or life as a dance with death; it's observational, surgical even, in its social commentary, with a slight whiff of the confessional. Unlike the references to the three travelers of Willowdale from "The Necromancer," this song takes the mythical and attempts to make it real, historical, and topical, not the other way around. But for all of the attempts to update an iconic nonconformist and drag him into the modern day, the world Peart and Dubois create around Tom Sawyer is shrouded in an aura of escapism and impressionism, catalyzing our imagination. And much like in Twain's novels, the river in "Tom Sawyer" represents freedom.

Literary critic Alfred Kazin wrote that Twain's two most iconic characters, Tom Sawyer and Huckleberry Finn, "never had to grow up. They remain eternally boys— the American boys of legend."

Arguably, the Tom Sawyer whom Lee sings of is Peart in disguise, just as Twain's fictional boy reflected the author in his youth. However, this tells only half the story. In his lyrics, Peart is describing a modern-day rebellious mind-set, not eternal youth, even if a child-like, blue-sky optimism burns through mists of skepticism (i.e., "Love and life . . ."). In addition, "Today's Tom Sawyer" retains the fictional youth's ability of persuasion, so much so that we don't notice his transgressions. And by refusing to use the word "I" in the lyrics (a Rand-ian slip perhaps), the song doesn't crater to personal confession but grows dynamically in strength, scope, and meaning due to its universality.

Although the persona inhabiting "Tom Sawyer" doesn't embody the economic, political, industrial, and military engines that power the United States or the whole of North America, we do get the nagging suspicion that the song is a hymn—and metaphor—for the conscience of a Western population (or certain segments of it) that have lived through despair, deceit, and disillusion but still chart a course and remain hopeful for the (near) future.

We've talked about Geddy assuming a role, even editing the words he was given in order to be a credible singer of Neil's lyrics. Likewise, Peart himself must don a kind of cloak of personality to properly gain access to the character he's writing about and perhaps rummage around Dubois' psyche, even his own. The result of this collision of opposites is a combustible bundle of visual flashes: a composite if solitary figure sailing down a river who possesses real-world experience *and* a sense of surrealism.

The rhythmic pacing and the use of active words suggest movement (catch, invade, drift, stride, trade, friction, and exit). Even more impressive is the way these images fuse via an economical use of phrasing. We're no longer just listening to audio: we're watching film.

## "RED BARCHETTA"

Like most of the material on *Moving Pictures*, the basic ideas for "Red Barchetta" leaped out of a jam—Geddy and Alex had several distinct sections and decided to fold them all into one piece. Luckily for the guys, Rush was rolling tape and caught many of the concepts that found their way into the finished song.

Peart dubbed "Red Barchetta" a sound track for an imaginary movie in the DVD *Taking Center Stage*. And like any good film, music is intrinsically liked with the images on-screen.

The striking lyrical imagery as well as the spirit in Lee's and Lifeson's playing individually and collectively, the precision of execution, the coordination between word and sound, and the emotion poured into the lines bring to life this filmic plotline whose story is told via wide-angle shots and close-ups.

More than any other song on the record, "Red Barchetta" captures the essence of the conceptual—the impetus for the record being written and recorded in the first place. It's social commentary woven into a cinematic plotline—the stuff of a perfect sci-fi movie.

Peart turbocharged the car in "A Nice Morning Drive," a short story written by Richard S. Foster and published in *Road & Track* magazine in 1973. Peart hot-rodded Foster's MGB roadster into a red Ferrari 166 and in the process reveals something about his once-hidden desires.

Although we acknowledge that some of Foster's phrases do come off the page, the very purpose of Peart's lyrics is to be a vehicle through which we cross into other sensory realms altogether. Peart's vision is more political and conceptually layered and deeper than the original story.

Foster's lead character's name is Buzz. We don't know the name of the narrator in "Red Barchetta," which goes a long way to making the experience of listening to the song a more universal one.

There are significant distinctions between Foster's writing and Peart's sci-fi lyrics. For one, there's no appearance of an uncle in Foster's original. But the uncle of "Red Barchetta" performs a similar role to that of Aunt Polly, who raises Tom Sawyer. At the least, the uncle is a fatherly figure for the vagabond main character of "Red Barchetta." And the idyllic setting painted by the music and the free spirit narrating the piece are reminiscent of elements of Twain's bucolic world.

But back to the issue at hand: The aggressive fellow commuters of Foster's tale drive larger, less energy-efficient, but safer automobiles. Those steering smaller, older cars not in compliance with modern safety vehicle standards are at risk of being targeted by road-raging psychos. The implication of Peart's lyrics is, however, that the alloy aircraft of "Red Barchetta" are manned *not* by villainous (even vigilante) motorists who view running smaller autos off the road as sport but rather by fascistic environmental emissions cops.

A reading of Foster's story reveals (or at the least gives the impression) that a frightened Buzz won't push his chances again. The unnamed autoist, perhaps a grown-up Tom Sawyer of sorts, of "Red Barchetta" will likely take another spin on an upcoming Sunday. Rush's refusal to label this type of rebelliousness as criminal, regardless of any future society's "motor law," was a stroke of genius. It was absolutely Twain-ian. It's as if Rush had asked, are we criminals for merely wanting to be free of authoritarianism?

The band (and many fans) has zeroed in on the track as being one of the record's most successful. Neil was especially happy with the song, having done a practice take just to ensure that Terry and Paul Northfield had the appropriate recording levels. After Neil did a preliminary track, Brown suggested he change one fill, and the next take is virtually what we hear on *Moving Pictures*. It's as if Peart's internal rhythmic clock was synced with a fantasy film reel that's being spooled—and projected on a screen—simultaneously with the scratch tracks pumped through his headphones, perhaps bit like an old-school Hollywood sound track being cut to image on a soundstage.

Lifeson's opening arpeggios introduce the track—we become acquainted with the titular car. It's a fade-in shot: The arpeggios, the throaty bass, the low tones of the

Taurus pedals, and the high-pitched synth notes have the combined effect of setting a scene or painting a pastoral picture. We envision sunlight; we can feel it.

The graduated decline of the bass notes puts us at ease—until the music revs up and takes us on a rip-roaring journey. The dust clears—spaciousness. We hear virtually nothing else but voice and guitar. Rarely had Rush been so minimal and yet so evocative.

At the opening of the track, Alex picks the notes of an A chord, then an F#m7. This is slightly reminiscent of the F#7 opening "Cygnus X-1, Book II: Hemispheres." Lifeson picks notes that follow a cyclical upward–downward trajectory. In the measure prior to Geddy introducing the vocals, Lifeson's notes subtly creep up the sonic ladder, setting the stage for this ultimately exhilarating song. This sunny turn in a major key befits the idyllic setting—a secret rural getaway. It's exegesis—an establishing shot if you will.

Lifeson's song-opening arpeggios drift from one channel and then another, finally settling in the center. The band follows suit: synth tones and cymbals are introduced left. We hear the metallic clinks of cymbal strikes (left), then the hi-hat in the right (and then, almost immediately after, audio in both), helping to create the song's stereo image, giving the audio a kind of spatial dimension.

Later in the process, the mix is what gives us the impression of a wide audio scope, matching and capturing Peart's wide range as creative ideas, rhythmic technique, and percussive textures.

At approximately 1:12, just prior to the second verse ("Jump to the ground . . ."), Lifeson's multiple guitar tracks fit together tightly like interlocking metallic gears. Notes and chords are skillfully blurred to become as one performance. Rush had hinted at this kind of feel in the past, but there's something about how seamless it all is here.

For fleeting bars, the music seems to float, levitating us with it: elements that feel independent of one another are nonetheless intrinsically linked in helping to ground the entire matrix. It's a compositional technique and effect Rush would take to new heights with "Vital Signs." Try this to test what I'm saying. Listen to the first verse (starting at 0:45) and focus your mind on one of the elements of the sound, whether it be bass, guitar, drums/cymbals, synth drone, or vocals. While concentrating on one part or pattern, you feel the music begin to slip away from you just as you sense your mind sailing to someplace else.

There's also a kind of brief split of the audio picture following the first verse: the keys in which the guitar and bass perform create dissonance, as if the listener had been fashioned with the audio equivalent of three-dimensional glasses. A pity Rush didn't explore this in greater depth for themselves and music listeners, but this tonal bisectionalism does hint at the kind of dissonance typically found in classic hard rock as well as heavy metal chords heard throughout the 1980s well after *Moving Pictures* appeared.

Although "Red Barchetta" does not have acoustic guitar, the division between these two feels—pastoral and mechanical or metallic—was a bit more dramatic and drastic, and the transition Rush uses in "Red Barchetta" is much more seamless—like an expert editor splicing together two razor-cut strips of thirty-five-millimeter film.

Skillfully edited, the track promises adventure around every corner. The dissonant, even nearly bitonal, quality of the section (beginning at approximately 1:15) represents the mixture of lawlessness, freedom, and excitement the driver feels untethered to restrictions and conventions. It sounds like a battle of keys—E fighting F for supremacy, which manifests in listener disorientation.

Later in the song, in the tires-screeching section (beginning at approximately 2:26), the eighth-note feel of the music has an enormous impact on the listener: the band is locked in with mathematical precision.

Beginning at approximately 1:39, Geddy's shift from reserved voice to growl helps fuel a feeling of nostalgia and pump up the song's emotion quotient. We as passengers experience every thumping of the heart, every hairpin turn, as we travel alongside the driver on his ride to freedom.

The vocal performance puts the song over the top as Geddy adds one more line to his résumé. He's no longer a bassist, vocalist, and keyboardist but also the lead actor for this film, striking a credible balance of empathy, exhilaration, and nervous excitement. At the same time, Geddy's tenor voice is calming, strangely quiet, and controlled, befitting the placid country scene described in "Red Barchetta."

"Well, I'm getting old," Geddy told *Music Express* in January 1981. "I can't just scream all the time. It got to the point where my voice was purely an instrument, an effect. I guess now I'd rather sing, utilize my knowledge of melody and technique—a feeling everyone in the band shares, probably from having forced ourselves to play more than one instrument each."

"Red Barchetta" is a strange if wonderful hybrid of mechanical precision and exhilaration, even eroticism. Amid the description of the classic red speedster—the gleaming metallic hardware and the well-crafted materials of the vehicle's interior—we catch a whiff of pornographic detail in imagery of the sleek aerodynamic chassis. The atmosphere as aphrodisiac is effective, driving sensations of whipping through a windswept rural landscape, bordering on the erotic and verging on orgasmic.

"Red Barchetta" is revved up in more ways than one. The song's emotional quotient cannot be suppressed—from an ineffable longing of the narrator for a time and place he never knew (what Germans call *Sehnsucht*) to a very real fear of being caught by the environmental police for driving an unauthorized vehicle. The song catalyzes an outlaw instinct in us.

Still, re-creating the sensation of motion is nothing new for rock or its parallel genres. As passengers, we zoomed along a German expressway to Kraftwerk's "Autobahn" and were transported by rail courtesy of "Trans-Europa Express" (or "Trans-Europe Express"). Fellow Germans Neu! offered a ticket to a thrill ride titled "Hallogallo," which hugged the pavement in similar motoric fashion. As we logged mile after mile with Kraftwerk or Neu!, we morphed from passenger to operator to the actual motor.

A slightly different and more layered phenomenon occurs with Rush.

In the "speeding section" (i.e., "wind . . . in my hair . . ."), Geddy's voice sounds almost robotic. However, a deeper dive reveals that the driver—we—are being infused with a sense of relaxed concentration, of single-minded purpose. In short, we experience a form of samadhi. This feeling of peace is a melding of man, machine, and nature. The lack of separation is directly proportional to the blurriness of the landscape encasing the bullet as it careens through the countryside. Everything has fused.

This prototypical "heavy metal thunder" motoring down the open road is much more human than its German Krautrock predecessors. Somehow, Rush has it both ways: we are the engine and yet thrill at driving it. An emotional layer is placed on top of the driving current of the song.

Keeping this all on track is the linear direction of the narrative flow, which reads like a sci-fi screenplay. "Red Barchetta" has nothing like a traditional refrain in the sense that certain key phrases reoccur in timely fashion. There's no real lyrical hook. Peart didn't write it that way. Certain sections of verses sound similar (and even a word or two do repeat) but not on the order of anything close to be a traditional chorus. In this (and perhaps the only) respect, "Red Barchetta" progresses along a linear path, like a car driving from point A to point Z.

Then why does "Red Barchetta" feel so round and complete?

One way to explain this is to follow the repetition of some of the chord structures and notes being picked for the song. Lifeson applies the same or similar chord sequences for certain verses, and in some cases, these make repeat showings. For instance, Lifeson plays notes in the A chord, then moves to F#m7 to A/G for the prominent verses (i.e., "My uncle has . . . ," "I strip away . . . ," and "Suddenly ahead of me . . .").

There's a practical purpose to this since the lyrics operate as a prog rock story and not hook-laden pop. The reoccurrence of chords and certain arpeggiated notes affords the song a semblance of coherency.

The application of suspended chords in the reflective interlude, "Down in his barn . . ." (1:45), is an independent episode, outside the normal flow of action. The car is not only representative of a time that once was but also a longing for a world now gone; the mood here is nostalgia and melancholy tempered by the excitement of discovery. And, much like the river in "Tom Sawyer" and Twain's novels, the Barchetta represents escape, conveyance, *and* real-world peril.

At approximately 1:25 (through 1:30), what I call "warble guitars" ("Jump to the ground . . ." and "Drive like the wind . . .") create an off-axis feel, reflecting the narrator's world shifting and about to spin out of control—the sonics are bitonal.

Some have noted the tip of the hat to Led Zeppelin in Lifeson's playing in this song. Indeed, there is this, but it is not obvious. This section does bear a minor, passing resemblance to Jimmy Page's riffing in "Heartbreaker." Lifeson's swagger and sonic dips, courtesy of string bends, is one way the Rush guitarist pays tribute, perhaps even subconsciously, to one his major influences. And it's done without betraying the purpose of the song or Lifeson's own creative voice and progress he's made as a musician.

At 2:11, the bass becomes a lead instrument. It's a subversion but an appropriate one. The least likely lead instrument takes front and center as this relic, the red Barchetta, this outlawed vehicle, takes to the open roads.

Geddy's bass playing overall is lyrical, hyperactive, and full of ringing notes. It also contains the occasional grace note, glissandos, and minor slides along the strings as well as significant movement around the fretboard and intriguing and evocative relationships in terms of guitar chords/notes. Despite Geddy's sledding across the frets, bordering on the rare slur, the performance overall offers the song clarity due to its precision; each note is well articulated and, dare it be said, on the whole "clean."

Perhaps because of the bass's uncanny definition, Geddy's four-string seems to be exceptionally loud as well not only in "Red Barchetta" but also in other spots on the entire record. Ordinarily, this would create sonic imbalance, but especially in this song, the industrial nature of the bass tone suits the lyrical setting. In an odd way, the mind links this metallic bass tone with the humming of motorized, oil-based engines typical of twentieth-century automobiles.

During the "Chase," or "Speed," section, at approximately 2:30, Lifeson chops out what sound like repetitive D notes, underpinning the section with mathematical precision, like wheels spinning around the pavement of an infinite road. Although it's obvious that Lifeson multitracked in this section, he likely doubled (or tripled) the syncopated eighth-note pattern that appears here—the only time such an orderly pattern appears. It's a true centerpiece of the song, propelling it ever forward and implicitly revealing the driver's need for speed. It evokes a strong image: The camera follows the Barchetta heading for a distant point on the horizon.

Some of the song's greatest imagery lies in Alex's solo, which was shaped not only by a delay effect but also by a wah-wah to cocoon the listener. This pronounced, nasally tone evokes images of a tunnel, either manmade or some form of natural wind phenomenon.

The version of the song everyone is familiar with fades out and ends circa 6:09. But the track likely kept going in the studio premixing and ended abruptly with a guitar chord following the arpeggios. Deciding to fade out was another good call from the crew, greatly benefiting the song and contributing to the diverse feel of the record.

Below I've attempted to break down the sonic and cinematic elements of "Red Barchetta," citing the musical and visual motifs, instrumentation, and time of what I deem are the pivotal audiovisual points in the song.

### Table 1.  "Red Barchetta," frame by frame

| Visual/Musical Motifs | Instrumentation | Time |
|---|---|---|
| "Riff A" denotes the introduction of the song. Whenever we hear the Riff A motif, it's in association with the Barchetta or the basic concept of the song. | Gtr. Arpeggios (Riff A) Lifeson plays harmonics <br><br> Synth–Taurus pedals lay down whole-note bass tones <br><br> Bass <br><br> Clinking of cymbals | 0–0:19 |

*(continued)*

## Table 1. (continued)

| Visual/Musical Motifs | Instrumentation | Time |
|---|---|---|
| The haunting arpeggios ("Riff B") tell of the legend of the Barchetta | Bass lead (couples nicely with the A to Fm#7 etc. note progression)<br><br>Gtr.: Arpeggios/harmonics ("Riff B") | 0:19 |
| "Riff C" evokes the image of the Barchetta cruising along unobstructed country roads, unprovoked ... | Guitar ("Riff C")<br>Bass<br>Full drums | 0:32 |
| This section reinforces the notion that the narrator/driver recounts tales his uncle regales upon him, about the farm and the way life used to be. The narrator is speaking "into the camera." This intimate moment then shifts to a wide-angle shot as the lens is pulled back ... | Vocal: "My uncle has..."<br><br>Interestingly, references to "uncle" are either accompanied by a sunny A chord or often trailed by one throughout the song.<br><br>Arpeggios ("Riff C") | Approx. 0:45 |
| Perhaps the pinnacle of Rush's ability to be plaintive and pastoral in an electric rock setting | Vocals: "and on Sundays..."<br>Guitar ("Riff C")<br>bass<br>drums | 0:58–1:11 |
| The narrator hitches a ride with, what appears to be, a freight train, out to the country to see his uncle. | The dissonance of the music reflects turmoil, excitement<br><br>a slight dissonance in bass and guitar tones | 1:12–1:24 |
| The off-axis feel of the guitar reflects how the narrator's/driver's world will soon spin out of control... | Warble Gtr.<br>(string bends) | 1:24–1:30 |
| Intensity level rises: our narrator knows what to expect once he arrives at his uncle's place | Excitable (Major) Chords | 1:30 |
| Pushing himself off the freight train and getting a running start | Vocal: "Jump to the ground..."<br>Warble Gtr. | 1:32 |
| Exhilaration of anticipation; awaiting the turn of the ignition key | Excitable (Major) Chords | 1:43 |

| Visual/Musical Motifs | Instrumentation | Time |
|---|---|---|
| The car is not only representative of a time that once was, but the longing for a world now gone; the mood is nostalgic tempered by the discovery and suspense of the narrator's impending ride | Vocal: "Down in his barn..." <br><br> Gtr. (Incidental) <br><br> A mix of chords, both suspended—mainly a suspended C—and major (G, A, F, C) | 1:45–1:46 |
| The Barchetta is unveiled and we hear "Riff A," again: the arpeggios/harmonics, which opened the song | Music breaks down <br> Gtr. Arpeggios / slight harmonics <br> Reprise of Red Barchetta Theme ("Riff A") | 1:56 |
| Ged's vocals almost seem distant when they re-enter the song at approximately 2:00. The wall of sound threatens to overtake the vocals. This is not by accident, as an unveiling of the car reveals the weight of history now resting on the narrator's shoulders. | Vocal: "I strip away..." | 1:56–2:00 |
| The shining car—what was and what is. | Bass <br><br> Gtr. Reprise of Red Barchetta Theme ("Riff C") | 2:01 |
| Lifeson cedes the lead to bass, here. The least likely lead instrument takes front and center; the relic, the red Barchetta, is about to hit the open roads | Bass lead | 2:10 |
| Chaos, excitement, lawlessness | Mess of sound: cymbal wash coinciding with vocals ("tires", "gravel," "weekly crime") | 2:20 |
| Tear out, burnt rubber | Heavily efx gtr. in conjunction with whammy bar (creating ascending notes) | 2:26 |

(continued)

**Table 1. (continued)**

| Visual/Musical Motifs | Instrumentation | Time |
|---|---|---|
| Speed Section, includes "tracking" or "traveling" shots. We get a sense of the camera following the car, heading for a distant point on the horizon | "Speed chase" Chords (Majors) – multi-tracked guitars – underpinned by eighth notes<br><br>Vocals: "wind … in my hair…" (2:41)<br><br>The time flips back and forth between 4/4 to 2/4, quickening the pulse of the song | 2:30 |
| Rush's use of descending notes seems ironic, since the narrator is on a "high." Can be interpreted as the driver's attainment of total bliss and a shedding of modern-day "consciousness"<br><br>Close-up shots of the interior of the car and the eyes of the driver … | Vocals: "adrenaline surge…"<br><br>Peart's drum fill, which descends in pitch, shadows descending guitar notes. Peart moves from higher pitched toms, on the left side of the kit, to lower, on the right, and ends his fill on the snare, grounding the section | 2:57 |
| Driver communing with nature and machine – the human, environmental, and mechanical are one. | Bridge<br><br>Vocals: "well-weathered leather…"<br><br>Some Major Chords and Flats depicting transitional state and transformation of the driver | 3:00–3:15 |
| Car skids out | Vocals: "Every nerve aware…"<br><br>Shattering/screech effect (efx trail skates from left to right channel in stereo image) | 3:16–3:20 |
| Roaming free | Nasally "tunnel effect" Gtr. solo<br><br>Time signatures flip back and forth from 3/4 to 4/4, building excitement, keeping us on edge – a precursor to the chase.<br><br>Bass solo<br><br>Roundhouse drum fill | 3:21 |
| Caution: Confrontation Ahead… | Reprise Warble Gtr.<br><br>Synth – Taurus pedals | 3:42 |

| Visual/Musical Motifs | Instrumentation | Time |
|---|---|---|
| Climactic point in the plot; action in imminent | Excitable (Major) Chords<br>Synth – Taurus pedals | 3:53 |
| A test of man and machine – a liberating drive becomes a race for freedom | Link between Geddy's bass line and driver's subversion, again | 3:54 |
| | Vocals: "Suddenly..." | |
| | Gtr. ("Riff C" – Barchetta Theme reprise) | |
| A ride born of mischievousness, turns nearly terminal | Vocals: "Go screaming through the valley..." | 4:14–4:20 |
| | Bass | |
| | Gtr. ("Riff C") | |
| | Mess of sound, again: cymbal wash coinciding with | |
| | vocals ("another joins the chase...") | |
| Instability and uncertainty on the outcome of this adventure | Bass and Gtr. slight dissonance | 4:21–4:39 |
| | Gtr. Warble | |
| | Peart's use of flams (at 4:33) giving the sensation of being stymied or stuck in the mud – appropriate for the predicament in which the narrator finds himself (i.e., being chased by two metallic police hover craft) | |
| Action is ratcheted up and coiled like a cobra set to strike | Gtr. Warble (continued) | 4:41–4:46 |
| | Vocals: "Drive like the wind..." and "Straining limits..." | |
| A brief glimpse of hope | Vocals: "...desperate plan..." | 4:50–4:53 |
| | Excitable Chords | |
| A temporary resolution; a truce ...<br><br>The driver looking over his shoulder; and a high-angle view of the wreckage of the alloy aircraft<br><br>Destruction all around, yes, but our hero gets away | Vocals: "At the one-lane bridge..."<br><br>Gtr. Chords (Incidental Reprise) Mix of Major and Suspended chords | Approx. 4:53 |

(continued)

**Table 1. (continued)**

| Visual/Musical Motifs | Instrumentation | Time |
|---|---|---|
| A pyrrhic victory?: Outlawed sportster and its driver are victorious, temporarily; they've averted total disaster but not danger; the drive is a detour—a single act of defiance, effectively protesting draconian traffic laws | Vocals: "Race back to the farm..." to dream with uncle ...<br><br>Drum fills<br><br>Gtr. Chords<br><br>Mix of major and suspended chords | 5:00 |
| Our narrator can't escape an oppressive regime, but he can thrill to episodes of individual freedom... and keep alive, not only the dream of the Barchetta and a distant time, but the actual machine of the past... | Gtr. Arpeggios (Reprise Riff A – The Barchetta Riff)<br><br>Bass is a bit more expressive than it was in the opening of the song, marking the miles traveled, a destination reached, lessons learned; Geddy enriches his sound, playing partial chords | 5:11–5:33 |
| The double "hits" or taps indicate the dream is still alive and kicking...<br><br>The ghostly "Riff B" reflects the dreamlike existence of the Barchetta: the car does not get driven very often. It lives as a shadow of its former self, as does the society of which the narrator is a part. A better world, one that does not outlaw Barchettas, exists mostly in fantasies... | Double hot or tap (bass and kick drum)<br><br>Gtr. Arpeggios /harmonics ("Riff B" Reprise)<br><br>Synth – Taurus pedals | 5:35–5:48 |
| Beginning of fade out | Snare<br><br>Gtr. Arpeggios (Reprise and slight variation on "Riff A" and "Riff B") | 5:49–5:57 |
| Near full fade out to black – the nephew and uncle dreaming as the scene dissolves ... Scenes from a memory.<br><br>Is the whole thing a waking dream? A sci-fi scenario that collapses, as the camera pulls in for a tight shot of the eye of the narrator? | Mix of guitars; Slight Reprise of opening "Riff A"—the Barchetta Theme. This recitation reinforces the image of the car, and the dream/hope of what the car represents ...<br><br>Gtr. and bass in sync | 6:01– |

# "YYZ"

Imagine flying in a small plane from Quebec, after finishing recording at Le Studio, and heading home. As the aerodynamic glider, a small private plane, circled Toronto Pearson International Airport, Morse code identifying the airport call letters Y-Y-Z is transmitted out to the pilots from the control tower beacon:

(-.—/-.—/—..)

The incessant beeping tapped-tapped-tapped-tapped its way into their collective psyches:

(-.—/-.—/—..) . . . (-.—/-.—/—..)

Musicians who had shut down cognitive responses after long recording sessions or refused to keep their antennae up for musical stimulation would have missed the subtle if not literal signals.

Not Rush.

With the beeping continuing, Neil chimed in, "This Morse code pattern would make a great rhythm part someday."

Fast-forward to the tour for *Permanent Waves*, and the band is doing their daily sound checks. Peart began playing the Morse code pattern on his bell or ride cymbal, and Geddy would join on bass. Before long, Peart and Lee had worked out the serpentine rhythms of the opening for "YYZ" (or, as some Canadians pronounce it, "Y-Y-Zed").

Assembling the instrumental at sound check jams created a cohesive instrumental, one ignited by the band's flirtation with the sensitive aeronautic instrumentations of modern flight.

These inspired jams gave rise to a number of ideas. What followed logically was the riff that closely aligned with the cadence of the Morse code pattern. This pattern was actually broken up, and the Lee and Peart heard it as being in 5/4 (or 10/8, depending on how one counts). Peart would later transfer the pattern to crotale bell for the band's upcoming record, *Moving Pictures*.

Rush had expressly desired to compose a shorter instrumental than what they'd done in the past, namely, with "La Villa Strangiato," which was a mash-up of unused compositional components. "YYZ" doesn't feel this way at all. Its rhythmic flow is undeniable—the result of Neil and Geddy deliberately writing the thing as a groove-based nonvocal track.

Some might peg "La Villa Strangiato" as being more technically demanding, perhaps based on the endurance level required to play such an extended track live, but "YYZ" is the instrumental Rush had been chasing for years—and continued in hot pursuit of, as evidenced by "Where's My Thing?," "Leave That Thing Alone," and "The Main Monkey Business."

As was the order of the day, a minimalistic approach hits the sweet spot, and the result was the four-minute-and-twenty-four-second "YYZ." This was to be a denser, more compact instrumental. No easy task. As they'd done for *Hemispheres*, a challenge was thrown down and had to be met.

Lee pounds the C–F#–C note grouping of the 5/4 Morse code opening riff until the bass drops to play the low note of the octave (at approximately 0:29); then the bass is double-tracked (0:43), significantly beefing up the sound in what might be considered the "verse" section of this instrumental.

The irony in Rush not being considered a heavy metal band is that Lifeson and Lee play in unison a so-called demonic triad, the devil's interval, often associated with gothic metal. This triad of notes, or tritone ("flattened fifth"), has been used by various artists and composers over the decades and centuries, including Black Sabbath, Jimi Hendrix, King Crimson (especially in the band's interpretation of Holst's "Mars," slyly titled "The Devil's Triangle," from 1970's *In the Wake of Poseidon*), as well as nineteenth-century classical and twentieth-century masters from Wagner to, quite famously, Leonard Bernstein.

Some have theorized that in the Middle Ages, one would be get "locked up" for employing this tritone in one's compositions. But adherence to this notion is likely historical revisionism. There were codified musical modes that the Roman Catholic Church thought acceptable in celebrating the glory of God, and anything that rested outside this was frowned on. However, some maintain that one could invoke the devil and make Satan actually materialize by playing notes arranged in a certain manner.

Whether Rush was running with the devil or not, the flattened fifth is the basis of the opening riff of "YYZ." Rush had used minor keys in riffs before (Led Zeppelin–inspired "A Passage to Bangkok"), but in some instances, these felt exotic or Eastern. However, the combination of C–G♭–C phrasing in "YYZ" lends the opening section of the song an overwhelmingly sinister quality. To make things even stranger, the riff is in 5/4, animating a St. Vitus dance of staccato rhythms hopscotching across the stereo image in both subtly complex and irresistible ways. Once the song settles in 4/4 time, much of it becomes rooted in jazz and, more precisely, blues—that devil music.

The ascending and descending riff, in 12/8, adds a Middle Eastern, almost Spanish, flavoring until Lee and Lifeson play a funky precision riff in 4/4 in simultaneity. (Some sources I've consulted with broke those measures in 12/8 into a digestible quarter-note rather than eighth-note feel.) Alex then comes over the top with the main melody, a lead line littered with sharps, which, to these ears, are along an E-major scale.

On bass, Geddy plays variation on a theme, hitting some of the same notes as Alex but working largely in the cellar (again, what sounds like minors to Alex's majors), enveloping what Lifeson is throwing out there. The track maintains a kind of cohesion as it builds its a two-pronged sonic assault: one from the upper and another from the lower register.

Some of the sonic properties of the music made by the German progressive bands of the 1970s were referenced in the section on "Red Barchetta." By contrast, Rush's gravity-defying "YYZ" was wired to convey pre-vehicular jitters and the jolt or cultural shock of touching down at destination points rather than the act of transport itself. Rush's approach is a much more aerial and, dare I say, humanistic view of travel from, say, Kraftwerk's repetitive, electronic-robotic *Die Mensch-Maschine* esthetic.

Rush explored aspects of sailing the skies as much as the terrain of the internal landscape and the inevitable impact—even side effects—of experiencing different modes of transportation. "A Passage to Bangkok" did this too in its own way, but the wordless "YYZ" captures the mental and physical exhaustion and emotional euphoria cultivated by Peart, our erstwhile Tom Sawyer, and his musical friends during their travel adventures.

Being on the edge of a city and rushing to some exotic place (also well as returning home from said location) coincides with the statement and restatement of the main musical theme. Despite the guys' individual technique stitched into the fiber and fabric of the song, this quality doesn't detract from the song's thrust. We feel the tightness in our bodies, the suspense and uncertainty, and the sensation of traveling, of running late and entering a transitory state.

The trading-fours (swapping-licks) section of the song acts as a representation of the time the band actually plays onstage. Bass and drums engage in what was once known in the jazz and blues worlds as cutting heads. So there's elasticity in

Rush's approach that allowed the song to breathe. This funkiness or jazziness can be traced directly back to the band's interest in jazz-rock fusion around this time, which includes bands such as Weather Report, featuring fretless bass maestro Jaco Pastorius, and Percy Jones's and Phil Collins's hyperactive Brand X.

Rush embarked on an evolutionary process to develop as songwriters as well as grow more adept on their respective instruments with an eye toward becoming more intuitive creative voices. The band's raison d'être shifted constantly, and "YYZ" was one of the inevitable outgrowths of their creative development.

Through riffing, melodic phrasing, a pursuit of technique, and a little assistance from studio technology, the band had the opportunity to flex some muscles, craft a tight instrumental with a high degree of musical interplay, and allow not only a measure of improvisation but also their influences to shine.

Where does this concept come from? We could go back to primitive forms of prehistoric music for one. But, as a modern concept, the home of trading fours likely has its roots in both the classical and the jazz tradition.

"I don't believe that there was ever a moment on those Rush records, maybe *Caress of Steel* [laughs], that the band was overplaying," says Jason Bittner (Shadows Falls and Overkill). "It wasn't, 'Listen to the drummer overplaying.' No, 'Listen to everybody overplaying. Listen to everybody overplaying together.' That's the point. They are making music by doing this."

One of the pioneers of the fusion genre of the late 1960s and early 1970s, guitarist John McLaughlin, discussed in a past interview with me the fiery passion required of artists who choose music and specifically jazz as a career path. In referencing the Mahavishnu Orchestra's influential 1971 record *The Inner Mounting Flame*, McLaughlin related that one's passion was tantamount to embarking on a spiritual journey of self-discovery.

"In India, they talk about the soul being a flame the size of your thumb," McLaughlin told me. "Itself, fire is a very mysterious [thing]. I think it also refers to aspiration, but I think passion is a closer word to it despite the strange connotations that 'passion' can have. I don't believe you can really be a musician without being very passionate about it because this is what makes you a musician in the first place. It's difficult, and you have to master your instrument, especially if you're a jazz musician. You have to figure out who you are; you have to create your style, and to do that, you have to know about yourself. It is a long, arduous process. You've heard references to jazz musicians—'They're smokin',' 'They're on fire.' These references, you find them not only in music but in spiritual matters. It essentially represents your spiritual aspirations."

In short, the members of Rush were coming into their own with "YYZ," in some cases seemingly performing the impossible. At the outset, some of the guys could not fully play the track without woodshedding. It's the "St. Francis of Assisi Rule of Music." St. Francis of Assisi is quoted as saying that on undertaking an endeavor that seems unattainable, one should start by achieving the necessary, then move to the possible. Once you arrive at that point, "suddenly you are doing the impossible."

Terry Brown once told me that he thought the playing on "YYZ" was "astounding" but said that the song certainly was "pushing the guys *way* over the limit. Geddy really couldn't play that when he got into the studio. He had got all the ideas, but to get it to his fingers and get it out the speakers was really hard."

In the first break (1:43), Geddy's fingers spider across the fretboard, even mixing in partial chords, as he glides up the neck. The part is brilliant, but, yes, it's also overdubbed. Geddy clearly punched in: He did not play the "YYZ" bass track in one go.

Via cross fading, Geddy's bass runs for the second break (1:56), what some fellow four-string instrument players consider the Holy Grail Rush bass lick, were also punched in. Lee slides up the neck and then descends, letting his fretting hand travel across all the strings. The third break (2:10) is marked by rolling, ascending runs and harmonics that seem casually tossed in (F# and C).

Granted, Lee is considered a great bassist and was prior to *Moving Pictures*; he even employs harmonics in "Different Strings," but the bassist of "YYZ" seems more in command than the one who recorded *Permanent Waves*. Lee almost had to become a different player to have achieved what he did on the record, almost as if we are hearing two different bassists.

I asked Brown about Lee's vital transformation, and he simply told me, "He just did it." This succinct response is as Zen as it gets. It's almost meditative. And a high level of concentration was certainly needed to complete the track.

Case in point: Peart intimated to *Modern Drummer* magazine that when it came time to record his drums and since he knew the song pretty well by this point in the production process, he did not have any scratch or guide tracks to play along to. It's difficult to believe.

As outrageous as this may sound, in my conversation with Paul Northfield, the lead engineer on *Moving Pictures* indicated that Neil was playing to a click, which may explain the confusion.

When Rush opened for Frank Zappa and Peart saw Terry Bozzio playing furiously, he interpreted what Bozzio was playing as triplets; this influence can be heard in Peart's drum break at approximately 1:49.

As indicated, the band did not play together live in the studio, and they cut the track in one take. It's all the more astounding, Brown might say, that the song retains a level of earthiness and gnarly technical turns. Indeed. The rhythmic thrust is maintained throughout. The bass and drums are in sync, and their combined impact generates a compound, or conglomerate, lead instrument.

Yet an integral part of the instrumental is when Lee and Peart trade fours. For the fills the right-handed Peart plays, he leads with his left hand as he plays orderly triplets and manages to take a swipe at a cymbal or two.

And it's not just execution: sonically, "YYZ" is impressive. Peart's kit here sounds so resonant. Peart had heard drummer Mark Craney (Jethro Tull and Jean-Luc Ponty) playing on a Gino Vanelli live album during the song "Brother to Brother" and liked the sound of his drums. Craney used open-back toms, and microphones were placed inside the shell for his booming sound.

Phil Collins, another influence on Neil, was using open toms and Rototoms as well around this time both with Genesis and Brand X. Collins's sound on the 1978 Genesis studio album . . . *And Then There Were Three* . . . especially seems evidentiary.

"We took off all the lower heads on the large toms and then miked them up from the inside, which is more in fashion in the '70s, where people were having single-headed drums," says Paul Northfield. "They are easier to tune, but they are not as resonant. It made life easier [on the studio], but it was not as musical a kit as a double-headed drum kit."

"In some ways, the combination of intense power and sophistication was, particularly for Neil, a strength and weakness," says Paul Northfield. "What he thought about drums changed the way people approached playing them. A lot of younger progressive drummers would regard his parts as if they were a mountain to climb. But he drove the whole direction of intense power and sophisticated thinking and put that into drumming, and maybe that didn't really exist before him. I think that is his legacy. We lived it by recording him."

Perhaps this was a leading question, unfair when I asked it, but I posited to Lifeson once: in the battle between technique and feel, what wins on a Rush record? "Feel, always," Lifeson said. "We have always been kind of anal about our records and how we recorded them in the past, and we were very disciplined. But I think really it comes down to feel more than anything else."

Lifeson even intimated that he tends to "play things that I naturally go to" rather than force ideas and have them be contrived.

As always, Lifeson was given free rein to *feel* his way around the track. Why not? Geddy and Neil had their spotlight; now (at 2:22) it was Alex's turn at the microphone.

Lifeson exhibits a similar kind of fluidity as Allan Holdsworth did throughout the late 1970s. The faint traces of "In the Dead of Night" by prog rock supergroup U.K. and "One of a Kind, Part Two" and "If You Can't Stand the Heat" by Bill Bruford's band are echoed in Lifeson's pull-offs, string bends, finger vibrato, and busy runs in general, approximating the tone and approach of Holdworth's "outside" soloing.

It appears, at least to my ears, that Lifeson slips just outside the chord structure for a brief few seconds to play some "outside" notes not tethered to the foundational key.

"Holdsworth—especially at that point in his career—was just hearing and playing things that to this day have him cited by guitarists the world over, including me, as being truly next level," says Eric Barnett of Fred Barchetta and Points North. "I can relate to Alex here, myself. I can try to play what Holdsworth played but can't comprehend how he created what he did and how he was able to make such outside playing still sound so melodic and fluid. But it inspires me to stretch, and so here and there, I'm able to get out of my comfort zone and bring in an influence that might not be as natively in my toolbox. That's what I hear all over *Moving Pictures*, and 'YYZ' and 'Limelight' are both great examples of that."

Lifeson plays "outside" in another respect: with a sense of freedom and nomadic aplomb.

Jazz-rock artists—and we can loosely include Rush by way of "YYZ" here—have for years incorporated scales and rhythms from all over the world, whether it was Africa, the Caribbean, South America, Asia, or Europe. In addition, while the likes of Peter Gabriel and Talking Heads were being seduced by the enchanting polyrhythms of Africa and South America, Rush too, magpies they were, had been scanning the planet for musical inspiration. Within this context, we are transported across an ocean (and time) to a different place.

Lifeson's guitar solo is swept up in this tide of global musical fusion. To wit, "YYZ" may be to date the most overt example of Aleksandar Živojinović expressing himself through the Middle Eastern and Eastern European modalities that snake through his performance here. They manifest, perhaps, in honor of Lifeson's own Yugoslavian ethnic heritage.

Lifeson's appearance in the 1973 film *Come On, Children*, directed by Allan King, seems relevant here. For many reasons, interestingly enough, he was not a stranger to the camera; he was in moving pictures before he made the album of the same title.

On camera, we see Alek, a budding rock star who feels compelled to rebel against his family's wishes. They want him to forget music and build a more stable career and not quit his schooling. Both Alek and his parents seem to be working either end of the same point: having the freedom to be mobile and secure in himself.

On the verge of "making it" on a superstar level, the globe-trotting guitarist, now known as Alex Lifeson, has been true to himself. He squeezed out one of the greatest guitar moments on Rush's greatest single record, which is indebted to his past and musical tradition. At the same time, Lifeson tips his hat to the diversity of one of his English guitarist heroes. Jimmy Page's "CIA" guitar tuning, a fusion of Celtic, Indian, and Arabic styles, can be heard in Led Zeppelin songs such as "Four Sticks," "Friends," "Kashmir," and "No Quarter."

Led Zeppelin's musky travelogue "Kashmir" resides largely in the realm of the imagination despite its title. "YYZ" is similarly cloaked in mystique, even if to a lesser extent. Lifeson's personal heritage adds an extra layer of authenticity, perhaps a truly personal connection, to his brand of "Eastern" music, one thinks.

Lifeson's solo seems to hint at the whirling, alacritous violin runs we hear in Balkan gypsy music. This is far from academic, however, but Lifeson's playing roams a bit through several stylistic territories. Although we would be hard pressed to call it a re-creation of traditional Bosnian folk or Romani music, maybe that's the message of "YYZ": pinpointing a location on a map—if indeed this is possible regarding any music's origins—wouldn't serve such a global song.

Of course, the concept of cultural imperialism doesn't escape this writer, but heading too far in this direction misses the point: Artists absorb influences and don't collapse their creative antennae when crossing a border into a new world, either geographically or spiritually.

Indeed. Peart's near-Latin ride-bell cymbal/snare pattern is based on a form of paradiddles and alternate sticking pattern and not only speaks to the globalism of the track but also is the band's raison d'être: rhythmic fluidity in Rush's compositions.

Like progressive rockers from Britain, the Canadian Peart internalized an influence, reinterpreted it, and spat it out differently from the way he'd heard it. What emerged was a newfangled invention, a hybrid of the musician's known skill set and "the other."

"At the time, I didn't know anything about Latin feels and Latin rhythms, so I just heard it as 'The Neil Peart Ride Pattern,'" says Brian Tichy. "I absolutely loved it. I initially thought he was trying to 'trick' the listener. Meaning when I first heard it, I thought he was playing the ride when he hit the 2 and 4 on the snare, which would create groups of three and five sixteenth notes, which would be very fast and difficult to play. When I realized he was not hitting the ride when he hit the snare, I was like, 'I think I can do that. He almost tricked me.'"

The iconic if deceptive "smashing glass" sound *wasn't*, but it does add to the song's sonic stew. There was no glass, and this explains the mysterious "plywood" credit next to Peart's name on the liner notes: Peart whacks plywood against the back of a stool.

Although the sound raises the specter of the Factory label's use of electronic experimentation (the modern techno-industrial movement's fertile crescent), it also evokes the whoosh of a thrashing whip or a stampede of Spanish dancers cracking castanets with flamenco flair.

"There's a definite school of thought that says rock should be pure and approached in a particular way," Geddy once told me. "We are fusion artists in a way; we mix up all kinds of stuff. Sometimes we get very technical. Maybe that is not in the same spirit that some critics believe in. . . . There's a place for our bombast in the world, and it is fun to do."

## "LIMELIGHT"

The star-making machine operates via a distorted and dysfunctional sense of the social contract. The recording industry, the media, and so on churn out (or promote) musicians, and in return, artists surrender any sense of privacy that noncelebrities often take for granted.

By March 1980, *Permanent Waves* had moved 500,000 units in the United States alone on its way to topping 1 million records sold in America by 1987. Radio airplay and headliner gigs were welcomed; at the same time, they had a corrosive effect on Peart in that fan obsession (even stalkers) and a general invasion of privacy constituted a new kind of unnerving norm. *Moving Pictures* would surpass *Permanent Waves* in every way possible, and Rush became an instrument of the very concept and celebrity-birthing machine they sing about in "Limelight."

Peart was determined not to be at its mercy.

Perhaps in an effort to make sense of the world, Peart turned to the classics. The Shakespearian quote referenced in the song, "all the world's a stage," from the play *As You Like It* hints at the many roles we play—the masks we wear—for "outsiders." However, at the same time, Peart's interpretation of the line "merely players" serves to diminish the concept of fame and the inherent phoniness of it all.

There's a wider universal plan, according to Shakespeare (and Peart): We're cogs in the cosmic wheel. You might receive earthly adulation, but you *ain't* special: you're a character in a divine play just like the rest of us. The organizational principle of the universe is the great equalizer.

"Limelight" might not directly challenge Andy Warhol's "fifteen minutes" theory, but it does undermine the notion that anyone would want fame in the first place. What little tolerance Peart had prior to *Moving Pictures* had apparently evaporated, and in its place came isolationism and self-exile from the public square. Peart seemed to use as a mantra the Humphrey Bogart quote "All you owe the public is a good performance."

What we're hearing and reading in "Limelight" is public psychotherapy—a kind of coping mechanism, perhaps even some validation for Peart's stance. Still struggling with his newfound fame, limited as it was at the time, Peart crystalized his philosophy with "Limelight," making the song both confessional and prophetic.

Peart told writer Gary Graff of the *Detroit Free Press* back in 1982 that he shaved his signature moustache because his face became too recognizable. "[Fame] was something we weren't prepared for when it came," Peart said.

It's always a dance, a balance, between the celebratory aspects of playing music and the darker aspects of fame. When Peart joined the band back in 1974, his first show with Rush was in front of 10,000 people, opening for Uriah Heep and Manfred Mann's Earth Band in Pittsburgh. Peart may have resisted the urge to self-glorify and be treated as a celebrity, but he admitted to getting a surge of electricity sensing the excitement in the venue. This internal struggle involving the seductive power of adulation went unresolved for years. Some might say it never was.

Universality is what makes "Limelight" work, one thinks. That's why it's surprising to know that initially, Peart had written the lyrics in the first person until Lee suggested some alterations be made. By changing the original line, which read, "I must put up barriers . . . ," for instance, to "One must put up . . . ," the song transforms into something instantly relatable. What Lee and Peart did was turn the idea of "making the personal universal" around 180 degrees. This transition also helped Geddy assume a role and easily slip into the voice of the lyric writer.

"We are low-key people and not very image conscious, and we never chased that kind of lifestyle and publicity," Geddy Lee once told me. "We think like musicians and act like musicians. Some . . . of us are more fiercely private. Neil, for example, is a very private person and withdrawn guy, and that is the way he chooses to live."

"Always very private," former cochair and co-CEO of the Atlantic Group Val Azzoli, who also worked for Ray Danniels, told me once. "Never came to parties. He was never the rock and roller in the band, you know? He wasn't a schmuck; he wasn't a bad guy. He was very respectful of the other two guys."

Growing celebrity is a double-edged sword. Led Zeppelin shunned the spotlight (for a time) and were not always available to the press for interviews. While Rush was accessible, keeping portions of their lives rather hidden from the light of day only meant their fan base spent more time wondering about them. As private as the Rush guys were about their personal business, this act of self-preservation created, perhaps inadvertently, an aura around the band that might not have been there otherwise.

To the outside world, the guys appeared down to earth but were also building a bit of mystery. Although "Limelight" wishes to distance its creators from fame, the very basis of the song, how it was recorded, spoke to the unreality of the mythic, exalted, liturgic rock show. When cutting the tracks for "Limelight," Rush literally envisioned themselves performing onstage.

Taken at face value, Rush was playing for the camera (the recording apparatus and studio setting). They were performing in their own indie film that cast themselves as the stars. In actuality, the band did just that for the concert film *Exit . . . Stage Left* for a crowd of nearly 10,000 people at the Montreal Forum in March 1981. Imagining the lights and heightened sense of awareness added to the energy of the track.

Having said this, as prophetic as the lyrics were, the sonic qualities of "Limelight" make it one of the most important songs on *Moving Pictures* and in the Rush catalog in general.

Lifeson decided to try a different make of guitar to capture sounds that may not have been totally possible with the equipment he'd been using in 1980.

Throughout "Limelight," Lifeson had created fresh, electronic textures. He had used effects (a guitar synthesizer on *Hemispheres*) and recorded plenty of overdubs to make his musical statements in the 1970s, but on records such as *Hemispheres* and *Permanent Waves*, he'd used primarily Gibsons for his main guitar sans vibrato bar. For years, Lifeson had been identified by his Gibson ES-335 and, to a lesser degree, the Gibson 355. Those types of Gibson were at one time associated with artists such as Jorma Kaukonen of Jefferson Airplane and Alvin Lee of Ten Years After—the very essence of 1960s electric rock guitar and something Lifeson could not fail to be influenced by.

But back in 1980, Lifeson wanted a new guitar for a new decade. Gibsons were largely out; custom Fender Stratocasters were in and became Lifeson's vehicle to translate the sounds he was hearing inside his head onto the recording tracks. Whistling vibrato, sonic delirium tremens, as well as the extreme bending of notes can rarely be easily created without a tremolo arm.

*Moving Pictures* was the coming-out party for these custom Strats. Ultimately, there were three custom Fenders that Lifeson used: an arctic white body with a black pick guard (later dubbed the Hentor Sportscaster), a black custom Strat (Porkflapsocaster), and a red-bodied guitar with a mirrored pick guard, which does not appear to have ever been given a name. Some dubbed it "Red."

"With *Moving Pictures*, that was when the Hentor was introduced to the world," says Freddie Gabrsek, an Ontario-based luthier who has worked on Lifeson's guitars, reverse engineered them, and sells replicas of the custom instruments with portions of the proceeds going to charity (http://www.freddysfrets.com).

Prior to officially handling the spec-tech work on Alex's guitars, Gabrsek, through his relationship with a mutual friend, had the opportunity to take the Hentor for a test drive and was knocked out by the sound of the instrument. "I have always been a Strat player, but it had a voice like I've never heard in a Strat before," says Gabrsek. "In the back of my mind, that stuck with me—how good it sounded."

Why?

"In the 1970s, Fender used northern ash instead of swamp ash in their ash guitars," says Gabrsek. "Northern ash is the same species but heavier. People generally do not want to strap a boat anchor around their neck if they are playing all night. Because of that, that was one of the reasons the thing sounded so great. Every other Strat I played was a traditional alder or swamp ash or something like that. It had a different voice. There is no excessive, harmonic bloom [with northern ash]. You hit a note or a chord, it slaps you in the face, and then it's gone. It does not have this weird overtone after the fact."

Veneman Music, in the Washington, D.C./Virginia area, first worked on the custom Strats, but Lifeson had since had alterations made to the guitars. A factory-issued pickup in the Fender near the bridge of the guitar was later switched out for a Gibson humbucker to achieve a chunkier tone. As late as the mid-1980s, the black Strat, what Lifeson dubbed the Porkflapsocaster, also had a humbucker near the bridge. There is some debate as to which custom Fender Lifeson uses in "Limelight," but the official video for the song shows Lifeson playing the black Strat; in the concert film *Exit . . . Stage Left*, it's the arctic white one.

In conversations with Paul Northfield, he recommended using the video as a guide, but Gabrsek explains that Alex was always "very coy about divulging specs."

Gabrsek, who was building a run of Hentors at the time of our interview, says that "there were even online clubs showing off their own versions of Hentor Sportscaster that they made. I looked at this and said, 'Nobody has this right. Nobody had the wood correct, nobody had the fretboard material correct, and nobody had quartersawn maple necks; nobody knew about the wiring.'"

After the mid-1980s or so, Lifeson was rarely seen with the custom Strats. I once questioned Lifeson regarding their whereabouts, and he said, "They're retired. At home."

As of 2021, Lifeson was exploring plans to auction off many of his guitars to raise money for charity.

Usually, any aspects of a popular record are enshrined in fans' memories. The musical instruments Lifeson used on *Moving Pictures* might appear to some as a collection of talismans, imbued with the power to generate special tonal qualities that few can explain how or why.

But, apparently, the tools of the trade were not sacred to Lifeson. He was in hot pursuit of a sometimes elusive but esthetic value rather than a magical object with vibrating strings that possessed paranormal powers. "Real magic" may have been spun not through manufactured pieces of equipment (even customized ones) but through the guitarist's fingers.

I specifically referenced Jeff Beck, someone I knew Lifeson was influenced by. "It comes down to the hands, doesn't it?" I asked Lifeson. "That's what I've always said," Lifeson told me.

Elements of Lifeson's guitar sound make his tone transparent and yet robust—virtually unique to him and the time frame.

Guitarists for decades have chased this sound, as if it were the Holy Grail Rush guitar tone. "'Chased' would be a wonderful way to describe it—because I don't think it's anything that can ever be 'caught,' arguably even by Alex himself afterwards," says guitarist Eric Barnett of Points North and Fred Barchetta. "There's an amazing liquid quality to it on the record—a magical convergence of his playing and a crazy amount of gain and sustain that somehow translates into singing clarity."

Rush alchemy at work again.

Much of Lifeson's tone and attack during the *Moving Pictures* era was influenced by celebrated fusion/progressive rock guitarmeister Allan Holdsworth of Tempest, Soft Machine, Bruford, and U.K. fame. "Points North opened for Holdsworth a few times before his untimely passing, and having seen Allan up close, there's definitely a straight line to draw there tonally," says Barnett. "In my opinion, the phrasing of 'Limelight' also pays homage to Holdsworthian concepts as well, the intervallic playing, for one, although more 'inside' and melodically conventional than Holdsworth. If not the same long legato runs, there's almost an absence of audible pick attack, where the notes sing more like a voice than a guitar."

"Alex would have been using a Marshall with a two-channel module and not one with super multiple overdrive channels and such," says Northfield. "Those tended to come later. Marshall 100-watt amps. He had two running in the studio, I think."

In addition to the Marshall wattage, the song was powered by the multitracking approach that Brown, Northfield, and Lifeson took to the album. Six tracks, three per channel, were layered, including the killer opening riff.

"It would have been very precisely layered and carefully tuned so it doesn't sound as chorus-y," says Northfield. "The blend would have been one track dominant and two tracks 'tucked' back a little bit so you get the fullness of multitracking but articulation of a single track. I'm sure that is why people who want to get that sound may have had trouble."

Another aspect of the recording for which Lifeson reflected a Holdsworth influence was in the way the Rush guitarist cut his tracks—this according to a conversation I had with recording engineer and producer Adam Moseley, who was present for some of the recording sessions for the first U.K. album, featuring Holdsworth.

"That was the case with *Moving Pictures*," confirms Northfield. "Alex would have been in the control room doing his guitar performance. The amps would be in the studio with a long cable driving the speakers and stuff. It's amazing I have any hearing left from that era."

The main guitar riff of "Limelight" is a hybrid creation: Lifeson plays notes along the E-major scale, transitioning into a dampened B chord. Various chordal shifts mix with fretted notes, and by the time we enter the first verse, Lifeson blurred the lines between arpeggios, strumming, and chordal playing—throwing in, among others, a G#-minor suspended fourth chord.

The timing of the piece is another kettle of fish. Some have counted the opening section as bars as 3/4 followed by 4/4, but others note the entire section, up to the first verse, as being in 7. Similarly, the start of the first verse can be written in 6 as opposed to two bars of 3/4 followed by a bar of 4/4 and a bar of 2/4.

Granted, although the band is not juggling bars of 19/16 followed by 21/8, 13/8, and 7/4 into 9/8 or some such bewildering rhythmic configuration, one must marvel at the guys' mastery of metrics here: The combined effect of all these changes seems to take on a life all their own. The song is restless, yet all three of the members of Rush pacify the beast and pass through odd time signatures with ease (and Geddy does so as a singer as well). It's all very smooth—this despite Neil ratcheting up the intensity by playing one of the most unusual drum patterns to ever open a rock song.

Peart uses his double-kick to play triplets—a neat little trick he learned from watching Tommy Aldridge.

"To me, the catchiest, most badass intro fill Neil does, which makes no sense, as far as the riff he is playing over, yet upon first listen, at least to me, sounded completely perfect, is the intro to 'Limelight,'" says Brian Tichy. "It starts off all big and mighty with the toms on '2' and '4,' then he throws in a triplet on the kick, followed by snare flams and then an off-beat cymbal choke to wind it up. Rush and Neil teetered the fine line of potentially overplaying/prog rock, but it was catchy and hooky enough to get on radio; it was above-average musicianship done in a tasty enough way to maintain an arena following."

"Neil introduced real power into progressive, intricate drumming arrangements," says Northfield. "There may have been others, but that was the thing that blew everybody away. His parts were really complicated, and sometimes there were songs that he would rarely play the same bar twice in a row, like in a song like 'Limelight.' It was always these highly arranged drum parts but then played with intense physical force."

Following suit, Lifeson freely changes tone and feel throughout the song. In the refrain, for instance, he plays arpeggiated "glassy" suspended major and minor-sharp chord riffs that are brought to life via a chorusing effect; heavily distorted chords enter soon after.

Geddy's bass notes often act as grooves in a gear, sometimes syncopated with Peart's snare beats, sometimes "resting" and leaving space for Peart's snare beats, and at other times complementing Lifeson's chords and single-note runs. As is often the case with Lee, he's able to take the lead while also reinforcing the structure of the song—all while maintaining the bottom end, very much like his early rock idols: John Entwistle of the Who and Chris Squire of Yes.

"Limelight" also displays Lee's range as a vocalist. Lee's dramatic reading of the lyrics (1:54) fittingly coincides with the song's reference to the Western world's most celebrated playwright, Shakespeare, and is underscored by Peart's showstopping, sixteenth-note sextuplet snare drum fill.

Geddy's voice climbs the ladder, hitting higher notes in the fourth stanza ("All the world's indeed . . ."); this alters the complexion and perception of the passage, elevating it to a kind of bridge section and enhancing our understanding of the lyrics.

But perhaps the song's greatest sonic delight is Lifeson's guitar solo. It's less a performance-based solo than abstract art existing beyond the parameters of the natural flow of the song. Its slo-mo action is the musical equivalent of being intravenously injected with some form of sedative. We feel drugged.

It's fiendish in that it coincides with the text (and subtext) of our surrendering to fame and being intoxicated with the idea of celebrity.

Synth supports Lifeson's elastic runs, acting as a rudder for the entire section. The 3/4 time offers the perfect frame for the floating fragments of sound Lifeson creates, like the timeless qualities of Debussy's *Snowflakes Are Dancing* (in 6/8).

Rife with fretboard slides up and down the neck, not to mention "up-and-down" picking, string bends, and sonic dive bombs, the solo that Lifeson performs with the assistance of vibrato bar is enhanced by reverb and delay effects.

Very little of Lifeson's style screamed hair metal guitarist. However, the Bach-like mathematical precision and repetition of grouped notes during the riffing section of the solo (slightly) hints at the picked scalar runs of neoclassical metal years before this subgenre was popularized.

Via whammy bar and looped delay, Lifeson creates a trail of repetitive electronic quavers (3:12). This standing wave takes center stage as the song's main sonic event. The controlled oscillation spirals into the background as Geddy reenters on vocals. Although faint, the electronic whistling continues until heavy chords reappear (3:30), recalling those first heard at approximately 1:09 into the song.

The musical instrument technology and gadgetry applied here contain shades of the feedback squalls that guitarist Adrian Belew commanded as a member of David Bowie's band on the 1978 live album *Stage*.

However, all things considered, Lifeson's playing is like a tutorial on how to play progressive hard rock electric guitar; it's both technical and impressionistic. Further, the meditative (narco-meditative?) aspects of the solo point to David Gilmour perhaps more than most other progressive or psychedelic rock guitarists. Arguably, "Limelight" is Lifeson's "Comfortably Numb": a musical moment embodying everything the guitarist is about and likely for which he'll be remembered.

"'Limelight' is and always will be in a class of its own," says Eric Barnett. "Alex has said in interviews that it was his favorite solo as well."

Geddy's nomadic bass line warbles and waddles up and down along what sounds like E- and B-major scales. Playing yin to Lifeson's yang, the bass leaves deep imprints in the muddy depths of the sonic range while the guitarist's notes quaver and spiral through the air.

As the song speeds towards its final lap, Peart unleashes rounds of rousing fills, framed largely by flams and double-kick triplets—a monster performance that brings the song to a rapturous, rumbling end. If this were happening onstage, the guys would take a quick bow, and Peart would wave to the crowd from behind his drum throne, and off he goes.

This studio "performance" left many breathless, maybe even the band itself. Skillfully evading rock star kitsch and collecting all the tension building throughout the song's duration, the climax accelerates the listener—and the music—toward orgiastic release.

Cinematic songs: The visionary and accessible tracks on Side I of *Moving Pictures* complement the filmic qualities of the music on Side II.

"The thing that blew me away when we were doing *Moving Pictures* was when we finished 'Limelight,' and the drum fills at the end; they are like multistroke rolls around the kick," says Northfield. "I thought, 'That is insane.' It is so powerful."

Author Susan Fast's observation about "Stairway to Heaven" and its placement at the end of the original side 1 of *Led Zeppelin IV* is applicable to "Limelight" in that "the song was followed by silence that allowed for reflection."

We're at the halfway mark in our journey, and had we been spinning the vinyl format version of *Moving Pictures*, the LP would need to be flipped over. In cinematic terms, the cue marks are visible: we've reached theatrical intermission. The projectionist threads a celluloid strip in preparation for the second act and readies a

*Moving Pictures* Side II: Darkness and Light

second projector for seamless transition between reels (in this case songs). This short respite allows us to survey where the band—and we—have been and where all this may be going.

# CHAPTER 9

# CINEMA PARADISO: SIDE II

"The Camera Eye" was the first song to be written for *Moving Pictures*. Odd, actually. The band's commitment to streamlining their songs and being more immediate seems to belie their instinct to record an epic track.

Even more confusing if a little intriguing, Rush was fixing to pursue a song based on lyrics Peart wrote, inspired by Thomas Hardy's short stories, collectively known as the *Wessex Tales*. If *Sir Gawain and the Green Knight* was inappropriate for *Permanent Waves*, then Hardy is a complete anachronism in the time of *Moving Pictures*.

Quickly abandoned.

Next?

Peart had also read John Dos Passos's novelistic trilogy *U.S.A.*, which includes individual works *The 42nd Parallel*, *The Big Money*, and *Nineteen-Nineteen*. Throughout the series, Dos Passos injects recurring passages titled "The Camera Eye."

"The Camera Eye" sections of the novels, as described by author and editor E. L. Doctorow in his introduction to the series, slipped in subjective details of the narrator's (Dos Passos's?) childhood and kept them independent from the rest of the text. Each one of the three books encompassing Dos Passos's *U.S.A.* series is a triple novel. Autobiographical scenes are threaded through myriad parallel plots. The eleven-minute "The Camera Eye" bears an unlikely resemblance to the unorthodox structure of these books.

Dos Passos heard the voices of everyday, turn-of-the-century Americans and documented them, pursuing their personal histories, even when their existence ran to ruin—especially when their fortunes ran aground. We're privy to the private lives and dreams of ordinary folk, who "live to the pulsebeat of their times," reads commentary for the Signet Classic edition.

Peart's own transcendent episodes in London and New York note the manic rhythms of metropolises but offer a much more meditative experience than that of Dos Passos's novels. Peart stands amid a tapestry of humanity and observes it. He is apart from this environment and yet a part. This split-screen effect, subtle as it may be, overlaps conceptually with the literary technique Dos Passos infused into his *U.S.A.* novels.

Although "The Camera Eye," on the surface, always seemed the odd song out on *Moving Pictures* given its focus and length, in retrospect, the personal observations are aligned with a celebration of the individual—an individual's experiences—that rests alongside "Tom Sawyer," the antiauthoritarianism of "Red Barchetta," and the self-exile of "Limelight."

As a "farm boy" from Canada, Peart had nearly always championed cities as a destination spot, and this was crystalized in the dichotomy of "Subdivisions" from 1982. Despite what some might objectively label as long-standing, glaring problems and urban decay, Peart accounts for all experiences there.

Elements of the lyrics comprise a kind of diegesis but are also anti-diegetic: the characters in this movie are oblivious to some of the sights and sounds, but the narrator off camera, detached enough from the action, sees a much broader band of imagery in these urban settings.

But there's a larger message here about being programmed and ignoring one's surroundings. The robotic repetitiveness of humanity flooding through the streets of London and New York has its musical corollary in the buzzing, chirping, and squeaking (if not organic) synthesizer threaded through the entire track.

In both instances, whether he is looking at New York or his one-time home (London), Peart is lamenting a lack of vigilance. Acknowledging the failure to capture fleeting moments falls dangerously close to lyrical despondency.

"I wore the record out," says drummer Jason Sutter (Cher, Marilyn Manson, P!nk, and Chris Cornell). "'Tom Sawyer,' 'Red Barchetta'—*Moving Pictures* has a kind of pop side, but then there is a lot of weird, dark shit on that record. Very melancholy. Strange, dark, impenetrable. Even considering things like *Caress of Steel* or *Hemispheres*, which is similarly dark. At that point, the early 1980s, I really believe that things like the 'The Camera Eye' and other songs on that second side really confused us. I didn't know what any of that was. It was so over our heads."

"The Camera Eye," as indicated, was the first song written for the album, but it still needed some finessing to massage it into shape. Not unlike "La Villa Strangiato," which was the end result of different sections stitched together in the studio, "The Camera Eye" was constructed through editing.

"They would not have done that in one take, from beginning to end," says Northfield. "As I remember, it was done sectionally. Rush were mostly playing live in the studio. They came from a period where they did twenty-minute songs. So those were not done in one take. They would play the first couple of minutes or a minute. Depending on the particular section, it may or may not be challenging or relatively easy to record . . . and so you would sequentially go through the song. You might use the opening of one really great intro and then the body of the song from somewhere else and then add in pieces that seem to be better from different parts. It may be three or four edited parts to do a five-minute portion of the song. After it's all edited together, invariably, then the bass and guitars would be recut."

One of the strengths of "The Camera Eye" is its flow relative to other long-form Rush inventions. Whereas earlier multisectional compositions had their musical components refracted by metrical complexity, here Rush largely forgoes math equations and fractals and keeps the foot just over the accelerator to maintain forward thrust.

The combined impact of its electronic pulse, driving beat, and repetitive rhythms apes a loop-based minimalist esthetic derived from German art-rock artists of the early and mid-1970s.

Young German rock bands felt compelled to forge a new identity. They'd been bombarded and burdened by the split between East and West Germany. John Weinzierl, guitarist of Amon Düül II, went as far as to tell me that the psyche-prog band "didn't want to have an English name, necessarily, and placed umlaut dots to point out that we are Germans."

What Lee, Lifeson, and Peart were doing may have had some precedent in the music of Harmonia, Tangerine Dream, Amon Düül II, Kraftwerk, or Guru Guru. The electronic experimentation in "The Camera Eye" recalled shades of the humanistic aspects of electronic experimentation German producer Conny Plank infused in his studio work with some of Germany's greatest creative minds from the early to the mid-1970s. Although more active and unpredictable, there is here a measure of impressionistic art, something almost Cluster & Eno–esque about Rush's electronic passages.

Geddy had referenced Genesis when describing the synthesizer in the song, grappling with descriptions of the sonic properties available via the Oberheim. But if we compare the synth sounds in "The Camera Eye" to anything in British progressive rock, it might be the knotty, hybrid, ambient/classical sequences Eddie Jobson created with a polyphonic synthesizer on the U.K. 1978 debut.

Closer cousins are Peter Gabriel's second album and the Who. Gabriel was himself seemingly influenced by Pete Townshend and his early 1970s electronically generated biorhythmic patterns. "The Camera Eye" claims kinship with the Who's "Baba O'Reilly" and "Won't Get Fooled Again." Although the pumping, driving keyboard rhythm Geddy rocks is closer to "Chopsticks" than Chopin's piano Mazurkas, there's more than meets the ear. It's infused with the "pulse beat" of the city.

"The Camera Eye" is simply a texturalist's dream. The song's opening lays on a matrix of hypnotic, repetitive, synthesized, and electronic bleeping-blurping sounds. The synth research-and-development bug that bit Roger Waters and David Gilmour via the Synthi-A syntheszier also took hold of Alex and Geddy by way of an Oberheim.

"There were some really interesting sample-hold patterns that make it sound complicated, but you are just holding down a chord, and [the keyboard] is making those [vocalizes bleeping] sounds," says Northfield. "That is all filtering. Geddy was using the Oberheim. He didn't consider himself to be a keyboard player, but he and Alex were looking for interesting sounds. So, between them, they would play around on the Oberheim and . . . hold two keys down, and suddenly you have this soundscape, harmonically simple but texturally interesting."

The random (or seemingly random) jumble of noises is sufficiently complex as to create fresh sensory phenomena nearly every time we hear it. It breathes; it's organic. Still, this was the era of *Star Wars* and *The Empire Strikes Back*, so these machine-generated noises seem to recall the protocols of the droid language used by C-3PO and R2-D2 to communicate with one another. They perfectly pick up on the lyrical theme of an orderly, nearly robotic, rush-hour crowd in the concrete jungle.

"The Camera Eye" atomizes Rush's sound and takes it to its most microcosmic and microscopic, releasing a certain amount of energy—generating a new being. The action is virtually biological, chemical, physical, and, you won't be surprised to know, visual. Sonic cells cleave and separate, divide, and collide. What we hear in "The Camera Eye" is less fusion than fission.

There's great cinematic quality etched into the composition. At 0:11, amid car horns honking and the commotion of city traffic, a street hawker calls out, "Fresh fruit," from a sidewalk kiosk. The audio snippet was taken from the 1978 feature movie *Superman*, starring Christopher Reeve as the Kryptonian and Margot Kidder (Lois Lane). It's brief, but it occurs at approximately 48:12 into the two-hour-plus film, when Kal-El's alter ego, Clark Kent, arrives at the *Daily Planet* building in Metropolis for the first time.

Peart's rudiment-based snare rolls at the opening of the song feel less like martial beats in a rock setting and more like a movie sound track for a suspense thriller.

Although the militaristic snare figures set the tone for "Countdown," echoing shades of "Jacob's Ladder," "The Camera Eye" moves, appropriately enough, beyond this slightly restrictive feel.

Panning the synth at the opening has the effect of creating a wide-screen visual image. Immediately, we hear a "split," a sonic blossoming, an aural equivalent of the sun breaking over the horizon, as synth notes are panned to one side of the stereo image (0:15). When the main musical synth line is finally introduced (0:45), Alex echoes the low C note performed by Geddy just seconds earlier on keys.

With the synth chirping along, Neil plays his rudiment-based military-like snare rolls. Alex scrapes his pick across the string, creating a metallic sound, only to quickly leave this texture for chiming arpeggios. A deep-pocket military groove by Peart, performed in sync with Lifeson's slashing of muted strings, almost in Sun Records/ Johnny Cash rhythmic "choo-choo train" style, invokes movement and suspense.

There's a lot happening in that short space. The song blossoms with two cymbal crashes (1:32–1:33) as Lifeson strums major chords while breaking loose with a wide-open suspended C chord: lots of overtones here and sonic layers built up to a majestic level. A C# note is being sustained through this section (beginning at 1:33). The fusion of synth and strings is so seamless that it smooths out the musical proceedings and creates the impression of infinite space.

Peart switches around his sticks and uses a traditional jazz drumming grip rather than matched to play the rudiments-based patterns opening the track. Kick drum, snare, and cymbal work are coordinated and dance a bit. As the music simmers, Peart plays the bell of the top cymbal of an open hi-hat, followed by a triangle.

At 2:20, the excitement ramps up. Where the drum fills are placed in the mix gives a sensation of distance and space. Sometimes, Peart's tom runs sweep across the stereo image, with a stray tom stroke or two materializing in the left channel. At other times, the fills largely hug the parameters of an audio channel and move from top to bottom in the vertical space—or what feels like vertical space. Once again, we can explain this in filmic terms: the production crew framed this all perfectly and chose the appropriate aspect ratio to frame this music movie. They scaled it precisely to include various sonic elements of the audio image.

Lee plays (let's call it) the superchirpyturbo-happy riff, something less C3-PO and more Sly and the Family Stone's "Hot Fun in the Summertime." The dual-note synth lead that Lee pounds out (G# and G) is supported by harmonious flashes of tones appearing and sprawling out underneath it, acting as undergirding. When the bass enters, a piercing, blanketing synth tone (moving back and forth between C# and C) sets up the introduction of the vocals and Alex's chord sequence, beginning in C.

"I remember that the most complicated keyboard parts on 'The Camera Eye' [hums the superchirpyturbo-happy riff] dah-dah-dah-dah, where he would have actually played one or two chords," says Northfield. "It was very simple from a playing point of view. But it is the use of, at that time, new sound textures, and so that was the inspiration."

The synth also provides a rudder for what could have been a much bumpier audio ride. Because of the use of keyboard, "The Camera Eye" retains a kind of "smoothness" or consistency, almost as if a looped sound was threaded through the entire track.

"I did an album with Porcupine Tree called *In Absentia*," Northfield says. "Richard Barbieri, his great strength as a keyboard player, working with power rock stuff, was his textural approach. He achieved beautiful sounds that made everything else sound great. That is what, I think, you're saying when you talk about 'smoothness.' Even though there was a wall of guitars, they were not mega-distorted guitars. There was distortion, but it was not on the same level as we tend to use now. [Lifeson's playing] is coming out of more of a blues-based guitar playing. The amps are not cranked to '11.'"

Everything seems smoothed over. Even the time changes are somewhat modest for Rush; the song moves into a half-time and 3/4 feel from 4/4 quite often but never, in my estimation, more "difficult" time signatures—9, 13, 17, 21, and so on. Perhaps it's wise that Rush did not fiddle with too many odd times or time-signature changes, as it would have mucked with the forward-propelled groove.

Lifeson's throaty guitar tone makes an appearance once again, a perfect foil for the clean, chime-y synth tones that have assumed the background. We hear both rhythm guitar and sustain, partially due to layered guitar tracks, which recalls an electric violin, and the sound subtly wavers under Lifeson's nimble hands. It creates the feeling of the entire section pulsating.

At 2:44, Lee's resonant bass plays the basic lead line (C#–G#–C#–A♭ (or G#)– F#–F), shadowing Lifeson's guitar; followed by the three-note sequence, C–F–G.

Meanwhile, Peart generates a series of fills throughout the instrumental synth passages that keeps us on the edge of our seats. The first round (2:26), synced with the synth, involves single strokes and triplets until Peart controls a conversation between snare flams and tom flares. Peart plays with time and feel to the point that it sounds as though he is slightly out of time—the rhythmic equivalent of a guitarist introducing dissonant notes, fighting the root chord, and making the C-3PO/R2-D2 synth passage that much more alien.

Scatted fills comment on the cycling, bubbling synth groove. It is, in its own way, a piece of call-and-response. Peart's fills at 2:26 and later at 6:49 are variations on a theme. Neil improvised them in the studio, leaving some space to be creative after meticulously working out the basic rhythmic patterns of the song. Peart was never comfortable improvising much in the studio or onstage, so this is a surprising turn, an instinct that he'd nurture much later with producer Nick Raskulinecz for records such as *Snakes & Arrows* and *Clockwork Angels*.

After a series of takes, Peart chose the best of the bunch, and these were edited into the final print.

"Those fills rule," says Brian Tichy, "and the final fills that end those sections are on another level. They almost sound polyrhythmic, but they're cool phrases that accentuate the 'in between' parts of the bars and beats. The latter of those section-ending fills is like the big brother of the two. It's storytelling, almost like closing or finishing a book, which gains us access to Neil's thought process. He gives a tip of the hat to the fill we heard the first time and adds to it the second time. It's a little busier, yet it follows a similar accent pattern."

"Some of those patterns have similar feels but they are not exact," says Jason Bittner. "He comes in on a different beat for each cycle, or he's playing slightly different drums or leaving something out. Really, those fills are probably some of my favorites on that record."

By 3:19, Lifeson's guitars sound like a flurry of agitated bees flanging about. Lifeson changes tones again (3:20), repeating the main riff but using a ghostly flange to change the mood and feel. There's an immediacy and mystery here that perhaps only a flange can provide. When Geddy's reverb-soaked vocals enter the first verse around the 3:38 mark, we hear overdubbed acoustic guitar, complementing the tone of Geddy's bass. Soaring keys hold down root notes (4:17) as Lifeson's gutsy, distorted tone carries the song.

Much of the song is defined by its forward thrust, but nuance exists here too. For instance, consider the instrumental section, bridge, or pre-chorus after the first verse and what could be considered the song's refrain ("I feel the sense of possibilities . . ."), beginning at approximately 4:03. Neil manages to be subtle in his unsubtlety.

When the song kicks off circa 4:19, Neil plays hard, as he always did, but his sense of storytelling and phrasing is sublime.

At 4:41, when Geddy talks about the roving band of humanity being "oblivious" to light rainfall, the bass resonates with extended sustain under his vocals. The reverberation is so overwhelming that it feels as though the bass is feeding back, then it cuts off abruptly. The percussive notes he performs following this are quick, staccato cellar-dweller sonic pulses punching their way through the verse.

Each time Geddy and Alex cycle through their riffs, Neil chooses to accent different parts of the measure with his crash cymbals. These cyclical rhythms may not be difficult to master per se, but the art is in the conceptualizing of the patterns on the fly and shifting of the feel of these percussive passages through the use of accents. Each round or series of crash cymbal strikes tells its own story.

At 5:59, Peart rides on both the hi-hat and the ride cymbal. He plays quarter notes on the ride and splits this pattern by hitting the snare on the downbeat with his right hand. He keeps his left hand on the hi-hat for steady patterns and accents. A heartbeat-like kick drum pulse, using eighth-note beats, pulsates through this unusual pattern.

Electric guitar, what sounds like bass pedals, and the famous Geddy Lee synth growls once again (6:09) offer support. A breakdown occurs, where musical fission leads to disintegration, circa 6:38. The song does rebuild itself, of course, with the help of the superchirpyturbo-happy riff, the second round of those Peart pseudo-"polyrhythmic" fills, and Lifeson's grinding guitar riff.

By 7:27, we're in London: Geddy reintroduces vocals, and the bass surprises. At moments, Geddy's playing is lyrical, at others funky and rhythmic. Geddy occasionally slides up and down the neck (starting at 7:20), and his figures seem to hug the section's basic keys, but a few stray notes do give the impression of bitonality.

As the music plays on, at 8:54, the voice of recording engineer Paul Northfield injects a question: "Hello?" Geddy replies in a mock Cockney accent, "Wot, Guv?" (possibly, "Morn, Gov"). The verbal exchange appears in the London section of the song, subtly commenting on the setting but also occupying its own space—picture within picture.

Lifeson mimics various orchestral instruments of a classical symphony (beginning at 9:16). At times, he makes his guitar screech like a scratchy violin, at others the dull roundness of a cello (9:24). When the strings take their bow, Lifeson's sound then assumes the tenor of a horn.

Seemingly informed by the blues, even the fiddle playing of bluegrass, Lifeson wrings out every possible emotion he can through string bends (beginning at 9:19), working in a fair amount of sonic dissonance—something almost so far removed from human that it recalls cat wails and bird squawks. Mixed with Celtic, bluegrass elements, and country and western, the solo's backbone is structured from the raw emotional material of speed metal, which had not really become a "thing" yet in popular culture. Lifeson then ramps up the excitement with what sounds like string bends and pull-offs (around 9:51).

Alex has said many times that "Limelight" contains his favorite recorded guitar solo on a Rush studio record. The "Limelight" solo is successful in large part due to its pacing, its texture, and how it helps to reinforce the lyrics of the song. It also heavily relies on effects and hardware, like the vibrato arm. It's the sound of a young guitarist exploring from his perspective the new wonders of the Fender Stratocaster (or in this case a custom Strat) and telling the world about his discovery.

How *very* "2112."

The solo's outro is as important as how it enters—"The Camera Eye" hits the spot in ways the other solos on the record don't.

Lifeson's fingers may sound as though they are flying over his fretboard, but the guitarist struggled to even conceive of the solo and then to play it passionately and fluidly. At one point, he had to exit the studio to collect his thoughts. It simply wasn't coming. After returning, Lifeson did several takes, and in that batch of tracks, he'd found what he'd been looking for, just letting things rip. He squeezed out a series of notes that is simply lightning in a bottle.

Guitar and bass are in sync. Geddy shadows the guitar riff introduced earlier in the song (at approximately 2:44), keeping the pacing of the whole thing rather funky. The song, then, transitions back into the refrain about "possibilities" and "hard realities."

The static-y sound of guitar amp feedback (10:21) buzzes with the transmission of 1,000 radio transistors. Synthesizer noises repeat and beep until we are held suspended in a timeless void: the modern meets the past, and we hear the bell clock of Big Ben tolling at 10:50.

"The Camera Eye" fades into the mists of the London evening. There's a pause and then silence for a few brief seconds.

## "WITCH HUNT"

After the last buzzing and repetitive warbles of "The Camera Eye" subside, we hear the twinkling of a child's toy, a sound sequence that Peart once described as "haunted child."

Just in the first few seconds of the song, we realize that Hammer Films and Roger Corman had nothing on Rush.

The combined effect of the instrumentation, the incessant pounding of gong bass drums, and the growing dissonance is creepy; it cocoons the viewer in a mist-shrouded atmosphere dimly recalled from mid-twentieth-century horror films.

"Witch Hunt" hints at violence; it vividly displays the face of evil but never exhibits pornographic gore. You can visualize the moonless night; the disorienting, almost uncomfortable close-ups of faces morphing amid the lapping flames; the smoke rising; and a wide lens shot transforming into a slow pull-away, revealing more and more detail of the scene.

Tiny pockets of twinkling percussion set the spin tingling: drones and singular tones, voices of angry townspeople—it's a dizzying array of sight and sound as synth washes dive-bomb the audio picture. Incessant gong-drum pounding martials the audio along to its inevitable, hellish place.

"'Witch Hunt' always made me think of fire and a witches' coven–type meeting deep in some woods somewhere," says bassist John DeServio (Black Label Society), who toured with Rush on their Roll the Bones tour as a member of Vinnie Moore's band.

Indeed. You'd rightly dub the foreboding, moonless night of "Witch Hunt" sonic noir if only the colorful musical wash and flame-lit facial features of the song's villains weren't so vivid. As it stands, Rush may have done more to out-occult and scare the bejesus out of middle America than any horns-flashing hooligan working in heavy metal could.

Lee made it clear in a Rush biography, *Visions*, that he and Alex, after reading Peart's lyrics, had envisioned a kind of storyboard, one that broke down the action scene by scene, with the intent of creating an audio movie.

"We worked very carefully with that in mind," Lee said. "We looked at it very cinematically, which we've done in the past, but this time we did it totally."

The level of realism and menacing makes the scene simultaneously frightening and yet also somewhat surreal. We're sucked into celluloid delusion in a nightmare universe that resembles the real world.

Nothing that Rush wrote after *Moving Pictures*, with the possible exceptions of "Red Sector A" or "The Pass," whether it is "Manhattan Project," "Distant Early Warning," "Nobody's Hero," "Losing It," or "Between the Wheels," comes close to the psychological stranglehold this sinister sonic weed has on the mind of the listener.

Why might this be the case?

The account Peart describes might be fictional, but it recalls historical events we easily unearth from the catacombs of our collective memory. We've lived it on some level as a people. The fear and anger are palpable, visceral, and primal. And while the time periods associated with witch hunts and witch trials in the Western world were for the most part centuries ago, Rush doesn't resort to sinking into a sonic morass by presenting musical curios of the fifteenth century and colonial 1690s. That would be a little too literal.

Instead, Rush keeps the song in the modern. Indeed. Unlike Rush's treatment for "Madrigal," the Canadian trio shrewdly does not fall back on these historical trappings but remains firmly planted in the modern. Some might disagree, but the electronic and analog–digital nature of the recording places it much later than 1980–1981. Adorning the track with a few twenty-first-century production touches, "Witch Hunt" could have been released yesterday or could be issued tomorrow.

Psychologically, it falls somewhere between possessing the ability to make the hairs on the back of your neck stand up straight and being a buzzkill.

Swiss psychoanalyst Carl Jung explained in the *Symbolic Life* that "it is becoming ever more obvious that it is not famine, not earthquakes, not microbes, not cancer, but man himself who is man's greatest danger to man, for the simple reason that there is no adequate protection against psychic epidemics, which are infinitely more devastating than the worst of natural catastrophes."

"Witch Hunt" describes a mass fever dream, a virus infecting the minds of the misguided. It's Jung's "Shadow" rising: the dark recesses of our personalities and soul resurfacing, a part of ourselves we usually keep safely locked away. "Witch Hunt" happens when a population uncovers its collective shadow. Perhaps no one is immune to the madness of prejudice or mass psychosis fueled by fear.

The characters in this dark play have succumbed to collective evil, circling on a downward spiral fueled by mass hysteria. As listeners, we too must confront the evil, the "other," this shadow, inside us. Despite its remit on groupthink, "Witch Hunt" is a point of personal reflection.

What do you see?

We can better answer this question by examining why Rush recorded it in the first place.

"Witch Hunt," as most Rush fans know, was the intended last section of the one-time three-part saga known as a song trilogy titled "Fear." As we've seen, Dos Passos was fond of trilogies, as was an American author Peart had read, Theodore Dreiser—part of a wave of interest Peart had in modernist literary figures, what he would have called "new world writers," such as F. Scott Fitzgerald, Ernest Hemingway, and Henry James.

The impetus to commit "Witch Hunt" to tape was manifold. An elderly friend of Peart asked the drummer/lyricist if he agreed that it was fear, not the pursuit of love or money, that drives human beings. Peart didn't want to believe what his internal voice was telling him at first, but on pondering the question, he deemed the declaration fairly accurate.

Peart set himself to work. He'd been thinking along the lines of a trilogy, but the catalytic conversation he'd had with his friend sent the thing into hyper speed. Peart envisioned the three-part musical series but hadn't written down all the details.

"The Enemy Within," Part I, which would appear on *Grace Under Pressure* from 1984, speaks to paranoia instilled in us by the powers that be. Part II, "The Weapon," warns us of the mechanism that weaponizes fear, and Part III, our "Witch Hunt," riles up the locals and projects fear onto unsuspecting strangers. (Rush later returned to "Fear" and added a fourth installment, "Freeze," for 2002's *Vapor Trails*.)

This trilogy of "Fear" seemed to rear its ugly head at the appropriate time in modern history. Jim Jones and the Jonestown Massacre were still fresh in the collective consciousness, and although the carnage in French Guyana wasn't the result of a witch hunt, the tragedy presents a cautionary tale about groupthink. In the ensuing years, scholarship indicates that not all of Jones's followers voluntarily drank poison: some were forced at gunpoint. Still, how many had blindly accepted the teachings and instructions of Jones and hung on his every word?

Even earlier, the Manson "Family" murders, the disturbing images of the Vietnam War being beamed into living rooms across North America, the deadly chaos of Altamont, the deaths of Jimi Hendrix, Janis Joplin, and Jim Morrison—all sent shock waves through the decade, their repercussions being felt as late as 1980.

"It was a bit of an ugly time," reasons Marty Morin (ex-Wireless). "It was like a leftover from the '60s, and everybody was getting burned out and getting into a lot of drugs and stuff. I think the toll of drugs showed up in the '70s, and we found out we were not invincible."

The general dour societal mood made Neil reflective: he thought back to his youth when he was ostracized or discriminated against because of the way he looked. In the late 1960s, Peart couldn't walk into a restaurant and sit down and order a meal if he had long hair. In addition, societal setbacks in the fight for justice and civil rights helped to spark Peart's creativity. Via pixelated images transmitted through his television screen, Peart observed the riots tearing apart nearby Detroit in 1968, a precursor to a larger realization that the hippie dream of enacting sweeping cultural changes had on some level failed.

Quoted by a daily newspaper in the American South, Peart alluded to censorship encroaching on free speech in Canada as one possible reading of "Witch Hunt" as well. Infringement on personal liberties and freedom is a recurring theme of the record.

The lyrical line "Those who know what's best for us . . ." is laced with double meaning. It's likely the only statement that both the misguided vigilantes and the supposed "witch" can agree on. The unfortunate target of public violence hopes for a mechanism or deus ex machina to deliver salvation. The problem is that the righteous mob alone believes it is the hand of God; subversion is everywhere—in books, films, immigrant communities, and the unfaithful—and it must be eradicated.

In real terms, though, ethnic cleansing and genocide marred (some might say derailed) the history of the twentieth century. It's difficult to overlook what Lee's Polish parents endured during World War II at the hands of the Nazis, but they had survived and could tell their children to succeed and exceed expectations. It also instilled the notion that no one—no government, no single person or leader, and no deity or supernatural entity—is tasked with saving you.

Ayn Rand would approve, one thinks, and a sliver of atheistic objectivist past is presented here too in a metaphoric state: just because the collective hive mind believes that a certain action is moral does not make it so. In Rand's 1957 novel *Atlas Shrugged*, the main character, John Galt, put the altruists and moralists on notice when he said, "You have been using fear as your weapon and have been bringing death to man as his punishment for rejecting your morality."

In the case of "Witch Hunt," we the listeners are predisposed to recognize that the mob is evil regardless of its self-serving moral certitude. Collectivism may in and of itself be a form of evil or witch hunt misguided by irrational fear and cemented by amoralistic decree.

Marrying the various creepy aspects of the song with Peart's lyrics seemed like a shoo-in. First impressions are often wrong, however. From the earliest days of the band's writing/preproduction period, "Witch Hunt" was earmarked for one of the band's fabled "production" numbers—a cinematic journey starting with the grotesqueries of the opening scene.

"They were always doing a song that would be fully experimental, where they regarded it as a studio song that they never intended to play live," says Northfield. "It was experiment, and they could go nuts. I think that was the motivation with 'Witch Hunt.'"

Helping to frame the image of an unruly mob, the boisterous crowd was recorded somewhat unconventionally.

On a dark night in November 1980, as snow flurries floated in the cold Quebec air, the guys in Rush, the touring crew, and studio personnel left the warm confines of Le Studio facility, carried with them a microphone (some reports say two), and assembled in the parking lot of Le Studio.

With a microphone (or microphones) set up some forty feet away from the studio, Peart assumed the role of master of ceremonies, egging on the impromptu hell-raising chorus into a blind rage and beseeching them to root out perceived evil in their community and destroy demonic influences lest they corrupt young minds.

The rumbling of vocal rambling went on for nearly half an hour, with the crowd performing take after take, each successive turn being more outrageous than the last. But they pushed on in the bitter cold and tried to remain warm through exaggerated physical movements and the effects of a bottle of scotch. Ever more hateful mantras surfaced with each fresh swig.

This was an interesting motif. Where could this have originated? We can't overlook the fact that this was not the first "mob rule" the Anthem label had cooked up.

Interesting precursors in the Anthem label universe are Max Webster's "The Party," from *Mutiny Up My Sleeve*, and "What You Make It," cowritten by Marty

Morin, from Wireless's 1979 studio album *Positively Human, Relatively Sane*, which was initially intended to be an instrumental. Sound effects and lyrics that reference the album title were added later. Both tracks were produced by former Max Webster bassist Mike Tilka.

"We wanted to make it sound like we were at a party," says Morin. "We had all our friends come into the studio and clink glasses and hoot and holler."

"They were a fun group of guys, and they loved to party, drink, and sing," says producer Tilka. "I put them all up in the studio and let them sing along to the track, hit beer bottles, and clap their hands. That is a one-take, right-before-you-mix-it energetic thing-y that we put on the record."

Whatever the impetus was for Rush recording crowd noises, Peart whipping the small gathering into a faux fanatical frenzy, was far darker than Wireless's romp into the arena of the audiovisual.

Indeed. Never let it be said that "Witch Hunt" lacks originality and production value. On listening to the chilling nursery-type chimes we hear at the dawning of the song, it might be tempting to conclude that the spooky (even creepy) mood Rush creates is due largely to Lifeson's use of slight dissonance. The basic notes we hear at the opening goes something like this: G–G (one octave higher)–C#–D–A–A#–F#–G–G (high) and so on, folding over on itself.

That "Witch Hunt" boasts such spine-tingling musical elements is not all that surprising: it's to be expected, one thinks, in a piece of cinematic sonic horror. But if all this is to be expected, why is the song so haunting?

Gilbert Ryle's concept of "ghost in the machine" might be relevant here. When the nature and arrangement of the musical elements are aligned in a certain order, a dark consciousness manifests itself. In addition, it's as if the music has been infused with what W. B. Yeats called "Spiritus Mondi." Rush, either through compositional forethought or on some subconscious level, created music that had a life of its own and imbued it with a kind of "spirit." In short, there's something *living inside this track*.

Why do I say this?

At 1:08, Alex's guitar tone hisses a sibilance we usually link with roving feral black cats; Lifeson's choice in tone not only comments on the uproar heard at the opening of the song but also excites our primal fears. Juxtaposing minor, suspended, and major chords in the verses, the guitarist further sends shivers up and down the spine of the listener.

Strangely, repetition in this song never becomes monotonous and is quite unnerving. The cycle of Lifeson's chords (essentially, G minor, B flat, D minor, and C) has a weird effect in that it focuses our mind: we are being led down a path to the inevitable. Truthfully, there are slight variations to what Lifeson plays; sometimes, a minor is replaced by a major, and the order in which chords appear changes slightly. But when a change does occur, there's a downward shift in pitch. Whatever brightness exists or existed evaporates. This descension coincides with Peart's darkest lyrics on *Moving Pictures*—those depicting hate and violence.

Geddy's voice is doubled here and treated with a slight delay (2:16). As such, we immediately receive a visual. The tracks soar and fade—one of the many touches of the cinematic in this song. The soundscape veers toward the split screen, and this section reinforces the song's spatial qualities. Geddy's voice appears dead center of the mix, parting the musical action: Lifeson's chords continue to play, and Peart's choreographed, multitracked percussion bang away on this side and on that side.

By expanding the audio field, Brown and crew fill in spaces along the sonic spectrum that some of us didn't even realize existed. It appears as though the sound moves left and right and, impossibly, vertically, up and down, in the stereo picture.

To great dramatic effect the drums in the first half of the track are multiple performances edited together. Beginning at 1:35, the fills are highly syncopated, and at times, Peart sounds like a one-man drum line or the choreographed barrage of the Drummers of Burundi. It's this non-Western, ethnic flavor that Peart would pursue throughout the 1980s and 1990s. Back in 1980, it's sufficient to say that Peart's cannon-fire–like drumming retains the timbre of conga or other so-called ethnic drums.

In the program for the Moving Pictures tour, Peart described how he performed the drum part twice: in the first verse and then adding percussion on separate tracks for the second verse. Peart keeps us guessing, beginning at 2:11, confusing us as to which drum he'll hit next—or, more exactly, which drum we'll hear in the stereo mix. Even after repeat listens, Peart's halting figures seem fresh and elegantly electroacoustic.

With the assistance of Brown's panning techniques and by striking drums in dramatically different ways in order to give the illusion of depth and dimension, Peart produces percussive sounds that crop up in various positions in the stereo image. The banging and clanging evoke the clinking of metallic weapons and a rumbling of a heavily armed horde—an approaching, marauding caravan winding its way through a village to seek its intended target.

Rush and Brown decorate the track in this way, because back in 1980, Rush never intended to play "Witch Hunt" live. However, as musical instrument technology vendors made strides in their research and development, it became technically possible for Peart to play the cowbell pattern with this left foot, for instance, triggering sound and essentially keeping metronomic time. In other words, technology caught up with the visions of Rush and Terry Brown.

"I don't know where the original idea came from—whether it was Terry's or Neil's—but we did a completely different drum sounds for the song," Northfield offers. "Neil, I think, used the same kit. All his drums were double headed, apart from a few smaller ones, and we took off all the lower heads on the large toms and then miked them up from the inside. It made life easier [in the studio], but it was not as musical a kit as a double-headed drum set. I do remember changing the miking and changing the drumheads for that song specifically because it was going to be a track that they would not play or never intended to play."

Northfield remembers more about the drums for "Witch Hunt." "After playing the basic track of the drums, Neil went over it again, and I seem to remember that he played more or less the same thing," Northfield notes. "I am thinking that maybe the idea was he wanted to double-track the toms 'Because everybody else is double tracking. And I never get to double track the drums, so . . .'"

Whether Peart was half kidding or not, the sound of the drums is menacing. They also complement and stress artistic concepts that have been running through *Moving Pictures*: split-screen effects, multivoice music, and the general concept of bitonality; the sound grows dynamically, pushing the audio spectrum wider and wider as each second passes.

Exactly what components created the drums sounds here has caused a little bit of confusion over the years. Does Peart use a Simmons electronic pad, an entire Simmons electronic drum kit, or a SynDrum (or SynDrum-like) single electronic drum pad?

Peart admitted in the DVD *Taking Center Stage: A Lifetime of Live Performance* that he did indeed use Simmons pads (triggering an electro-tom sound). Interestingly, recording engineer Northfield vaguely remembers a single-pad electronic surface, such as a SynDrum, but he is not certain.

"I don't remember much in the way of electronic drums," says Northfield. "Neil may have had one drum pad, but he did not have extensive electronic drum kit."

"I don't think he was using Simmons, but Neil still managed that A Flock of Seagulls electronic drum sound," drummer Jason Bittner adds.

Paradoxically, some of the song's brightest tones account for its most sinister. Rush roped in art director pal and Ian Thomas Band keyboardist Hugh Syme for synth duty. The sonic dive bombs that Syme generates with synth drone on, starting around the 0:44 mark, and develop into a full-blown filtered sonic spiral, inducing a kind of disorientation.

Aside from this being perhaps Syme's finest hour on a Rush album, the glassy-glossy texture of the chiming synth is deceiving. Strangely, when played on a keyboard, the basic line of Syme's parts don't reveal anything particularly demonic in the actual note formation. Isolated for its wider musical context, the tone might suggest lightheartedness. Yet there's something about the pacing and arrangement of the notes in this context that collectively induces a kind of paranoia—both in the tension ratcheted up by the lyrics setting and in one's own mind.

If Rick Wakeman's pipe organ solo in Yes's "Close to the Edge" was a sound track for a liturgical, transcendental progressive rock experience, similar to the Hammond organ in Procol Harum's "A Whiter Shade of Pale," then Syme's work is the polar opposite: It's relentless, even oppressive—wind gusts pumping through the machinery of pipe organs at a black mass.

Syme's piano playing on the previous studio album for "Different Strings" had a certain definition and clarity, and we the listeners are endowed with a real sense of the wood and wire of the piece. However, there is no disinfectant here. The toxicity levels of Syme's input approach maximum strength.

Additionally, Geddy's bass commands the foreground (at 4:13) and serves a dual purpose. Its tone is melancholy, as if lamenting the observer's impotence in stopping this sad chapter in human history from progressing—or repeating. Is there nothing the speaker can do to prevent this misjustice? Does the speaker himself fall prey to the seductive power of groupthink?

Allowing the bass to take center stage in the first place—the bass, an instrument that is traditionally the undergirding of any rock band—reinforces the subversiveness of the setting. Geddy's lines are so deliberate and steady that they seem directed at the mob's single-mindedness and self-appointed moral superiority. The bass is effectively "the other," or, in Jungian terms, representative of the what's lurking in our subconscious (i.e., the shadow).

As the bass notes recede, Syme's synth tones claim the sonic foreground once again; Taurus pedals sustain the bottom end. As the audio decays, we're made keenly aware: no one, not even the speaker, it seems, is saved.

The arc of the album's track sequencing tweaks our psyches, alternately suppressing and building pressure. The unpurged orgiastic tension generated here seems intentionally claustrophobic.

Over the course of *Moving Pictures*, we've felt the fleeting pyrrhic victories against the impacts of authoritarian rule ("Red Barchetta"), the eerie effects of the demonic triad expressing travel anxiety ("YYZ"), a form of social isolationism ("Limelight"), and psychological despondency ("The Camera Eye").

Then we arrive at this monstrous thing, visionary in every sense of the word—technically, musically, and in its production.

We can point to similar productions, one thinks, by Martin Hannett, done around this same basic time frame (1979–1981) for Joy Division, U2, New Order, and Orchestral Maneuvers in the Dark. They simultaneously glow and exponentially veer toward gloom and doom. This dynamic portentousness makes listeners uneasy, even those familiar with the tracks. It's a similar bewildering, shadowy quality that "Witch Hunt" possesses—or that possesses "Witch Hunt."

It's the final track, "Vital Signs," that becomes the record's spiritual and emotional savior, uplifting us with its message of personal identity. The record rises on the boundless possibilities and promises on the New Wave horizons, setting the stage for Rush's ascension as a synth-based group in the era of techno-rock New Wave.

## "VITAL SIGNS"

Spiraling out of the blankness and bleakness of "Witch Hunt" is an emissary from the future, like a sonic satellite spinning toward us, rescuing us—and *Moving Pictures*—from our primordial past. The spinning savior takes the form of modern rocker "Vital Signs," an omen foretelling what was to come for Rush through the 1980s.

The 1988 movie *Cinema Paradiso* seems oddly relevant here regarding "Vital Signs" and *Moving Pictures* as a whole. The tagline hyped the "everlasting magic of the movies." We've allowed Rush—the actors, directors, producers and projectionists for this cinematic musical journey—to help shape a kind of theater of the mind through track sequencing, editing, sound mixing, and storytelling techniques. Although it did appear just minutes before that the darkness would consume us, we are nonetheless left with the classic Hollywood ending. Movie magic.

Themes of individuality, self-empowerment, attaining personal courage, and maintaining one's integrity and determination—all conceptual threads "2112" had forced under the microscope—come roaring back with wide-screen relevancy in 1981.

"Vital Signs" also speaks of a kind of self-realization and tolerance. "Witch Hunt" preaches tolerance too by presenting the madness of mob mentalities and how it ultimately must force good people toward introspection and finally action.

It's no accident that the darkest song on *Moving Pictures*, maybe in all of Rush's catalog, was set on a collision course with the band's radical new approach to music. "Vital Signs" is the antidote—the yin to the yang of "Witch Hunt."

Depending on what source or format you consult, "Witch Hunt" and "Vital Signs" clock in at virtually the same time: the songs are only a second or two apart in duration.

Bookending this album was imperative. Had Rush ended the record on either "Witch Hunt" or "The Camera Eye" (the latter was seriously considered for the closing track), the balance of the record would be thrown off. Yes, ending it all with the eleven-minute track would, on some level, be symbolic of where they had been in years previous. By leaving us with "Vital Signs," however, Rush appears to be embracing a new direction. It's the difference between looking back over the shoulder and considering the distant horizon and its endless possibilities.

Although there had been hints at this musical transformation on *Permanent Waves*, Rush had not up to that point synthesized all the various elements we hear in this song (reggae, programmed synth patterns, funk, New Romantic synth pop, and New Wave rock). It may be the best New Wave song Rush ever wrote—even considering the fact that the band spent the next four studio records and a subsequent live album attempting to perfect a synth-pop sound filtered through their progressive rock tendencies.

For that matter, Peart has admitted that the explosive fills he plays in the song were informed by King Crimson's Michael Giles and his manic schizoid roundhouse phrasing. The sixteenths on the hi-hat were inspired by something he'd heard on a multigenre track by Godley and Creme (of 10cc fame), 1978's "Sandwiches of You."

"Vital Signs" 45 rpm

What's important here is not Rush's encyclopedic knowledge of pre-1981 rock music but rather that they were brave enough to introduce these various non–hard rock influences into a largely metallic musical context—with virtually no commercial impetus to do so. "Vital Signs" is the record's most unusual song and is the inevitable destination of the band's continued streamlined sound.

The mixed feelings Peart describes in the lyrics actually relate to the function and form of this song—the actual structure of the music. The band was not certain of how fans would receive this new direction, one informed by New Wave. Although it was in many ways programmed music—literally machine music—these devices were operated by very human hearts, hands, and minds.

In the program for the Moving Pictures tour, Peart said that his lyrical work for the song "derives from my response to the terminology of 'Technospeak,' the language of electronics and computers, which often seems to parallel the human machine, in the functions and interrelationships they employ."

By equating the human condition with the functions of a machine, anomalies are increasingly distrusted as outliers or human error. The "random sample," the outliers, is what keeps us special. The line "deviate from the norm" means simply that we have to view our circumstances from a different perspective in order to be rejuvenated—to survive and become nonconformist in order to achieve our true potential—to steal a phrase, to be all we can be.

"The impulse is pure" captures our drives to be different, which can be attained if not corrupted by external forces. "Soft filter" is a reference not only to cigarettes and changing habits but also to a type of camera lens. In essence, the double meaning urges us to see life from a different perspective. Determination, almost dogged and mechanical, helps the passionate achieve their goals.

The tech jargon *seems* to foretell of the rise of machines and the inevitable homogenization in mind, body, and spirit that's likely to occur in a completely computerized society.

But perhaps we're stressing all this techno-speak too much. Introducing the idea of machines and computers is, in movie terms, a red herring. Metaphor shouldn't overrun or muddy the message: "Vital Signs" is about individuality and not losing your personal characteristics (your vital signs) even in the face of authoritarianism or bureaucracy managed by teams of computer software programmers. It's about how we can interface with technology—and all aspects of life—and still retain our humanity.

In *Rocking the Classics*, author Edward Macan describes the apocalyptic hippie view of a "nightmarish technocracy," and, as we've seen, Emerson, Lake & Palmer's social commentary on oppression, in their "Karn Evil 9: Third Impression," is a good example of this.

Even though it cedes ground to technology, Peart's message carries less overt cynicism about our automated future. Inasmuch as "Vital Signs" rescues *Moving Pictures* from going too dark, it does the same for the doomy-gloomy *Brain Salad Surgery* wing of the progressive rock subgenre. By the same token, themes of self-realization that run through Yes's *Close to the Edge* and, to a degree, *Tales from Topographic Oceans* have been upgraded via techno-speak to reflect a more contemporary meditation on the human spirit.

In short, "Vital Signs" is post-postmodernist prog rock, fusing styles without succumbing to the succubi of 1970s excess—and a perfect marriage of conceptual theme and musical execution.

Here's why.

Each member of the band sets his own course musically and rhythmically at the opening of the track, yet the precision and dynamics of their parts couple well with the techie lyrics and actual electronics used to shape the track.

As the song fades in, Alex's guitar chords repeatedly ping-pong from the left to the right channel as the programmed synth pattern maintains center balance—a centripetal force that cycles and spins through the stereo image.

"The only sequencer on the record was used for 'Vital Signs,'" says Northfield. "That was a sequencer that Geddy had, and he used one in his rig. It was a very elemental sequencer that you could, maybe, program a sequence of sixteen notes in a one- or two-bar sequence. It was more like programming an old drum machine than it was sequencing or programming you'd do in a workstation these days."

Lifeson's chopped guitar chords come to the fore, and the song's face emerges from the shadows of the dimly lit proverbial sonic hallway. Slyly, the guitar diverts attention away from the hypnotic effect of the repetitive keyboard figure. Crashed cymbals (timed with kick drum) shatter the atmosphere (0:11) as Lifeson's string of chords, composed of minor and flats, ends with a cutting, almost threatening A♭6 flattened chord, helping to smash the pristine sonic revelry.

Lifeson's staggered-rhythm approach, introduced just prior to Geddy singing the opening lines of the first verse, requires the listener's brain to go through mental calisthenics in attempting to follow the pattern of upbeat and downbeats.

Lifeson alternates the feel of his playing by allowing the pattern he plays to slightly change from measure to measure. Over four measures, Lifeson's chords fall on beats 2 and 4 of the first measure, beat 2 of the second measure, beats 1 and 3 of the third measure, and beats 1 and 4 of the last measure. This four-bar pattern cycles up to 0:46. Lifeson also strums some chords twice, adding more rhythmic complexity.

Peart's precise, metrical, danceable sixteenth-note hi-hat patterns (punctuated with accents) complement the rolling rhythmic patterns of both the sequencer and

Geddy's bass and vocals. At the same time, splash cymbal accents (synchronized with a single kick beat) are "isolated," adding a subtle creative (or human) touch.

It is no surprise to find that Peart used an electronic click track as a guide during the making of *Moving Pictures*, but he hardly needed to use one here, as the programmed sequencer easily performed a similar duty.

On his Fender Jazz bass, Geddy shadows the sequencer, his fingers migrating across and up the neck. You would think the part was recorded once and looped if it were not so funky. Actually, Geddy repeats a two-bar pattern that includes eight notes per measure until the bridge, when we hear Lifeson chuggin' eighth-note patterns. In essence, Geddy's bass notes alternate and cycle too. This kind of rhythmic hide-and-seek is patterned on the sounds of reggae that had been wafting out to the boys at least since 1979–1980. Indeed. Peart underpins the song's feel through the metallic pinging and clanging of timbales, instantly recalling Caribbean and Afro-Cuban styles.

All the parts are sliding and moving, some in tandem, some as complements, and this kind of tongue-and-groove rhythmic pattern is indicative of African music, even electric Chicago blues of the 1950s. Dare we say, it also hints at Brian Eno's ethno-techno matrices defining the late 1970s and early 1980s music by Talking Heads.

Clipped snare beats snap at Lifeson's crashing chords (and Geddy's vocals). These sliding musical/rhythmic components never quite sync yet strangely interlock, anchored by the repetitive synth sequence.

The song feels as though it switches into half time (2/4) following the "atmospheric disturbance" verse. I tried counting out four beats per measure across this section, and the music breaks down easier with a 2/4 bar in there. The drums, when overlaid on this short section, are a different story. This might be down to how beats are grouped, but they feel as though they are in 6/4 for the same section.

Circa 0:48, Lifeson's driving eighth-note feel is reminiscent of the wind-whipped tunnel sequence of "Red Barchetta." Lifeson then breaks with this solid rhythmic approach and shifts to crunchy chord shapes, now in sync with Lee singing the phrase "external interference."

To punctuate the ending of verses, Lifeson uses the A♭6 chord mentioned above, but at 1:38, he switched to a major seventh (A♭maj7). It's an interesting chord because it signals finality. However, although I detect no real dissonance in it, there's something unresolved about it that lends an air of suspense. As this chord fades, it leads into the C minor–A♭ chord sequence first heard at 0:17, the off-beat pattern we mentioned earlier.

It's fascinating that such subtle shifts highlight how sensitive the music is to the words. In the refrain, Lifeson plays a series of chords but applies one he had used only once previously in the song: a Gm7 chord. We hear it when Geddy sings about "reverse polarity" and again when Lifeson's chords correspond with the appearance of the word "deviate" and later "elevate." Like some form of runic inscription, the notation calls attention to certain lyrical phrases.

After playing a largely rhythmic role in the song, Geddy's bass takes the foreground for a melodic solo at 3:07 that is underpinned by synth. The synth roots around in C and Geddy's slides up and down the bass neck, pluming and descending with a kind of lyrical arc, hitting notes in accordance with a C-minor scale. You could say that Geddy flashes his vital signs, speaks his piece, and then reports back to duty, serving the song and once again providing support in the bottom end.

Even the lyrics have a kind of internal rhythm. The structure of the song is organized in couplets: two verses followed by a refrain. This pattern is repeated with some slight variations. For instance, the word "deviate" is slyly swapped out for "elevate." None of this takes into account Geddy's post-3:00 ad lib outro singing, in which he repeats three of the lines for the "chorus."

The first lines of the first, fourth, and fifth verses end in words that rhyme or are close rhymes; ditto for the second, third, and sixth verses. Near rhymes that link both verse and refrain are immaculate and solidify an already compact song. Internal rhymes also exist.

In addition, subtle shifts in phrasing are apropos of the song's musical and conceptual themes. No two stanzas are identical, not even the refrain or chorus couplets (stanzas 3 and 6). And for such an orderly song, it allows Rush to go slightly off the rails near its end. Talk about a New Wave anthem dedicated to individuality.

It always sounded to these ears that in the outro, Geddy conflates (jumbles?) his words. If it is a faux pas, it is a wonderful mix-up. The line beginning at 4:03 contains a phrase that we don't instantly recognize. It's either the word "revelate" or possibly "evelate"—neither word appears in the English dictionary. It's likely the intended word was "elevate." If nothing else, this vocabulary scramble underscores the message of "Vital Signs": be yourself.

## DIGITAL DISASTER?

Perhaps it's appropriate that "Vital Signs" was the last song to be written for the record. As the album drew to a close, it was the tech who gave the band the most fits in crossing the finish line.

"Some things are indelibly imprinted in my brain, like what the console was, the tape machines we were using, preamps we had, because I remember what was in the rack and what they did," says Paul Northfield. "When the E series arrived, it was ergonomically sophisticated, and so mixing complicated stuff became easier with a console like that, which was an important part of the process."

In 1980, Le Studio installed a forty-eight-track Solid State Logic (SSL) mixing console with video interlock for their studio. "Le Studio went through various evolutions with the Trident console and then with an SSL-E series consoles, which is how we recorded *Moving Pictures* and what console we mixed on, with some outboard stuff," says Northfield. "We had a small eight-channel Neve sidecar [mixer], which was used for kick, snare, and some bits and pieces; you only had a stereo 'out' on it. I think other than kick and snare, everything else was done using the console preamps.

"That's surprising because an old SSL-E is not a sonically particularly great signal path," Northfield continues. "It was a combination of that, with Studer A-80 tape machines, which is what the record was recorded on—two A-80s. So the album was recorded forty-eight-track."

The tracks were "mixed down" to a three-quarter-inch Sony digital machine rather than what would normally have been an analog two-track tape device, which inevitably compromises audio fidelity on some level.

"We mixed the record to a digital format, but it was not a good digital format, not by today's standards," says Northfield. "It was Sony's first sixteen-bit digital stereo system. We had this digital mix-down system because Terry and the guys brought it in. It was one of the first stereo digital recorders, a PCM 1600. There weren't many in North America at the time, maybe half a dozen."

Compared to an analog mix, the audio living in the digital environment was much clearer on both the high end and the low end with none of the degradation you'd expect from an analog format—precisely what a record such as *Moving Pictures* needed to underscore its sparkling audio, nuance, and complexity.

Rush was on the cutting edge for the recording and later mixing and mastering processes, but issues arose regarding the communication between all of these various digital and analog machines. Neil Peart wrote in the Moving Pictures tour program, "In a massive electronic freak-out revolution, the digital mastering machine, the mixdown computer, and one of the multi-track machines, gave up their collective ghosts one after the other, driving poor Broon [Terry Brown] to distraction, and setting us two weeks behind in the end."

"Peter Jensen, who owned [the Sony PMC digital machine], had to come to the studio and fiddle with a screwdriver to cut the noise because it had a fluttery noise floor," says Northfield. "It had to be adjusted for every song. Every ten or fifteen minutes, we had to get the screwdriver out and tweak it. It was that kind of cutting edge [laughs]: I think 'bleeding edge' is how we refer to it now."

Northfield continues, "When you consider that everything else about making the album was analog, that one digital thing, at the end of the chain, and because it was the last thing in the chain, it all worked together very well."

This episode helped to inspire "Digital Man," a song on *Signals*. When it came time to decide who was going to make the trek out to Le Studio and who would stay on location, living and working side-by-side with the band, it was deemed unnecessary to bring a dedicated digital mixing/mastering specialist with them. (They wouldn't need a bed for the so-called digital man.) As it turned out, Rush would indeed need a digital man—in more ways than one.

But, as Northfield explains, the issues weren't all confined to the digital realm. "We had incredible difficulties with the interlock of the tape machine, oxide falling off the tape, Ampex 456, as we got to the mixing. The oxide would cake up on the heads of the tape machine. After three or four passes, you'd have to clean the tape heads because they would have brown all over them. We were, at a certain point, worried about too much deterioration. We, fortunately, did make it through, but a few other people had exactly the same problem: it was a bad batch of Ampex 456."

This was not all: As magical as the recording was, the mixing and final stages of the production process was hell on earth to birth *Moving Pictures*.

"The console was starting to do weird mix changes because it was an automated console, and after a number of passes, we would start to see faders moving," says Northfield. "At that time, the automation systems didn't require that the faders move up and down. They used what is called a voltage-controlled amplifier—VCA—that adjusted the volume level. . . . That was all recorded into the computerized part of the console. The console would play back the movements that you recorded. But because of a problem with grounding and noise into the computer buses, it was starting to produce movement on the faders."

It's almost as if the Trident "Ghost" from England migrated across an ocean to follow Rush up to Le Studio for the recording of *Moving Pictures*.

"The interlock systems were not working very well because all forty-eight-track analog machines required use of a machine to lock them together—a time code track on each track, one on each machine, so forty-eight tracks were actually forty-six usable tracks," Northfield says. "Sometimes it would take twenty seconds for the machines to lock up, so you would have to start the tape twenty seconds before the music. Part of that was because the Studer A-80s didn't have the powerful reel motors that were on the Studer 800s. You've got big reels that weigh a ton with motors that are trying to lock two tapes together. So we had a combination of poor interlocking system and a brand-new console."

Bleary-eyed and frustrated through these technical glitches, the band walked away from it all for a few days as the technical crew worked furiously to get everything in line. Before they did, as always, the band's dark humor, which manifested during their *Caress of Steel* moment back in 1975, helped to make light of the techno bombs going off in all directions. Bunker mentality be damned.

"The tape machines and the interlock system were referred to as Huey, Dewey, and Louie," says Northfield, "Huey and Dewey being the tape machine and Louie being the interlock system. Albert, after Albert Einstein, was the computer that started to lose its mind. The comedy aspect of Rush being Rush tended to make it a little less torturous. And it was torturous."

A computer going haywire is reminiscent of the HAL 9000 computer from Stanley Kubrick's *2001: A Space Odyssey*. Considering that Albert, like HAL (for heuristically programmed algorithmic computer), had "lost its mind," Northfield said, the cinematic comparison seems to fit.

If we have not beaten this metaphor to a pulp already, just as Bowman evolves into the star child at the ending of *2001*, so too Rush would emerge from this unforeseen, challenging technological process with what can be dubbed the best progressive hard rock album in history, recorded by a band that had been primed and reborn for the 1980s.

"But by the time we had finished the album, we were trashed," says Northfield. "I was. Alex and I. I got the most drunk I've gotten in my life. I think he has gotten a lot more drunk than that before, but I almost became a statistic: 'He died on his own vomit.' We drank everything that remained from the sessions: there was some scotch or gin or something or vodka on the counter in bottles. It is not like everybody drank a lot, but during the period of making the record, we would have drinks on a semiregular basis. At the end of it, Alex and I drank everything that was left over, which was really not a smart thing to do."

The record was done. After its completion, Geddy drove back to his Toronto home from Le Studio in Morin-Heights in the middle of snowstorm. When he finally arrived at 4 a.m., he came home to an empty house: His wife and family were gone. They'd headed down to the Caribbean for a vacation, one Geddy was supposed to take with them. But Geddy explained that the record had taken longer than expected, and his family awaited his arrival. Geddy packed his luggage for his stay, got to the airport, and took his flight to freedom, no doubt with "YYZ" ringing in his ears.

The original digital mixes—what the band and production crew were listening to via monitors in the studio—provided the basis for the record's master. Due to the delay in mixing, the mastering needed to be scheduled for five days in New York, where the vinyl LP was cut from the master by Bob Ludwig at Masterdisk using, among other pieces of equipment, an NTP compressor, a Neumann OE-DUP equalizer, and a Sontec equalizer. In Canada, the master was cut at the Lacquer Channel in Scarborough, Ontario.

The production run for the album kept the machines at record pressing facilities humming. Columbia Record's famous Terra Haute location in Indiana, Presswell in New Jersey, and Keel Manufacturing Corporation on Long Island, among others in North America, churned out the *Moving Pictures* discs in record volume. These pressings rolled out of the plants and were eventually loaded onto a distributor's trucks, finally being placed into vinyl bins of retail record outlets.

For the Canadian market, and despite recent economic downturns, the LP was made of virgin vinyl stock, meaning that the record company did not use vinyl taken from reclaimed and discarded LPs, which could contain impurities and impact the fidelity and playability of the album.

"The whole motivation behind this campaign is to offer the consumer the best," Anthem's Tom Berry told *Billboard*. "For instance, the LP includes a four-color hardboard inner sleeve. This is a digital mix and virgin vinyl in Canada, and the price is only $9.98 list, which, compared to other audiophile recordings, is substantially less than the norm."

"The sound was compressed for radio purposes, and I would have thought—because very few rock recordings sound terrific when you convert them to high resolution because it doesn't have dynamic range—it would not have sounded terrific," says André Perry. "But it sounded terrific. The fact that it was recorded in analog, I think, saved the day. Today, you can listen to it now in high def, and the record really stands out. It doesn't feel like it is overly compressed."

Amid the interlocking analog/digital crisis, a film crew, led by director Bruce Gowers, arrived at Le Studio to capture the band in the studio for three promotional videos they were doing for the record: "Tom Sawyer," "Limelight," and "Vital Signs."

Gowers had worked in TV, in film, and on documentaries since the early 1970s, and by the middle of decade, he had found success with music videos by Queen, including the iconic "Bohemian Rhapsody."

"I did one music video with Queen, and my phone never stopped [laughs]," Gowers says. "That was how I got to come to America."

Gowers remembers coming to Le Studio for two to three days near the completion of the record. "They were in a great mood but were perplexed by the digital," says Gowers. "That was an ongoing theme throughout our short stay with them."

Mercury wasn't calling the shots on this. It was Anthem (and management company SRO), which had a good grasp on the imagery they wanted to promote. The videos act as time capsule and documentary with audio accompaniment.

However, much credit should be given to Gowers: where the camera focuses the eye, the images of Lifeson manipulating the whammy bar, a dog in the snow seemingly reacting to the music being played inside the studio, an audio-reactive pulse monitor, Geddy sitting between two congas while supposedly cutting a vocal track, the determination on Peart's face as he plays a long fill—it all left an indelible mark on a generation.

"The location was absolutely beautiful," says Gowers. "I think it was around Christmastime when we shot. The snow was right on the money."

Gowers remembers doing several takes with everybody to ensure they had enough good footage for the editing suite.

"We would do a take with Geddy on bass guitar, and then we would do a vocal take of Geddy," says Gowers. "Because they played so many instruments, it actually took a lot longer than a regular shoot."

Audio from the shoot is not, of course, what we hear accompanying the images: It's the finished studio tracks. The band does appear to be performing, however. For instance, Peart plays so hard at one point in the video for "Limelight" that it appears as though his headphones are about to slip off his noggin.

"Neil played those tracks, and when I say he was lip-syncing, I guess you could say he was finger-syncing," says Gowers. "He never makes a mistake in some of the most complicated drum fills, ever. Most rock drummers at that time could not have done that."

"They didn't want to act or role play," adds Len Epand, formerly senior vice president of music video at PolyGram. "They just wanted to play. They wanted to be what they were: musicians. Some of the worst videos are when you take musicians and try to make them actors and try to build some sort of narrative that is embarrassing or leaden."

"I don't think I have ever worked with a band that were so mentally and physically together as this band," says Gowers, who shot iconic promo videos for Rod Stewart, Bee Gees, Prince, Michael Jackson, Journey, and Supertramp. "Their arrangements were musically very complicated. It wasn't three-bar blues stuff."

# CHAPTER 10

# JOAN OF ARC AND FLAMING PIE PLATES

*Moving Pictures* premiered on CHUM-FM in Toronto with special guest Geddy Lee. CHUM announcer Rick Ringer was the master of ceremonies—the sonic projectionist for this collection of mini-movies, someone who had hosted other Rush album premieres prior to *Moving Pictures*.

"There was always champagne poured, and to this day, I still look back on those premieres as a highlight of my broadcast career," says Ringer.

Formats for radio had been changing for years, and by the 1980s, the media conglomerates were already beginning to move in, weeding out regional flavor through corporate homogenization. "[Broadcast premieres] represented a different time in FM radio, I think," says Ringer. "You don't get that these days on most stations."

Before the digital revolution, circa 1981, getting the exclusive right to spin an anticipated album was not just a cultural event—it galvanized listener enthusiasm.

"Don't get me wrong, even back then we had a set playlist," says Ringer, who had traveled with the band for two different tours. "I wasn't picking my music for my own show anymore. That was another thing that made these album premieres so special. It meant that we went off regular programming for an hour and half or so and just played the album and talked about it."

When "Tom Sawyer" was sent out over the airwaves for the first time, it was like virtually nothing Ringer had heard from the band before. "That song was something otherworldly almost," says Ringer. "You just knew Rush had taken the next step: 'Okay, you guys have done it.'"

*Moving Pictures* was singular in its ability to turn minds and change opinions of the band and its music. Where there was still some divided opinion about *Permanent*

*Waves*, with *Moving Pictures*, critics knew Rush created something of value even if from their perspective it was just this once.

Publications across Canada and America seemed genuinely surprised about the record's freshness. The *Pittsburgh Press* may have issued tempered praise for the band itself, but the writer recommended the disc nonetheless, saying the record boasts a "high-percentage of listener-oriented . . . songs," which "produces a good LP."

Even critics who were typically brutal on Rush in the past knew the band struck gold. The *Los Angeles Times* had to concede—and predicted that the record would "be a monster."

In the past, purple prose was the power juice that fueled the competition between rival critics when lambasting Rush for its perceived pompousness and pretentious lyrics. When faced with the genuine article (from their points of view), namely, an object such as *Moving Pictures*, it became a race to cram in as many insults about Rush in their pieces before rescuing the trio from utter humiliation with a kind word or two about their collective musicianship or songwriting (or something).

"The thing you can't control is how much time someone spends with your music—and the pen is in their hands," Lee told me. "So [critics] get the final word in some ways. But a good record will cut through that."

A *Vancouver Sun* reviewer who said he'd "rather have bamboo splinters stuck under my fingernails than listen to Geddy Lee shriek" told us that "Red Barchetta" is "the grabber" on the LP and that "if you must listen to Rush, listen to this."

In his review for the *Edmonton Journal*, Rush arch nemesis Graham Hicks noted the melodicism of "Red Barchetta" and the jazzy instrumentalism of "YYZ," which Hicks equated with "Return to Forever . . . on acid," and a "swingin', near-reggae" song "Vital Signs." Hicks called *Moving Pictures* the band's first record "deserving of serious critical attention."

And *Rolling Stone* magazine, in a piece penned by noted music journalist David Fricke, ran a favorable feature on Rush, their work ethic, and their latest record. And perhaps no surprise, the *Detroit Free Press*, based in a town presiding over a struggling and decimated automotive industry, singled out the auditory fantasy "Red Barchetta."

Ravenous reviews may have been in remission, but there would be repercussions in time for the band's tour: The vitriol returned with a vengeance as Rush swept through the United States. Both the major coastal papers—the *New York Times* and the *Los Angeles Times*—blasted, dumped on, skewered, buried, or were bored by Rush when witnessing and writing about their live performances and concert attendees.

The *New York Times* compared Rush unfavorably to Led Zeppelin, dubbed the concert little more than "ritual" for teenagers, and concluded that Rush was "rock music at its most macho."

This may be the single most misunderstood aspect of Rush's long-standing appeal. A fair portion of the audience throughout the band's career was made up of either aspiring musicians or professional ones at some level. Difficult to tell, but this may answer why certain fans were pulled into a hyperconcentration zone and felt an almost spiritual connection to the music—and also why magazine and newspaper writers often appeared bored.

"There are some bands, at least in my mind, I could name who inspired people to pick up an instrument," says Jason Bittner. "Led Zeppelin, as you said. Cream. The Who. They motivated people to take up an instrument. Of course, Rush did too."

In short, the record *Moving Pictures* had saturated—it was a film many wanted to see, especially those who had worked with Rush prior to *Moving Pictures*.

"I thought it was such a natural progression from the *Permanent Waves* album, and I was so jealous," says recording engineer/producer Adam Moseley. "I remember they brought it back to Trident [studios in London], but they didn't do much mixing there at all."

By March, *Moving Pictures* was starting to burn it up.

The album had hit the *Billboard* Top LPs and Tape chart, entering at number thirty-one. The following week, the band had climbed to the fifteenth slot. For the period ending March 21, 1981, Rush had nestled themselves within the Top 8 records in the nation.

*Moving Pictures* was blowing up at radio too and packing them in, up to the rafters, at arena venues; 15,000 ticket holders per show paid to see Rush perform at Maple Leaf Gardens in their hometown of Toronto over three nights. As the *Ottawa Citizen* pointed out, icons such as Frank Sinatra, George Harrison, and Neil Diamond had not matched this feat, having posted similar numbers but over only two-night stints.

As March 1981 drew to a close, *Moving Pictures* had reached number three on the albums chart and held steady in that position before succumbing to the fourth slot in mid-April. REO Speedwagon's *Hi Infidelity* and Styx's conceptual *Paradise Theater* were among those that stood in the band's way of claiming the top spot.

After three months, the record was still Top 10 and, in fact, was ascending once again in late May 1981. For fourteen of the first seventeen weeks that the band was on the charts in late winter/spring 1981, *Moving Pictures* stayed within the Top 10. And six months after it appeared, the record remained Top 40 in the United States.

It was a similar tale in Canada, where they were tracked by *RPM* magazine and went to number one in early April and remained there for a month. On *RPM*'s "50 Singles" chart, "Tom Sawyer" squeaks into the contention, debuting at number forty-nine. The leadoff track performs respectably, but "Limelight" broke into Canada's Top 20 and claimed a piece of real estate in the Top 100 Singles for 1981. It also made a stand on the *Cash Box* Top 100 chart.

"Limelight" was released as a single in March, followed by "Vital Signs," which appeared in the United Kingdom. By April 13, 1981, *Moving Pictures* had gone gold in the United States and would achieve platinum status just two weeks later. At press time, *Moving Pictures* has gone to sell more than 5 million units in the United States alone.

It was a banner winter/spring for Rush: *2112* went platinum, and in March, *All the World's a Stage* followed. Rush became the only band for the year 1981 to have three records certified platinum, in what PolyGram had coined "the great platinum Rush."

"*Moving Pictures*, and that era, was the crux of Rush's career because, before I got to work at the record company, they were a bit abstract and arcane kind of progressive rock

Although largely an albums-oriented band, Rush issued tracks from *Moving Pictures* as singles and B-sides, including (pictured) "YYZ," "Limelight," and "Witch Hunt."

guys," says Len Epand, "virtuosos who most didn't think would go too far into the mainstream. Lo and behold, they added the synthesizers and hooks, and away they went. It all came together at that time. They could have remained purely progressive rock and been a cult-y sort of band, but they branched out."

## BURNING AND DODGING

It wasn't just the music that spun a spell. It was some form of occult ritual for young music lovers to slice the shrink wrap that had been mummifying the LP object, protecting the integrity of the slick cover, for its long journey to the hot and eager hands of fans.

Opening it, sliding out the dustcover and record, was only the beginning of the mystic endeavor.

The red font used for the lyrics appearing on the LP dust cover lent the album an air of the esoteric. The lettering wasn't exactly hieroglyphics, but the crimson-blood red ink, set against the starless black background, bugged out the eyes. Squinting to read the words on both sides of the dustcover, including the dense liner notes, rewarded the dedicated with insights into who the band was—and what it was actually singing about.

Not many people knew at the time, but vinyl releases would, relatively speaking, soon become obsolete. Increasingly, album cover artwork did not have the same impact on a recording artist's public image. Musicians and rock stars alike understood the power of visuals. They were beginning to interact with their fan bases via newly released video placed in heavy rotation on MTV. It seemed like it happened overnight.

The video industry began changing the music business, and within a matter of just a few years, CDs began gobbling up market share. A rock star's visual persona was becoming increasingly defined not by LP packaging artwork and certainly not by the shrinking canvas of the CD booklet cover but rather by the medium of the music video.

*Moving Pictures* may have been the last great, even iconic, Rush album cover if not the last great pre–mass market CD-era Rush LP cover. As the album was being completed in the fall of 1980, visuals used for the front and back covers and inner dust sleeve were shot, playing on the pun of "moving pictures."

There's more than just a whiff of the self-referential here that would have made Pink Floyd and its go-to design firm, Hipgnosis, proud (or blush?). The observer is lost in a spiral of visual puns.

"Pictures being moved by moving men, and the people off to side are being moved by the moved paintings," says photographer Deborah Samuel, who shot the front and back covers of *Moving Pictures* and the black-and-white portraits on the LP dust sleeve. "The whole thing is a pun."

Being escorted into the building, ostensibly a museum (more about this in a moment), we see Cassius Coolidge's painting of dogs playing poker, titled *A Friend in Need*, from 1903 (a painting Peart wanted to include in the shoot), a framed photo of Joan of Arc at the stake (the "witch," referencing one of the tracks on the album, Syme's idea), as well as the *2112* Naked Man raging against the red star of the Solar Federation.

Legend had it that Syme could not locate a suitable painting of the Maid of Orléans—and he desperately wanted a "witch" on the cover to coincide with "Witch Hunt" featured on the record. He located a burlap sack and a heavy wooden post and recruited Samuel to portray the martyred saint. It was a kind of inside joke: Syme was the man waving on the cover of *Permanent Waves*, and now it was Samuel's turn in the barrel.

"When I shot Joan of Arc, I had a long cable release behind my back, and we had pie plates filled with lighter fluid, and Hugh would toss a match into them, and they would flame up, and I would take the pictures, from behind," Samuel says.

The deeper one digs into the creative inspiration for the shoot, the more apparent is the two (maybe three) degrees of Rush. For instance, one of Samuel's friends, Robert Gage, a notable Toronto hairdresser, portrayed the director on the back cover image.

"The two men holding the Joan of Arc picture were friends of Hugh," says Samuel. "Actually, the first three, from left to right, were friends of Hugh. Michael Baker is the fourth [moving] guy, and his daughter is on the extreme right side. I think she is screaming or something. The fifth guy was actually Kelly Jay [Fordham] from the band Crowbar. I was very friendly with his then wife. She is actually on the back cover [Kerry Knickle, former Canadian DJ, holding up clipboard (off to the left)]."

Flip the LP over: It's revealed that the scene parading through the front cover image is all being caught by a moving pictures film crew. As was the case for people populating the front cover image, this "production crew" was actually a close-knit community of friends and business associates tied largely to Syme, Samuel, and the band and its management company.

It seems fitting, then, that a Toronto architectural icon, the parliamentary building, acts as a backdrop for people with so many shared experiences in their hometown. And since it was a government building and the shoot took place on a Sunday morning, there wasn't likely to be anyone there.

"That building, at Queen's Park, is on the main thoroughfare in Toronto," says Samuel. "It sat at the top of the street, and cars would be diverted around this entire lot in a circle on both sides of it. For Canadians, it was very much a landmark, a very old classical building. I think we kind of thought of it that way. Also, for what we wanted to do for bringing trucks and equipment and a lot of people, it was well suited to that."

The classical architecture, the impressive arches, and the austere, almost foreboding facing give the structure the appearance of "a museum of sorts," Samuel says.

The vivid colors of the image—the bright red of the moving men uniforms, the corona of flames in the picture of Joan of Arc, and the pinkish hue of the Masonic stonework—seem hyperreal, adding undertones to an otherwise monochromatic gray. On some copies of the LP, the front of the building does indeed appear grayish. (Will the real Queen's Park stand up?)

"Depends on the time of day," says Samuel. "The kind of light, which was overcast because it was raining, would change the color a little bit than what it would be if it were a sunny day. The light fixtures were there, as part of the 'film set,' but the shoot was done through natural light."

From the roof of the truck used to transport equipment, Samuel set up her tripod and began shooting.

"I had a high angle on all of this and shot down," says Samuel. "I used a Mamiya RB67 medium-format camera using Ektachrome Color Transparency Daylight Balanced 120 film, with warm-up filters over the lens. I used an eighty-millimeter lens for the front cover and a fifty-millimeter lens for the back cover image."

As the shoot was proceeding, a film crew was also on hand. Taking the pun even further, a motion pictures crew, headed up by director Rodney Bowes, captured actual footage that was later used for Rush's live show. Bowes, a graphic designer, photographer, and video director, actually appears, just in frame, near the bottom left corner of the back cover photo of *Moving Pictures*.

"We were shooting live action, and the record cover was being shot in stills by Deborah Samuel," Bowes says. "We were filming the guys moving the pictures and the lady dropping the basket and the fruit falling out of it."

"I was teaching at the time, at the Ontario College of Art & Design," adds John Coull, who operated the camera as the shoot's cinematographer. "One of my students was Rodney Bowes. I think Rodney had just graduated. I don't remember the exact timing, but Rodney had contacted me, and we did a music video [prior to the *Moving Pictures* film shoot]. I'd shot a music video for Bob Segarini. Rodney gave me a call and said they were doing the album cover for Rush's *Moving Pictures* and had the idea of the pictures coming to life. So he asked me if I would put that together."

Coull remembers it being "super-low budget. We got an inventory of old lighting equipment from William F. White—it was just stuff laying around. I don't think we even paid rental money for that equipment because it was just spare inventory. So we just scattered lights around and made it look a film set. Had a small panel truck that we dragged all the equipment to this site with and put a ladder up against the side of the truck and climbed up to the top of the truck and used that as the shooting platform."

Like Bowes, Coull appears on the back cover. "I'm the fellow standing in the foreground with the dark brown winter coat on," says Coull. "That was sort of my payment for the job. [laughs] Rodney took a still shot of the scene, and we matched that. We had all the characters stand in the same position for the still shot, then called action, and they moved the pictures. The idea was that we would put a freeze frame on the beginning of the shot, something that matched the album cover. We had an optical house do that. It was a slow-motion start to bring it up to speed so that the picture would come to life."

When Rush toured the record, they used the film Bowes and the crew shot, projecting images onto a rear screen. "I remember seeing it in Toronto, at Maple Leaf Gardens [March 1981]," Bowes recalls. "I remember that night because I was shooting some pictures, and I put all my crap on the back of Geddy's keyboard, out of light. When Geddy was playing keyboard, he was right in front of me, but I am out of the light, so nobody can see me from the audience. I remember Geddy saying to me, 'Look, Rodney. Here's your big moment. Check this out.' I couldn't see behind him, on the screen, but the film was playing, and the audience reacts. The album cover came to life, you know? That was the first time I had shown my work to thousands of people at once, where I got an instant response to something I did."

"The highlight for me was that we got to go to the sound check for the concert, and then I was able to be backstage the night of the concert," says Coull. "Standing very close to the drums, for me a drummer, was the thrill of a lifetime. What we got to see was this magic moment where the lights all dimmed and the image of the album cover came up on the screen, and then it started to move and the audience went wild.

"My daughter had the album out and was showing it to my grandson, who is eighteen," Coull continues. "They were over for dinner and I said, 'Come, here, and have a look at this. That's your grandpa on the back cover of this album.' He said, 'Oh, I've heard of Rush.' My daughter put it on the turntable, and it was wonderful that a record from 1981 did not give you a cringey feeling that, 'Oh, gosh, I was involved with that.' There was no embarrassment. What a great album, and I'm proud of the fact that I'm on that back cover."

To complete the visuals for the album packaging, Syme and Samuel traveled from Toronto to Morin-Heights and Le Studio, where the inside LP dustcover images were to be shot. Individual photos of the band members on the inside dustcover jacket of the original LP format release have become just as iconic as the front and back cover imagery.

One of Samuel's strengths as an artist is her ability to highlight physical traits in intense detail without making them appear grotesque. Samuel maintains the overall integrity of the composition while also providing the observer an intimate look at the subject.

"I get a lot of e-mails from Rush fans," says Samuel. "The Neil Peart image is a big picture. When we were shooting it, we said, 'We want Neil to start here and end up here.' It was repeated a few times to get that. Alex started with a knee bend and moved up to the light. Geddy was jumping."

The time-lapse photos, or, as Samuel called them, "motion trail" images, were made possible in part via a device called a monobloc unit. For Lifeson's image, Samuel used a secondary light source as well.

"The monobloc is the strobe light head source, with dials on the light head to vary the intensity and number of flashes desired over a given time. So only this light source was used. You can time how many flashes you want over a period of a second or two seconds. It is depending on how many images you want to show up. With Neil and Alex, they would have had quite a number of images in a second or two. Geddy, I think, it was only three or four. It depends on whether you want eight flashes—eight images that are moving—or you want four images that are moving."

Samuel also used a processing technique of burning and dodging—controlling the exposure of certain portions of the photo to create contrast, making darks darker and brights brighter. "The pictures of the band were made using a Mamiya RB67 medium-format camera with an eighty-millimeter lens using Tri X black-and-white film," says Samuel. "The images were printed 'in the dark room,' and I would have used softening filters, like a black nylon stocking for part of the exposure, which kind of blends the tones. I didn't do it for the entire [process] because then you start to lose contrast. That's how you pointed out that you can see detail and not have it be grotesque. But I can dim down certain tones. I can lighten things up because it makes the eye move along the picture. Printing is a visceral process. It's creating the story, really, of how somebody looks at something."

Rush was so impressed with Samuel's work on both *Permanent Waves* and *Moving Pictures* that she was tapped once again for the photo for the cover photos of *Exit . . . Stage Left* and *Signals*.

"The album, the album art, it gelled something in time," says Samuel. "Maybe it was just its time and the band's time for that to happen."

With the record having been released on February 12, Rush took to the road on the February 17, opening their tour in Michigan. For the band, things had radically changed and yet had come full circle: Michigan was the first state the band ever played in the United States way back when John Rutsey was still on drums.

The multicity tour extended from midwinter through early summer. When they came home, they turned around and stayed out for virtually the whole rest of the year, playing shows into December 1981. Although Rush headlined many shows without an opening act, the likes of Max Webster and FM did offer support for various parts of the tour.

"Both bands were heavily influenced by the prog rock thing, for sure, so they were kindred spirits," says FM drummer Paul DeLong. "I know that Neil really admired Marty Deller's playing. In fact, Cam [Hawkins, keyboardist/vocalist] told me that Neil would be at his drums covered with a tarp, playing along during FM's set. And it's no coincidence that Geddy Lee would be standing at the side of the stage every night watching Cam play Minimoog. This definitely influenced the material that Rush would be writing."

Radio station programmers across the United States were adding music from *Moving Pictures* to their rotation. From Los Angeles to Pittsburgh, New York to

Arizona, and Boston to Florida and Texas, radio bigwigs and listeners alike were responding to the Canadian trio's new music. Rush was catching fire in America.

The band's dates at Maple Leaf Gardens on March 23–25 were scheduled to be recorded. And what would become the *Exit . . . Stage Left* film was shot in Montreal at the Forum on the following scheduled concert date, Friday, March 27.

Although the *Montreal Gazette* did not appear to approve of the brisk business Rush was doing via merchandise and refreshments prior to the concert, they nonetheless provided a detailed picture of an arena buzzing with activity inside and outside the doors of the Forum. According to the report, non–ticket holders for the event caused, in the paper's estimation, a "quasi-riot" due to their lack of ability to legally enter the building to see the show.

Mid-April offered a chance to escape the rigors of the road for a short window. The band was touring through the Southwest and was invited by NASA to observe the space shuttle *Columbia*'s maiden voyage—similar to what their one-time literary hero, Ayn Rand, had done before them for the Apollo 11 launch in July 1969 at Cape Kennedy. The band would write and record a song dedicated to the inaugural launch, titled "Countdown," which would appear as the closing track on 1982's *Signals*.

After months of being on the *Billboard* Rock Albums chart, having entered in March at number six, *Moving Pictures* was still in the Top 10 well into May and June. A sold-out show at Madison Square Garden in New York City on May 18 was capped off by an award ceremony held at Penn Plaza to acknowledge that *Moving Pictures*, *2112*, and *All the World's a Stage* had gone platinum.

What makes this feat even more astounding is that America was living through economic doldrums. According to a *Circus* article that ran in August 1981, on average, attendance was down at rock concerts relative to 1979, prior to the gas shortage. This didn't stop people from lining up to see Rush perform, however, and by the summer of 1981, Rush meant business—*big business*.

Just to give the reader an example of the band's reach and the tour's scope, on their Hemispheres tour in February 1979, Rush had visited Shreveport, Louisiana, not particularly known as a hotbed of progressive rock, and 4,000 folks came out to see them. Roughly two years later in April 1981, with the economy in the toilet and Rush supporting *Moving Pictures*, 8,000 people gained access to the Hirsch Coliseum.

To their credit and despite some of the extra costs associated with trekking across a continent (everything from gas prices to rental fees), Rush didn't appear to compensate for the added expenses by passing the bill along to their fans.

Paraphrasing a one-time PolyGram A&R guy, it's one thing for a rock tour caravan to steamroll into town during a recession; it's another when the town doesn't roll up to see the band. Rush's music evidently transcended all of this negativity and charmed fans' wallets open. Once again, Rush had defied the odds and were not victims of the industry's general downward spiral of dwindling concert revenues.

The numbers don't lie. The band's swing through California and Nevada pulled in dollar figures the band had rarely seen. The haul from a two-night stand in June at the Forum in Los Angeles alone was well over $200,000, and for a string of half a dozen dates in the West, including those in Los Angeles, the box office figures were north of half a million. At press time, those 1981 dollars from just a few shows equate to nearly U.S.$2,000,000 today.

Similar brisk business was done in the major cities of the East Coast, Midwest, and Pacific Northwest when the band swung through epicenters New York, Philadelphia, Pittsburgh, Cleveland, Boston, Seattle, and Portland.

Although they were performing as the headliner for the Permanent Waves tour that they embarked on in 1980, these were smaller venues and not the major sports arenas native to North America. Between sales of the recordings, merchandise, and touring, Rush climbed out of debt and had the opportunity to renegotiate with Mercury Records.

"You either eventually happen and you shouldn't be in the red then, hopefully, or you never get out of it because the record company has advanced you money or a private individual advances money, and if you never happen, you never recoup," says Mike Tilka. "With Max Webster, for instance, everybody thinks you're successful because people know who you are, or you're visible because you play Maple Leaf Gardens. But those things—and making money—are not the same thing. If you do get out of the red eventually, you hit that album or touring schedule, audience, or promoter relationship where all of a sudden you are making real money. Of course, [Rush] did."

SRO and parent company Anthem may have seen Rush's rise as a well-earned victory for a hardworking band. But no one at the company could have predicted this. Val Azzoli, who worked for Ray Danniels in the late 1970s and became Atlantic Records cochairman and CEO in the 1980s, told me once that "*Moving Pictures* just blew them up. I believed in what we were doing, they believed in what they were doing, and we were making a difference."

"In the Mood": As if tracking their musical progress, Rush released one of their earliest songs and their most modern, to date, as both sides of a single.

By the end of August, Anthem had released a single of "Vital Signs," b/w "In the Mood," in the United Kingdom and Spain. Although the song didn't and wouldn't do for Rush or *Moving Pictures* what "Tom Sawyer" or "Limelight" had, the band believed in the track and thought it a signifier.

With the coming fall, Rush revisited some old business: they had set aside the notion of releasing a live album prior to recording *Moving Pictures* but felt they could not put it off much longer.

Rush decided to peruse recordings taken from the band's shows dating back to June 1980 on the Permanent Waves tour in Canada and the United Kingdom (some

*Exit...Stage Left*: The gold standard of Rush concert films

from Scotland). Fifty rolls of two-inch tape were spooled for the live recording project, titled *Exit . . . Stage Left*.

The band's June 4–8 shows at Hammersmith were later made available with the fortieth-anniversary reissue edition of *Permanent Waves*. Only "Jacob's Ladder" was culled from a mid-February show in St. Louis, Missouri, at the Kiel Auditorium.

As the band was compiling the live album, making fixes they felt were necessary and generally gathering the appropriate songs, Rush began to believe that this double live record, to be titled *Exit . . . Stage Left*, was too pristine.

Some take issue with this assessment. For fans, there's still plenty of passion, rawness, and atmosphere here, differentiating these live versions from their studio cousins. A shortened but caffeinated version of "Beneath, Between and Behind" on *Exit . . . Stage Left* is perhaps the definitive iteration of the song. For a slightly different but no less adrenalized take, check out the live rendition recorded in Manchester in 1980 and appearing on the *Permanent Waves* remastered edition released in 2020.

"*All the World's a Stage*—a lot of the fans loved it, but the band were unhappy with the rawness," says chief recording engineer Paul Northfield for *Moving Pictures* and *Exit . . . Stage Left*. "Consequently, when we did *Exit . . . Stage Left*, that ended up being extremely overdubbed and really rerecorded. Almost the only thing that was kept were the drums and the live ambience. Other people love it for that because it is very precise, and it still had a live energy from the point of view of the bed-track recording. There was a lot of overdubbing and reinforcement and fixing and things like that."

Dedicated to Terry, "Broon's Bane," the minute-and-a-half acoustic intro to "The Trees" (which lilts in 6/8 and is built on arpeggiated notes in minor and suspended chords), qualifies as some of the best classically tinged guitar work of Lifeson's career. A bane, indeed.

Rush owed a lot to Brown, dating back to their earliest days, and in retrospect, the gravity of the piece proves more poignant when one considers what was just around the corner. More about this in a later chapter.

"Closer to the Heart," with the help of the audience (the Glaswegian Chorus listed in the liner notes), foreshadowed the wave of human feedback the band would receive in Brazil years later, as documented with *Rush in Rio*. A heightened state of synchronicity and interplay existing among the members of Rush had never been more evident in the live version of "Closer to the Heart." As much as each member has had a spotlight as an individual to perform onstage, this song is a synthesis of their interplay.

On the whole, there was an electricity even if there was more control exerted over the sound of the tracks in relation to *All the World's a Stage*. But this tight hold on the tracks creates a steady tension that still makes *Exit . . . Stage Left* a compelling listen. Because precision was the overriding directive of the mission, some intense performances were left on the cutting-room floor.

"The thing most incredible about Neil was, if he was playing something insanely complicated, then his feel started to come out," says Northfield. "You can't think when you're playing like that. You have so much going on that it is all intuition that's carrying you through. I remember mixing live stuff, and Geddy and I were working on it, and maybe it was something that was never used because maybe the guitars were out of tune or Geddy was not happy with his vocals for some reason. There's a lot of recordings of Neil that, on one particular night, he might have been on fire, and there are times that he displays jaw-dropping fluidity and feel. But it was within the context of something so complex that you don't even understand how anybody can play like that."

The concert film *Exit . . . Stage Left* is a different story altogether. The Wagnerian impact of the music, as well as the prismatic, almost hypnotic, and (at rare moments) Ganzfeld-inducing effect, was created by the lighting, courtesy of Howard Ungerleider. Clear light appears with a shock of silver beams as a hiss of crashed cymbals wash over us; the film is a must-see-hear-feel-taste synesthesian delight.

"Howard was one of the first to start using lasers and all that kind of stuff," says Rodney Bowes. "Very progressive lighting guy. I think Howard's lights were every bit as important as Rush's performance in those shows."

The amber, clear light, as well as red and blue color palettes (simultaneously "bugging out" the eyes and creating a three-dimensional effect), stress the spatial quality inherent to the visual work as a whole.

If the stage production doesn't dazzle you, maybe the performances will. The concert film portion of "Xanadu" should be viewed if for no other reason than to watch Neil's hands gravitate to all areas of the kit. For most aspiring drummers at the time, the drum solo included in "YYZ" had every bit the cultural impact in the progressive rock era that "Sing, Sing Sing," "In a Gadda Da Vida," and "Moby Dick" had on earlier generations.

"*Moving Pictures* is my favorite Rush record, but sometimes I'll say it really is *Exit . . . Stage Left* because it encompasses that time period in which my drums were set up, as close as I could, to Neil's arrangement," says Jason Bittner. "I would come home from school and do nothing else but play along to Rush, nothing but try to learn the 'YYZ' solo. I still think the kick and snare sound is great. I even told him so. He said, 'Well, thank you. My sound has evolved since then.' I was thinking, 'I know, sir, but I still think it is the best . . .' as he is signing my Slingerland Artist snare drum."

When listening to drum solos on *All the World's a Stage, Exit . . . Stage Left,* and *A Show of Hands* in chronological order, the evolution of Peart's ideas, the integration of electronic samples, and technique is evident. Rhythmic and musical concepts were developed, repeated, and restated, building toward a climax before bursting into a completely different idea.

Advanced equipment (for the time), such as an Akai digital sampler, a KAT percussion unit, a MIDI controller, and high-end electronic Simmons pads, generated some of Peart's most tribal sounds to date.

"I will say, one of the greatest parts of Neil's solo from *A Show of Hands* is his incorporating the electronic percussion composition 'Pieces of Eight,'" says Bittner. "I did something similar when I did the Modern Drummer festival in honor of him."

Peart gained momentum with his solo on *All the World's a Stage*, but his ascendance to the Drum God throne was complete with 1981's *Exit . . . Stage Left*. For some, Neil's solo in "YYZ" was the natural successor to Bonham's "Moby Dick," viewed as the gold standard of rock drum solos.

"Bonham changed drumming forever by the late '70s, and I think

Neil Peart's ever-evolving solo, tucked inside "YYZ," is featured in the concert film, *A Show of Hands*.

Peart changed it again [in the early 1980s]," says Dave Krusen (Candlebox, Pearl Jam, and Unified Theory). "He was such a huge influence on drummers in the '80s. Beyond that, too, I remember in the early '80s, we all wanted to play like that. His soloing was so different. He had such intricate parts but at the same time probably the best 'air drumming' drum parts ever. To me, that says a lot; it shows that [Peart] was always about the song, the music, more than he as a drummer. Ultimate band drummer."

"I think the drum solo on *All the World's a Stage* is great, but Rush was still up and coming in many ways then, whereas Zeppelin was huge by that point in time," says Brian Tichy, who played bits of Rush songs onstage at special events and at drum festivals. "Bonham got a ton of attention with 'Moby Dick.' But what Neil was developing in his solos, that he peaked with in 'YYZ,' was nothing short of brilliant."

It did have precedence, of course. Listen to the solo by Graham Lear, one of Peart's heroes, on Santana's double-platinum live release *Moonflower* from 1977. There are some rhythmic points of overlap in style and approach between Lear's chops in "Soul Sacrifice/Head, Hands & Feet" and Peart's drumming performances.

Lear had developed his technique and incorporated triplets with double bass and increased the number of toms in his setup.

"If you sense any similarities, you are probably hearing Whitey [Pentti Glan]," says Lear. "He was such a big influence on all the drummers in this area. He was the true drumming rock star in our area because the Mandala was so popular. Whitey was a special, unusual person.

"Whitey had an interesting setup," Lear continues. "He was the first, maybe the only one I saw, who took his bass drum, put tom-tom legs on it, and turned [the kick drum] sideways and had one of those pedals that would reverse upward. He put that underneath it and put the mounted tom on a separate stand. . . . His drum set looked completely different. The curtain would open, and Mandala would come out, and you would go, 'Wow.'"

Whether we are discussing Lear, Pentti "Whitey" Glan, Led Zeppelin's John Bonham, Buddy Rich, Gene Krupa, Cream's Ginger Baker, the Who's Keith Moon, or even Tommy Aldridge (Black Oak Arkansas, Whitesnake, Pat Travers, and Ozzy Osbourne), Peart seemed to grab a piece of what made these drummers great—and then added his own twist.

"A friend of mine from St. Catharines knew Neil," says Mike Tilka (Max Webster and SRO/Anthem). "I knew Neil because we toured with Rush. Neil was a bit of a sponge. That guy learned, and I don't think I knew a musician who practiced as hard as Neil. He *made* himself a good drummer. Some guys are naturals. I'm sure Graham [Lear] was probably a natural. I don't know for sure because I didn't know him when he was young. Neil was a schooled, a self-schooled but schooled nonetheless, listener. You're right. He would have listened to Graham; he would have listened to every-body, that guy."

"Neil used triplets and all those toms and the double kick," says Tichy. "When he incorporated all of those into the band's writing, he took it to another level. He really set another standard."

"What Bonham did was he played a drum solo that a nondrummer could relate to," says Jonathan Mover. "Similar to someone like Ringo, though Bonham had mon-ster chops and was one of the gods of Mount Olympus, he played a drum solo that anyone could listen, tap along, or air-drum to. It was more like a drum composition, rather than, 'I've got 10 minutes to show how fast I can play and twirl my sticks.' Gene Krupa did the same thing with 'Sing, Sing, Sing.' He captured the audience in a rhythmic way. That's very different from someone like Buddy Rich, who had the speed and ferocious chops that terrorized the listener because they could not believe or understand what he was doing. When you listen to a Neil solo, it's something you can follow along to–a song written for and played on the drums. The little cowbells . . . the concert toms . . . those elements gave Neil the melodic moments an audience likes to hear and can always relate to. Whether or not Neil designed it that way, I don't know.

"However he came up with the material, Neil went out there with these little compositions that people could latch onto and relate to, because they recognized them, like a song." Mover continues. "He had a wonderful way of putting it together and presenting it, and in doing so, brought the listener along for the ride. He gave the cake and the icing, and you got to eat both. If he really did design it that way, then he was even smarter than I know he was. And he was a very smart guy."

The live double record *Exit . . . Stage Left* was shipped on October 20, 1981, with plans to broadcast a live concert film in the United States and Canada. Incredibly, Rush released their best studio record and live album in the span of less than a year. It closed 1981 in the Top 20 of *Billboard's* Rock Albums chart.

The concert would air in different television markets from 1982 through 1983 and eventually be released on VHS format as *Exit . . . Stage Left* (later also on DVD).

"The Weinsteins, who started Miramax, and I were on a flight back from Cannes," remembers Len Epand, formerly of PolyGram. "The two brothers, Bob and Harvey, were there, berating me to try to give them, license to them, *Exit . . . Stage Left*. But I already had a deal with Embassy Home Entertainment. They gave us much greater licensing fees than what [the Weinsteins] were offering. The whole flight: 'Come on, license us Rush. Come on.' Nobody knows about that; I never told that story."

*Moving Pictures* and *Exit . . . Stage Left* were ushered into a world in which the videotape home market was just starting to gear up and MTV had been established. Although commercial LaserDiscs had been available since the late 1970s, within a few years, mass-produced, prerecorded VHS cassettes would storm the marketplace, and, of course, the CD format for audio changed the way we listened to the world. *Moving Pictures* rode the crest of these technological waves.

"MTV was iconic, and it was out there, inspiring everybody as well as the competition to do better," says Epand. "It enabled the artist and director to tell stories and market an act and sell their performance, which helped ticket sales. I used to say that video is reality through a lens and film is image making—larger than life."

The early goings of MTV were not exactly hospitable to bands like Rush, whose focus was on performance rather than fashion. While Rush wasn't in danger of ever being overexposed, PolyGram promoters who approached the all-music channel were still hopeful that some agreement could be reached. Getting on MTV, however, proved to be daunting.

"MTV was tough," Epand admits. "If it wasn't a huge hit yet, they would put it in some lunar rotation—three in the morning. [laughs] If the record started building, then they would kind of follow it up. It was only rare cases that it would go immediately into heavy rotation, if it was the latest Def Leppard or Bon Jovi or something."

By 1987, say, with Rush's "Time Stand Still" or videos shot for songs appearing on Def Leppard's album *Hysteria*, production seemed to reach critical mass. Artists learned from the previous six years or so of video making what to do and what not to do.

"We went through some really awful times figuring it out," says Epand. "Some really crappy videos were made to get to that point."

By November 1981, Rush was touring the United Kingdom, continental Europe, and the American South and Northeast, generating positive reviews, especially like the one from the *Daily Telegraph* for the band's three-night stand at Wembley Arena in London. With some reservations, the *Miami Herald* recommended *Exit . . . Stage Left*, saying it is "an accurate representation of Rush today" and worth a listen. By year's end, a single of "Closer to the Heart," b/w "Freewill," both tracks from *Exit . . . Stage Left*, entered *Billboard*'s Hot 100 chart in the United States.

Amid the accolades and commercial successes, the inevitable renegotiation occurred: Rush re-signed with Mercury/Polygram for global releases, except Japan and Canada.

Suddenly, Rush was in demand. They had celebrity status they could trade on, maybe for the first time, whether they liked it or not. This was never more apparent than with the comedy single "Take Off," released on Mercury/PolyGram in December 1981, leading a late holiday retail rally in places such as the American Midwest.

Geddy lends his voice to the comedy hit, "Take Off."

Rush were fans of the Bob and Doug McKenzie shtick—a fictional TV talk show they hosted on the comedy sketch series "Great White North" on *Second City TV* (*SCTV*). Rick Moranis and Dave Thomas, who portrayed Bob and Doug McKenzie on-screen, found their way to Anthem Records. Although the two hadn't seen each other in years, Moranis invited Geddy to sing on their lead track.

As the original Moranis and Thomas skit had done, this surprise comedy hit contains a high degree of self-deprecating humor. The manner in which the McKenzie Brothers express their gratitude to Geddy for agreeing to do the session is strange, funny.

Lee deadpans, "Ten bucks is ten bucks."

Produced by Marc Giacomelli, "Take Off" became a radio hit, and the album *Great White North* went gold in the United States—riding a wave of popularity enjoyed by both Rush and *SCTV*. Suddenly, every humorless joke about how serious members of Rush were had dated poorly.

Rush, *SCTV*, the lovable goofballs Bob and Doug McKenzie, and the country of Canada, as a brand, land, and exporter of creativity, further crept into the mainstream psyche and collective subconscious of a generation. But it wasn't just Rush that was innovative or hotter than the sun. Canada had a decade or more history of hard rock and progressive rock that was coming to fruition.

Toronto's Triumph saw success with *Allied Forces* in 1981 for Al Mair's independent Attic label (and MCA in the United States). Ontario's Saga struck gold with *Worlds Apart* (courtesy of the hit "On the Loose"). Halifax's own April Wine, signed to Aquarius Records in Montreal, pumped out memorable, riff-driven hard rock and struck gold with 1981's Mike Stone–produced *The Nature of the Beast*. Red Rider's *As Far As Siam* on Capitol combined hypnotic grooves, New Wave, and pop in the same year. Red Rider's lead songwriter, Tom Cochrane, demoed the hit song "Lunatic Fringe," a haunter with a hint of twang and blues, the night John Lennon was shot.

Loverboy's *Get Lucky* was so ubiquitous that it was vulnerable to mimicry and parody, and Gino Vannelli, who saw such great success with "I Just Want to Stop" (from 1978's *Brother to Brother*), kept rolling with the Top 10 U.S. ballad, "Living Inside Myself," from *Nightwalker*.

Canada's rock music industry coalesced by the late 1970s and saw a steady rise in talent and success. From Montreal to Vancouver, the innovativeness was self-evident. For instance, Robert Charlebois, French-language vocalist in the chansonnier tradition, released his 1972 self-titled release on the Barclay label and pricked up the ears of progressive rock enthusiasts, even fans of art rock/glam perpetrated by Brian Eno–era Roxy Music. Backed by a versatile band, featuring bassist Bill Gagnon and drummer Christian St-Roch, among others, Charlebois' music breathed and unfolded with audiovisual spectacle, cinematic in its scope.

Other names helped to expand the boundaries of Canadian progressive music. From Quebec, we heard multigenre music: folkie/proggy Beau Dommage; country/folk/classical sounds of rockers Cano; film score composer, Edith Piaf collaborator, and at rare moments the occasional progmeister Claude Léveillée; chamber prog ensemble Conventum, featuring guitarists André Duchesne and René Lussier; the more expansive and experimental moments of social activist Raôul Duguay;

symphonic folk rockers Le Temps; and Dionne-Brégent, a partnership forged by percussionist Vincent Dionne and keyboardist Michel-Georges Brégent, who had created a minimalistic and avant-garde hybrid of esoteric electronic soundscapes rife with cyclical patterns and (largely) orchestral percussion in the mid- and late 1970s.

On the West Coast in Vancouver, keyboardist/piano man John Mills-Cockell was experimenting with Hydro Electric Streetcar and also joined Toronto-based jazzy/folk soulful pop band Kensington Market for the Felix Pappalardi–produced *Aardvark*, their second album on Warner Bros.

The chameleon-like eclectic collective could morph into blue-eyed rhythm and blues/soul, something resembling *Pet Sounds*–era Beach Boys, country-jazz artists, psychedelic popsters, or an approximation of proto-progressive icons the Moody Blues. This musical freedom apparently wasn't enough for Mills-Cockell, who established his own band with the Toronto-based experimental electronic synth project Syrinx, which recorded for Bernie Finkelstein's True North label in the early 1970s.

"I became a fan of Syrinx when their performance of the instrumental 'Tillicum' was chosen as the intro to a late '60s weekly CBC TV show called *Here Come the '70s*," says Monte Nordstrom, cofounder of what was the Vancouver-based progressive folk-rock band Ptarmigan. "In March of 1972, Syrinx performed at the famous Le Hibou coffeehouse in Ottawa, where Ptarmigan had opened up for the legendary Lenny Breau a couple weeks earlier. We got to do a guest set as a duo that night in between their two sets. When the show was over, we all went to an after-party [get-together], and I had a good visit with synth master [Mills-Cockell], who was a very funny, intelligent guy."

Nordstrom's own Ptarmigan was signed to Columbia Records Canada, and their Paul Horn–produced, self-titled debut borders on meditative drone, migrating between psychedelic folk and progressive rock.

We can't name every progressive act in Canada that began making noise in the mid-1970s, but the above is enough to demonstrate that scenes existed, even thrived, north of the U.S. border and across the shores from England.

At the same time, some of Rush's contemporaries, whether we are discussing Kansas, Styx, Starcastle, Saga, or FM, were by the early 1980s shedding some of their progressive rock tendencies—or dissolving altogether.

While the odd Max Webster track might qualify as progressive rock (in broad terms), *Universal Juveniles* from 1980, as of this writing, was the band's last official studio album. Likewise, Montreal's popular multigenre progressive heroes Harmonium saw their final studio effort, *Harmonium En Tournée*, released in 1980—not long before chief songwriter Serge Fiori decided to step away from the band.

Rush held together and topped them all with *Moving Pictures*. As alluded to throughout this book, *Moving Pictures* achieved this through equilibrium, containing the proper ratio of melody, technical prowess, guitar and bass riffs, and application of synthesizers to reach a seamless and arguably earthy blend of hard rock.

Very few if any other North American (or, for that matter, European) progressive bands had the same success in fusing these elements.

At turns dense yet ambient, accessible yet musically complex, *Moving Pictures* sufficiently mixes various musical ingredients to become a new element. In short, *Moving Pictures* is the stuff of magical elixir, derived and synthesized through a ritualized integration—via technology-based recording alchemy—of creativity and technical prowess. It's a constant spring that offers sonic treasures, thought-provoking themes, and even a sense of spiritual healing.

# CHAPTER 11

# THE COLD WAR

Once *Moving Pictures* was unleashed, nothing was ever really the same again for Rush.

Afterward, solid efforts ensued, from 1982's *Signals* to 1985's *Power Windows* and 1991's *Roll the Bones*, but nothing captured the public imagination like *Moving Pictures*.

Music for the band's next studio record, *Signals*, was already coming together on the Moving Pictures tour, with "Subdivisions" and "Chemistry" being among them.

By March 1982, the band had finished rehearsing its new material and had in April embarked on a nine-date tour in which they'd played "Subdivisions" and "The Analog Kid." Legend has it that some of the material may have been earmarked initially for what would have been a Geddy Lee solo record. Plans were apparently scratched, and in the following months, from April through early July, *Signals* was recorded at Le Studio.

Brown had produced New Wave records, pop, and pop with punk elements, including Alfie Zappacosta's band Surrender and Hungarian native and Canadian resident BB Gabor. But back in 1982, Brown did not foresee and perhaps could not even have conceived of the level of programming that would encompass and envelop Rush's music. Soon, the entire architecture of Rush songs was being mapped by synth.

"New World Man," "Losing It" (in which creative minds and athletic bodies fade into oblivion), "The Weapon" (which continued on from "Witch Hunt" as part 2 of the Fear saga), and "Digital Man" were testaments to Rush's willingness to move on from the progressive-influenced hard rock to some hybrid of hard rock and synth pop with faint traces of prog.

One of the record's standout tracks, "Subdivisions," dissects suburban isolation and alienation—what it means to be an outlier in an environment shaped by a closed society's need for conformity. Those like Peart, who had either decided or simply needed to be "freaky," were objects of ridicule, derision, even violence. "[The album]

*Signals*, from 1982, took shape on the Moving Pictures tour.

is partly about me, in a way," Peart told the *Detroit Free Press* in 1982. "We all grew up in modern subdivisions. It's a unique thing that's part of the postwar cultural scene."

*Signals* did not perform as well as *Moving Pictures*, although it did go platinum in the United States and generated Rush's only Top 40 hit, "New World Man," which was heavily inspired by the Police. Some observers believed *Signals* to be a breath of fresh air. The *Los Angeles Times* claimed it was Rush's best work, cohesive and refined.

Music was changing rapidly, and as much as some fans might object, in retrospect, *Permanent Waves*, *Moving Pictures*, and *Exit . . . Stage Left* represented a bygone era: Rush's renaissance, golden age. *Signals* transported Rush to the point of no return.

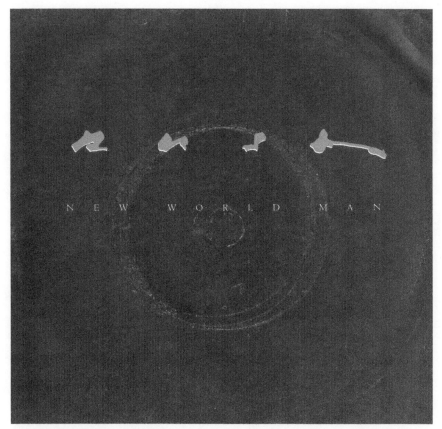

"New World Man": a single from the 1982 studio album, *Signals*, was heavily influenced by the Police.

While on tour for *Signals* in Florida in mid-March 1983, Rush met with Brown to discuss their collective future. It didn't take long for Brown to get the gist of where the conversation was headed.

"[*Signals*] was the last record we did," Brown told me. "There were a lot of changes going on in direction that I was not enthused about: electronics, a lot of keyboards, which I didn't really hear as part of the band."

"I really liked *Signals* but not as much as *Moving Pictures* and *Permanent Waves*," says Brian Tichy. "Probably because it was more keyboard dominated. I loved 'Subdivisions,' and 'New World Man' was cool, but the LP as whole didn't grab me as much as the other prior LPs. With that said, I like it twice as much now. It pops up in my car on my phone here and there."

"I saw the *Signals* tour, which was the first time I saw Rush," says Dave Krusen. "I always felt when a band changed direction, the new songs, at least live in concert, kind of stuck out from all the hits that came before. But Rush so easily incorporated new things into their sound because they seemed to always be pushing the envelope. Being so progressive, they had a blank check as long as they did it right, and I think they always did."

The obvious techno sheen applied to the post-*Signals* records was out of step with the percolating pop-prog potpourri they'd perpetuated for the previous six or seven years. Granted, reggae-fied pop and electronica or techno pop were more in line with the popular tastes of the early 1980s, but Rush was never supposed to be about such trends.

"Keyboards were not really my forte," Brown said. "Hence, the disappearance of me."

Jettisoned from Rush, Brown was set free in more than one direction. He has had an illustrious career as an engineer and producer, with and without Rush, collaborating with a diversity of artists: Klaatu, Dream Theater, Alannah Myles, Traffic, Fate's Warning, April Wine, Toronto, Voivod, Blue Rodeo, Cutting Crew, and others.

Alfie Zappacosta, when he was leading his band Surrender in the late 1970s, remembers working with Brown: "We got to meet Terry Brown, and we were never in a recording studio before. We were in total awe. He owned Toronto Sound, wonderful state-of-the-art studio. Terry counted on the musicians to bring that brainstorming part to the picture, and he would allow us to do what we wanted."

Working with Brown helped broaden Zappacosta's horizons as to what and what not to expect from the industry.

"It took a long time after that to see just how many different kinds of producers there are," says Zappacosta. "He let the leash go, and we threw together what we could. It was a learning experience."

Brown looms large in the Rush story. And he still orbits the universe both personally and through Rush's Six Degrees of Separation. In some ways, the Canadian music industry is a small world: Zappacosta's 2021 record, titled *Saved*, was released through Peter Cardinali's label, Alma Records. Cardinali, a bassist/producer/arranger who has recorded with a number of artists, was in the Dexters, the one-time house band for the now defunct Toronto venue the Orbit Room, co-owned by Alex Lifeson. Cardinali also appears on Lifeson's *Victor* record, the Rush guitarist's solo project from 1996.

Disengaging from Brown may have signaled wide-eyed confidence as much as well-intentioned self-delusion, leading to the nerve-racking recording and mixing sessions that ensnared the making of the 1984 record *Grace Under Pressure*, copro-duced by Rush and Peter Henderson.

If *Moving Pictures* and *Permanent Waves* before it exhibited signs of a coming deluge of New Wave songs, then *Signals* and *Grace Under Pressure* were tidal waves of unabashed synth-pop/prog, opening the floodgates for mid- and late 1980s techno-rock efforts.

Arguably, Brown could not have foreseen that Rush would invite a guest key-boardist on not one but two of their studio albums later in the decade—*Power Windows* (1985) and *Hold Your Fire* (1987). Then, again, perhaps he could.

"They needed to go through [that period] to be successful, and I needed to do some other things as well to be successful," Brown said with a laugh. "'Subdivisions,' I thought, was killer, but that was as far as I could see it going—as far as the amount of keyboards [used]."

"I mean, Terry Brown produced nine Rush albums including some of the heavy prog hitters like *2112*, *A Farewell to Kings*, and *Hemispheres*, so I get where he was coming from," says Eric Barnett. "I think you can say that *Moving Pictures* was the start of the Rush 'synth era,' but it was *Signals* that solidified the direction they were headed."

As the band parted with Brown, they went in search of a new producer. Steve Lillywhite, who had worked work with the likes of Peter Gabriel, U2, Ultravox!, and XTC, was top on the list.

To the band's delight, Lillywhite agreed. But something must have happened on the way to Le Studio because Lillywhite suddenly became unavailable. Perhaps help-ing the band shed its writing/recording process and public image was not something Lillywhite was prepared to do. Rush's sound had roamed a bit toward the New Wave end of the mainstream progressive rock spectrum, but they still had wide appeal with musos, aspiring musicians, and those who considered themselves hard rock aficionados.

That the production collaboration never materialized was, perhaps, a blessing in disguise.

It's possible too that in a bid to become hip in the age of New Wave, Rush was caught up in a maelstrom of musical and production possibilities—the wonder of what their careful art could be in the new decade, collaborating with Mr. New

Wave Producer, who could make their dreams come true from his position stationed behind the glass at Le Studio.

"I heard something about Simple Minds being the other project [Lillywhite was going to work on]," says Robert Di Gioia, formerly a recording engineer at Le Studio who had worked on *Grace Under Pressure*. "I don't think he would have been the right person for the [Rush] project, either. The term producer gets thrown around a lot; depending on what the situation is, it determines what is required of a producer or what is not required of the producer. It is a tricky thing to match up sometimes."

Another name was bandied about, and when the coast looked clear for his involvement, he too declined. This broken connection was due to scheduling. Some have theorized this producer was, in fact, Rupert Hine (the Fixx, Howard Jones, Saga, and Tina Turner), who would produce the band's studio records *Presto* (1989) and *Roll the Bones* (1991).

Rush were living parallel lives: The search for a producer continued, to no avail, while they were writing songs and playing live concerts. After weeks of preproduction, Rush had written and recorded demos for more than half of what would become *Grace Under Pressure*: "Between the Wheels," "Afterimage," "Kid Gloves," "The Body Electric," and "Red Sector A."

Then a dilemma: They'd planned on being finished with the album prior to having booked five shows at Radio City Music Hall in New York in September 1983. This wouldn't be an issue, except the band had to stop work on the record to prep for the concerts before taking the stage in September. New material from the upcoming album would be debuted, namely, "Red Sector A," "The Body Electric" and "Kid Gloves," and Peart, for his part, premiered a full electronic kit.

After their stretch at Radio City, more writing and recording of demos ensued. "Distant Early Warning," "Red Lenses" and "The Enemy Within"—part 1 of the Fear saga—were being sketched.

Still schizophrenically riding a dual course, Rush continued to conduct interviews with prospective producers, hoping to find the elusive golden-eared music man. During this turmoil, Geddy's son Julian lent an action figure to his dad, what the band had dubbed Roger Kneebend. It was placed on the band's recording equipment, presiding over the procession of prospective producers—a list that had grown to dozens.

In a dark humor reminiscent of the Down the Tubes tour, the thinking was that in a pinch, Kneebend could pitch in and maybe get a production credit.

If all of this weren't enough, Peart was reading newspapers every day—mostly Toronto's *Globe & Mail*—and becoming increasingly angered and dismayed over the state of the world: economic stagnation, Cold War proxy skirmishes between the world's two superpowers, environmental concerns, the failure of nuclear arms negotiations, the downing of Korean Air Lines Flight 077 by the Soviets in September 1983, and so on. He needed exorcism by poetry; he needed to write about it, ratcheting up an already tense musical environment.

Anger, disillusionment, insecurity, uncertainty, world-weariness—many of the negative or confused human states of being not only were discussed in Rush's new songs but also made up the flesh and bone of this recording project. Rush seemed just as outraged and confused as the rest of us at the time, and this was reflected in "Distant Early Warning," "Red Lenses," "Between the Wheels," and "Red Sector A."

In addition, personal issues were pervasive. Just as dysfunction had become rife among the band's friends and acquaintances, tragedy struck close to home. Recording assistant Robbie Whelan died in an auto accident in 1983, not far from Le Studio. The band dedicated *Grace Under Pressure* to Whelan, and the song "Afterimage" was written in his memory.

"Robbie was a sweetheart of a person, an assistant engineer, who had come from England," says André Perry. "The night before the accident, he came to Montreal with me. I was working on video, not a commercial gig but for charity. He died in our arms. It was a terrible thing. I don't believe in it, but if there is a heaven, he went straight there because of the charitable cause. If you want to believe in that headspace, he is out there looking at us."

It was all building toward something that could be purged only through flame. This was at odds with the pressure cooker needing to simmer down before it went combustible and *kablooey*. After meeting with producer/recording engineer Peter Henderson, something seemed to click. Henderson had worked on *Breakfast in America*, a major success for Supertramp circa 1979, a fact that was certainly not lost on Supertramp superfan and Rush manager Ray Danniels.

A mild-mannered guy and a solid engineer of great skill, Henderson captured the music as it happened. "Hugh Padgham had been to Le Studio a couple of times with the Police for *Ghost in the Machine* and *Synchronicity*," says Di Gioia. "He had gone on to do with work with Genesis. . . . He came back to do a David Bowie album years later. These are musically strong people who don't need anyone to tell them how to write their songs and how to play their instruments."

Just when Rush thought their prayers had been answered, chaos seemed to reign. Months of recording and overdubbing ensued; fourteen- to sixteen-hour days in the studio were logged. Geddy gradually and with increasingly regularity settled into the producer's chair as it became apparent that Henderson was a great technician but not quick to offer creative suggestions.

"It was one thing to have a million opinions when you know that you have one guy sitting there, who you trust, who is a father figure, who you ultimately trust to say, 'Yea' or 'Nay,'" Lee told me. "But when that [person] is not there and you're in the floating world for the first time, you have to step up and make those decisions. It was difficult."

In a way, Geddy's experience with Wireless, just prior to recording *Moving Pictures*, proved vital to taking command of *Grace Under Pressure* and retaining his sanity.

"Geddy took the bull by the horns, and if there was nobody else there to lead, he was definitely there to make sure that they got what they wanted out of it [the recording process]," Robert Di Gioia told me. "With three guys in the band, I think, maybe, they wanted somebody to lead and take them somewhere. There was one occasion that the three guys go out, do a track, and it felt really good, and they said, 'We love that take.' Alex: 'Yeah, that's good.' Geddy: 'Yeah, that's good.' Peter would say, 'Yeah, that's good.' Then Neil would say, 'Totally unacceptable.' Everybody would stop and say, 'What is wrong with it?' He would then point out one part of the song where there was like a triplet bass note thing and one of the heads wasn't as loud as he wanted it to be. To him, that meant it wasn't perfect. That is a tiny little detail that only he would have noticed. That was the way it was with Neil. If you were going to question Neil on something, you better have a damn good argument about why you think it should change or whatever; otherwise, he will get what he wants."

The grip was tightening. Geddy was claiming more and more of the producer's role, and he demanded more and more precision execution from his longtime friend and bandmate Alex. Lifeson would cut take after take, yet it appeared the coproducer was unsatisfied. Notes were passed back and forth to each other about what each one believed needed to be done for a track.

"It was a long, involved project that just wouldn't end," Lee told me. "It was a kind of insecure time for us."

"At one point in the process," says Di Gioia, "Peter [Henderson] asked, 'What's our budget for the album?' It got a bit of a laugh out of the band. Rush was the band and the record company, and the budget was whatever it took to get it done."

After poring over the minutia of the record, it became nearly impossible for Geddy, who was helping to spearhead the mix, to be objective about anything.

"We were working with new people," Lee told me. "So much of our records are experimental, anyway, so it was just a long tough road, and we were working in a residential studio in Quebec, and it was thirty-five degrees below zero. It was snow, and I hadn't seen my family in ages, and we never took days off."

"We would go to the studio and put in a long day, break for dinner at the guest house, then back to work," says Di Gioia. "I remember one night we had a very heavy snowfall, and Geddy went out and brushed off everybody's car."

Hello, Darkness, their old friend. The classic Rush gallows humor manifested again to help ease tensions. Due to idiosyncratic penmanship, Henderson's name was read as Hentor, and the ironic moniker "Hentor the Barbarian" stuck. Yet this strangely appropriate nickname for the gentlemanly Henderson captured the absurdity of the circumstances. *Grace Under Pressure* was a battle—a war—to cross the finish line amid brutal Canadian winter temperatures and white-out conditions, with tempers flaring amid a seemingly endless hair-pulling recording process.

"I could never make a record in that way, again, never," Lee told me. "So, it was a lot of pressure on our families, personal lives, and it was a pretty tense affair all around."

The band finally finished with the record on March 12, 1984. For years, Rush was confounded by the fact that the recording for the album had taken eight weeks—working twelve-plus-hour days—to record the basic tracks when they had already done much preproduction and with very little time off to lollygag from the moment they entered the studio in November 1983.

What Henderson got right was overseeing the fact that the guitars had returned somewhat to the fore. (Even if their impact was blunted by various effects Lifeson had used during the recording sessions.) And what some might call a homogenized sound indicative of *Signals* was gone.

"The making of it was a real test of the band hanging and being there for each other," Lee told me. "It took a big chunk of us to get the record done."

*Grace Under Pressure* was emblematic of the post–Terry Brown slog the band shoveled on a daily basis—at least in the short run. Rush's music developed rapidly throughout the 1980s—quickly skittering away from the magic of *Moving Pictures*.

On *Moving Pictures* in particular, the execution and the texture of the music, not to mention the timbre of the analog synth/keyboards, were purely and simply different. On later records, all those frequencies that were naturally occupied by synth gobbled up space normally reserved for Lifeson's guitar, and it became difficult at times to discern whether we were hearing strings or keys. (Guest keyboardist Andy Richards even admitted to using synth sounds that mimicked guitar on those mid-1980s Rush records.)

Fans could sense that keyboards had assumed an integral role in mapping the architecture of the band's music, fundamentally changing what Rush was. As such, Geddy was concerned about being able to reproduce the material onstage without adding an extra member to the touring ranks. That meant Lee made sacrifices for the "good" of the track so that three members could actually perform the studio material live without extra help. If there was a complicated series of notes he wanted to play on bass, best not to write an overlapping complex lead line for keys as well.

The opposite was true too. The bottom end—quite literally—was lost because the bass guitar wasn't always present. Of course, the band had access to Taurus pedals, which both Geddy and Alex stepped on when playing onstage, but pedals cannot replace the intricacies and melodicism of a bass's strings being plucked by human hands.

Rush even left its recording home, its Abbey Road, for a time after *Grace Under Pressure*. It is quite telling that the studio efforts directly following Rush's years-long stint at Le Studio, namely, the two Peter Collins–produced mid-1980s synth-era records *Power Windows* and *Hold Your Fire*, were recorded and mixed at various locations across two separate continents. It was as if the band had developed a taste for the international or universal flavor of Le Studio, and their thirst was quenched only by trekking to faraway locales.

Still, changing sounds so rapidly, risking it all to follow an artistic esthetic, was unusual for a commercially successful band. While *Moving Pictures*, followed by the platinum *Signals*, secured some level of audience support through the 1980s and even 1990s, by constantly tinkering with its writing approach and overall sound, Rush might have alienated a core portion of its audience.

But perhaps it was never just about pleasing a core audience per se. Although Lee was specifically referencing *Caress of Steel* when I spoke with him on this occasion, what he said holds true for the 1980s: "We have a remarkably loyal fan base, and the fans have to put up with our experimentation," Lee told me. "They expect us to experiment and look forward to what might come."

The listener can decide for him- or herself whether all of Rush's experiments have been successful. Few would argue to the contrary that *Moving Pictures* has withstood the test of time.

However, threading the needle between impulse and intellect was something of a professional preoccupation for Rush at the time. *Hold Your Fire*—and the process by which the record was completed—stands as a monument that seems to embody this struggle.

A criticism of Rush's recordings during this era was the "squashed" sound of the tracks and the many layers of overdubs, choking the mix. Peter Collins's production simultaneously demystified the progressive rock band while going nuclear on their sonic fingerprint.

Peart remarked once that freedom and responsibility are preferable to reliance on a machine. If this is the case, how could Rush have roamed so far from their roots, allowing the very framework of their music to be designed by programmable devices?

Did Rush become victims of their own pursuit of technology? Opinion seems divided.

"I think they embraced it," says Kevin Aiello of Points North. "It was the technology that allowed them to remain a three-piece band and be able to play the more complicated or layered parts to songs live. It also allowed them to stretch their compositional abilities. If it wasn't for Neil exploring and experimenting on electronic drums, first with Simmons pads then Roland, we would never have had an album like *Power Windows* or an absolute drum masterpiece such as 'Mystic Rhythms.'"

"I love the '80s material," adds Eric Barnett of Points North. "There's certainly some production elements that, in retrospect, might seem a little dated or odd choices. But that was part of what made them Rush—that evolution and willingness to take chances. When you talk about trying to reproduce songs live, anything in that '80s period from *Signals* through *Hold Your Fire* in particular is just crazy making. And some of their most emotionally connected songs, like 'Mission,' come from that period."

"*Signals, Grace Under Pressure, Power Windows*, and *Hold Your Fire* are still some of my favorites," says Aiello. "You can see the band coming into their own as songwriters. And, yes, I even like 'Tai Shan.'"

"The keyboards fully support the direction they went as a band," says Uriah Duffy of Points North. "They advanced through the years until *Counterparts*, where, I think, they dialed back a bit. They definitely did a great job of using new technology, stayed relevant with current sonic pallets of the time, and forged their own musical growth through the use of all this machinery."

"How they employed the technology onstage, using triggers, things had to be so precise," muses Monte Nordstrom. "It was almost like flying a jet airplane."

Rush wasn't particularly known for their hit singles, but in a bid to morph into something much more attuned to the times, Rush managed a kind of fringe main-stream appeal after *Moving Pictures*. After all, *Grace Under Pressure* went platinum, and so did its successor, *Power Windows*. But those that immediately followed, *Hold Your Fire* and *Presto*, went gold only in the United States, proving that Rush's market power, in America anyway, was slipping.

Ironically, as we were ready to leave the 1980s behind us, Rush had the oppor-tunity to work with Rupert Hine for 1989's *Presto* and 1991's *Roll the Bones* (which was, incidentally, the last Rush studio album to go platinum in the United States).

The seasoned British producer suggested the band return to its power trio roots. It was the first step in a long process of Rush reclaiming its rightful place as a pro-gressive hard rock band—a maneuver that gave way to heavier releases: *Counterparts* (1993), *Vapor Trails* (2002), and the conceptual *Clockwork Angels* (2012).

Rush has now officially retired, having called it quits in 2018. And the door may be irreparably closed for a Rush return with the passing of iconic drummer and lyricist Neil Peart in January 2020. They may be gone, but one of the hallmarks of their style was that they stepped into as many musical ones as possible. Fans celebrate Rush's willingness to attempt new musical ideas.

"They kept that going with 'Distant Early Warning,' 'The Big Money,' and 'Time Stand Still,'" says Brian Tichy. "They had found this balance of still sounding like Rush but sounding accessible enough for the masses."

"They took great chances, and I think the glue for them was their audience," says Jonathan Mover. "What a wonderful position to be in: here you are, a platinum band, and no matter what you do, you don't need to write for the public. You're writing for yourself and your fans. Every time you play Madison Square Garden, you know those same 15,000 to 18,000 people will show up for you. I think that was a big factor in the magic of that band."

It's largely these very public shifts in creative direction—growing pains one could say—that solidified the band's reputation as an agile if rare musical species willing to follow its muse and/or respond to the ever-changing marketplace. And it must be said that some of the material on *Power Windows*, *Hold Your Fire*, *Roll the Bones*, *Counterparts*, *Test for Echo*, and others contains similar filmic properties and spatial dimension as the classics on *Moving Pictures*.

Those overdubbed strings in "Manhattan Project" befit a Hollywood counter-intelligence spy thriller, the wide-scope expansiveness of "Test for Echo" hints at a million TV screens tuned to different channels, motoric rumbling in "Cut to the Chase" is propulsive and metallic, dusty African cadences of "Scars" are tribal and intoxicating, spiraling synth work revolving around "The Big Wheel" is dizzying, and the opening keyboard chords of "Second Nature" are evocative and pensive.

*Moving Pictures* laid the groundwork for these (and others) but also benefited from the special "X" factor: time, place, peak talent, production, and material. With *Moving Pictures*, the trio successfully underlined their hard rock roots but also applied keyboard technology without sacrificing aggressiveness. It would be difficult to make that claim about any other record released after *Moving Pictures*. It was and is the epitome of equilibrium.

"Part of why this music is still being appreciated is the sheer quality of the work," says Len Epand. "They call it classic rock for a reason. Younger generations discover it. I'm a guitarist, and I started as a rock guitarist. This stuff doesn't get old."

"When I went out on tour with Linkin Park and Chris Cornell, Linkin Park's front-of-house engineer would calibrate the sound system with 'Tom Sawyer,'" says Jason Sutter (Cher, P!nk, Marilyn Manson, and Chris Cornell). "A lot of times front-of-house engineers use Steely Dan because it has to be a well-produced song. But every morning at eleven o'clock, if you had a late night or whatever, the alarm clock was Rush's 'Tom Sawyer.' It would be loud and clear. It never got old."

"*Moving Pictures* is definitely one of my favorites to this day," says Rick Colaluca. "It was a turning point for the band in couple of ways. It definitely had more key-boards in the mix as well as a more radio-friendly sound. Hell, I've heard 'Tom Sawyer' in the grocery store."

"They had broken out with *2112*, and then they kept moving forward with *Permanent Waves*," says Rick Ringer, announcer at CKYC/CFOS/CJMU/CFPS, for-merly of CHUM-FM. "I think *Moving Pictures* represents a creative breakthrough for them and, obviously, a commercial breakthrough as well. Is it their best work? I think, to encapsulate a moment in time and a moment in a career, where they turned a corner toward that Hall of Fame induction, you would have to say it was *Moving Pictures*."

# OUR VIENNA (OR PARADIDDLES IN PARADISE)

## THE CAMERA EYE: THE FINAL REEL

Historians, writers, and journalists have long considered turn-of-the-twentieth-century Vienna, Austria, a fertile time for European science, psychology, architecture, dance, theater, and the arts in general. Various disciplines and philosophies coexisted, even coalesced, within the city circa 1900, prompting observers to conclude that the shining city on the Danube represented the pinnacle of Western civilization—the fount of our modern era.

Recent scholarship may have raised issues about this historical assessment, but the mythology surrounding the zeitgeist of early twentieth-century Vienna, what some refer to as the "City of Music" or the "City of Dreams," has been so ingrained in the Western psyche that it's unimaginable that this commonly held belief will be upended anytime soon. If nothing else, it proves that we hold dear our golden ages, bygone eras for which people long.

As I sit here watching the river flow outside the window of my office, I too am carried to another, perhaps better, time. Waves of reflections ripple out to me, carrying me back to my youth. Music, like a river, is a continuum that holds true transportive powers, and suddenly, I find myself back in the 1980s.

I remember a summer listening to *Moving Pictures* and hearing the compressed sounds of synth opening "Tom Sawyer" transmitted over the airwaves—the stark imagery and the river.

Rush was everywhere. Everybody was taking notice, even though, for many of the listeners who would become hard-core fans, they'd known little about them prior to this record.

As was inevitable when a rock group becomes popular, local bands covered the popular material. There was plenty to see and hear throughout the early 1980s, a golden age. It was my Vienna, and I suspect I'm not alone in feeling this way.

Memory is a funny thing—it ebbs and flows, and you arrive at the most unpredictable places. Suddenly, I pull another scene from my Rush highlight reel.

I'm at the Nassau Coliseum in Uniondale, New York, on December 9, 1987, attending a Rush show—what can be described as the pinnacle of mixed-discipline, progressive symphonic/techno rock. Watching three guys perform synchronized music live onstage was like witnessing choreographed, multitasking, high-wire sonic acrobats.

I'd been to Rush concerts prior to the Hold Your Fire tour and would catch the band many times after, so this was not an isolated occurrence. Yet at the Coliseum in December 1987, there was something in the air. No, I'm not talking about aromatic clouds sending smoke signals of mental escape. Well, okay, they were present too.

What I'm talking about is finality. One phase of my life was coming to a close, and I was transitioning to another. So was the band. Rush had referred to *Hold Your Fire* as an "arrival record," which translated to a soft shoe dance on the precipice of the unknown, effectively ending the band's "synth era."

The Hold Your Fire tour ran from late October 1987 through early May 1988 in multiple cities across two continents with few days off (aside from the 1987 holidays). By most accounts, it was a bit of a slog; the guys were away from their families, and Neil and Geddy were ill at different points on the tour.

After Rush came off the road, there was little in the music press about the band's future. Invariably, rumors circulated, and conspiracy theories arose. As time passed, logical human beings began to think that maybe there was some truth to the scuttlebutt that Rush was kaput or at least had taken an indefinite break. Surprising longtime fans, maybe even themselves, Rush emerged in 1989 with no less than a new musical direction, a new producer (Rupert Hine), and a new album, *Presto*.

And the surprises continued. When I saw Rush at the Nassau Coliseum for the Presto tour, in April 1990, something eye-opening grabbed my attention. No, it wasn't the monster-sized blow-up bunnies, one on each side of the stage. Well, okay, that *was* surprising and a bit amusing. I'm referring to something far more relatable than inflatable.

As Rush's show progressed, during the song "War Paint," clear light flashed briefly. This was an odd occurrence, as if the house lights had come up for a few seconds. It was illuminating to say the least. I saw Neil on his throne, basking in the lighting director's scaled-back design choice. His face was fully visible.

Then presto, like magic, Peart smiled.

I can't recall ever seeing Neil smile at a live concert before or after this. Stubbornly, it remains nestled inside the crinkles of my scrambled brain in this manner, signifying something of importance.

Later in the set, Peart was just as intense as ever. Variations of paradiddles skittered on top of Neil's electronic pads in "Scars." Simultaneously with those rudiment-based rhythmic figures, Neil triggered snare sounds with his feet. Impressive to say the least.

But it was that smile that has stuck with me the most. It was so unexpected, so human.

It seems that he was smiling as much for us as for himself. A private moment in such a public setting. Isn't this the very nature of true artists and creative souls? Isn't that what was addressed in part with "Limelight"?

Peart's intense onstage concentration—his ability to fuse brute force and, in some cases, high concepts—was something I'd always admired. Even if there were busier drummers in rock and jazz-rock fusion who were more technical in their own ways, there was something about Peart's dedication to literally putting his head down and performing patterns he'd worked out months earlier in the studio, reproducing them onstage nearly exactly.

Today, drummers can play paradiddles backward to a click track, blindfolded, at superhuman speeds—while simultaneously performing French pataflaflas with their feet on triple-kick drums kits. We can heap either praise or scorn on Peart for helping to create this "rock drummer as acrobat" archetype—or simply acknowledge that he was one template for the modern progressive rock percussionist. One thing is certain: Peart indirectly mentored drummers, teaching them the value of rhythmic composition, complexity, timbre, and storytelling.

And beyond music and drumming, Peart was the picture of health, personal strength, and prosperity, bicycling and traveling to exotic locations around the globe, an inspiration. Things were going well for Peart and the band. That was our first clue I suppose.

By the early 1990s, the bandanas Peart had worn onstage, along with his shaved noggin—wardrobe and hygiene rituals the drummer picked up as a world traveler—stoked wild speculation. Some fans let their imagination run away with them and thought Neil had been subjected to chemotherapy.

Awful fallacies.

Gossip reached a fever pitch in 1993 when phone lines lit up at a Cleveland radio station wondering about the vitality of their drum god—a status (or perception of status) that the Ayn Rand–weened Peart publicly shunned. Callers hoped against hope that the rumors Peart had contracted colon cancer were false. As it turned out, none of these *backasswards* speculations were true, and Peart rarely dignified these hysterics with a response.

Fans breathed a sigh of relief: paradiddle paradise lost, paradiddle paradise regained.

But fast-forward several years, and Neil's life in the late 1990s *did* take a horrific turn: Within the span of less than a year, he'd lost his daughter and then his wife.

It was around this time that I'd become a stringer for one of the New York City daily newspapers and wrote about Rush, Geddy Lee's solo record, and their return to recording and touring. I met some of the guys in the band and even got to interview them. Here I was, a schmuck from New York, occupying the "same frame" as the musicians I had seen onstage and in concert films dating back decades.

After coming off a hiatus, Rush clawed their way back into the mainstream psyche, first with *Vapor Trails* from 2002 and then the CD and DVD releases of the live offering *Rush in Rio*.

Rush was nearly as popular as ever, and they rode an almost unprecedented wave of encouragement all the way to their induction into the Rock and Roll Hall of Fame in 2013. After returning to the Rush fold in the early 2000s, Peart recorded and toured with the band through 2015 and later called it quits with Rush.

As unexpected as these turns of events were, nothing could prepare fans for what felt like a bolt from out of the blue. It all seemed to happen so suddenly and so recently.

Frequently, I'll receive e-mail alerts from an entertainment trade magazine. My e-mail system is a receptacle for all manner of film and music business–related items, including dreaded obits. After you've received hundreds of these earth-shattering bulletins, you become accustomed to them; you have a second sense about what the headline in the subject line is going to say—even before you finish reading it. You know the VIP named in the header is deceased.

One day in January 2020, I quickly scanned the subject line of an e-mail alert, and something felt horribly wrong. The name Neil Peart appeared in the header.

Even though every instinct was telling me otherwise, I said to myself, *It can't be.* I opened the message, clicked on the link in the body of the text, and started reading. In silence, I knew there was no denying it was true. I checked various news services, even *Modern Drummer* magazine's website, and they all were united in their reporting.

Unlike 1993, this was no cruel hoax. Neil Peart had passed.

Within minutes, electronic messages of a different kind, from friends and associates, came flooding in, expressing concern, confusion, even condolences:

"Dude, what the hell?"

"You OK, brother?"

"Will, have you heard?"

No one in this communication loop had uttered a spoken word. We were in mourning, suffering in the silence of cyberspace. I'm not ashamed to admit that I had taken some time to collect myself. So many people had looked up to Neil both as a friend and as a drummer over the span of decades. Losing Peart was like an intergenerational, interdimensional snafu.

This communal grief was accelerated by modern technology, linking people in ways unheard of prior to the digital age. It's a phenomenon, I told myself, that Neil himself might have written about.

Because his impact was so great on generations and in an attempt to make sense of all of this, I sought out a number of the people to speak with about their personal Neil Peart stories.

"I walked into the dressing room the first time I met Neil, and he took my hand, shook it, and said, 'I hear we have a mutual friend in [producer] Nick Raskulinecz,'" says Jason Bittner (Shadows Fall and Overkill). "It was probably as unawkward as could be. Before we met, I saw him walking in the hallway, and it took my breath away. He was so tall, and it reminded of the alleged footage of Sasquatch from the late 1960s, when he gets caught in the camera for a second. [laughs] 'I just had a sighting.'"

"They were some of the nicest people on the planet," says bassist John DeServio of Black Label Society, who toured with Tichy as members of Vinnie Moore's band on Rush's Roll the Bones tour in the early 1990s. "Everybody, including the crew, took great care of us. The first night of the tour, in our dressing room, was a bottle of champagne and a note inviting us to their dressing room to hang out after the show. Geddy held court, and we all gathered around like it was a sermon from Gandhi. Alex had a great sense of humor, and Neil was reserved but very nice. At one point on the tour, I actually played Geddy's bass while I jammed with Neil for like a minute. We jammed a samba—and I'll never forget it."

Although Neil's life was marked by tragedy, in later years, he'd built a new life, turning his personal story into something even more inspirational. Peart left his native Canada for a while, traveled on his motorbike, and was incommunicado with friends and family for long periods of time. When he returned, he left Toronto for good, eventually settled in sunny California, remarried, and maintained a second residence near Montreal.

"He healed from the loss of his first family, had a second family, and finally told the guys from Rush that he was done with touring," says Jason Bittner. "He said, 'That's it. I can't do this anymore.'"

In the days that followed the announcement of Peart's passing, songs like "Red Barchetta," "Vital Signs," "Limelight," "Mission," and "Losing It" haunted me. Something about fulfilling dreams, gaining command of the world around you, living life on your terms, the bell tolling—they were difficult to listen to, but I reflected on Neil's prodigious talents as a drummer and thinker.

From shock emerged a new perspective. Songs expressing incredible concern, world-weariness, sadness, and regret for unfulfilled potential hit like detonated emotional bombs. The opposite became true too: Here was the unmistakable sound of joy, which was somehow heightened since Peart's death. The endless pursuit of songcraft and the earnest search for technical perfection meant that Rush's art was far more expressive, even complex, than even I had imagined back in the 1980s—and far more human.

Weeks went by, and my life changed radically. The world appeared to be on the brink, and, personally, I was in the middle of a move, ready to leave my home. My mind wandered back to the early 1980s, *Moving Pictures*, the first time I'd heard "Tom Sawyer" over the airwaves—and that night in December 1987. I couldn't escape the feeling that maybe I was standing at yet another crossroads both on a macro and a micro level.

"You know I was talking with a friend of mine the other day," says Bittner. "I said to him, 'The world started to come to end the moment Neil died.' A month later, I was sitting in L.A. with COVID. Our whole band is convinced we had it. We had it, really, before we even know what it was. It blows my mind that I knew Neil and could consider him a friend. I miss him terribly, and I would have, even as a fan."

For the people who knew, met, and were inspired by him, Peart was their model of the scholar musician. Peart meant every word he wrote for "Limelight," but when he accepted you, that was it. You were "in," as they say.

"Everybody knows that Neil Peart does not want to meet you," says Jason Sutter. "More than that, he sure as hell does not want to talk about drumming. Through a series of events over several years, I got to know Matt Scannell from Vertical Horizon, who became a good friend to Neil. I drummed on *Echoes from the Underground* [2013], which also featured Neil. When Matt took me to meet Neil at the Nokia Theatre [Microsoft Theater, Los Angeles], Neil told me, 'I want you to know that I will forever hold you in the highest esteem as a drummer.' He said those words just like that. Neil was telling me things about the tracks because he sat with them, studied them, analyzed them in order to offer Matt notes on the record before it was released. He knows the tracks inside and out. He's talking about drumming. *My drumming.*

"When we leave the backstage area, and we open the door, there's a line of at least twenty dudes standing there," Sutter continues. "There was Chad Smith from Red Hot Chili Peppers, Brad Wilk of Rage Against the Machine, Taylor Hawkins of the Foo Fighters, Ray Luzier, Gregg Bissonette, Jose Pasillas from Incubus; Danny Carey from Tool was already backstage when I was there. I could go down the list of drummers. A who's who waiting to kiss the ring of the master."

"Probably the first time I met Neil, you know, I wanted to tell him how much he meant to me and how much his sound on *Exit . . . Stage Left* influenced me," says Jason Bittner. "Before I met him, I was talking with Mike Portnoy [Sons of Apollo, Transatlantic, cofounder of Dream Theater] and he said, 'Whatever you do, don't talk drums with him.' I said, 'Mike, I know. You don't talk about equipment.' I did not tell him this, but when I put on *Exit . . . Stage Left* with headphones, it feels like I am fourteen again; it's summer, I'm trying to build that kit, trying to play these songs."

"I saw Rush twice, and it was amazing," says Dave Krusen. "Peart's riser spun around, and you could see this massive 360-degree drum kit; it was crazy how he incorporated all of it. He wasn't just shredding fills: it was the way he orchestrated all the percussive parts so seamlessly that was so inspiring. Rush influenced all of us in the Northwest back then—great songs and musicianship."

"I was on a club tour with Vinnie Moore and John DeServio, who is now the bassist in Black Label Society," says Brian Tichy. "We were having a blast. Vinnie's manager said to us, 'Eric Johnson had to cancel his last two weeks opening for Rush, and you guys are taking over... starting in a few days.' We were all blown away. We played ten arenas with Rush, including Madison Square Garden, for two nights [on the Roll the Bones tour in 1991]. At the Garden, Neil came onstage while we just finished sound check. I asked him something about his kick drum, and he replied, 'Have you tried them yet?' I hadn't. He said, 'Go ahead.' He stood in front as I played, and he'd chuckle when I did something 'Peart-ish' or the semicircle toms runs. His tech spun the riser around, and I played all his electronic stuff, and he showed me the different sounds they got out of them. An amazing experience."

"You asked how Neil's playing or technique pertains to my drumming in Overkill or Shadows Fall, but Neil's influence is all over the place," says Jason Bittner. "It is not always blatant, but the hi-hat work, anything with splash cymbals, two-handed ride patterns, making a drum part complete and not varying it every night . . . it's all because of Neil."

As I write this, a river runs through my yard and the outskirts of my midwestern town. I'm reminded of the expression relating to time and tide. And now something that former cochairman and CEO of Atlantic Records Val Azzoli told me way back when seems prescient: he recalled that Rush's sound checks were always scheduled for 4 p.m., but "[Peart would] be there at 3:55."

Peart created an archetype, was ahead of the curve, and was nothing if not *beyond* punctual. Indeed. He left us too early. However, in his sixty-seven years on Earth, Peart changed the course of progressive music, rock drumming, and, dare I say, many lives.

One has to wonder what Peart would have made of our current day and age— our time. We've all changed much since our early years, and the last few have been exceedingly difficult on some. Yet we, each of us, feel compelled to hold dear our Vienna, returning to it because we have to.

If he's looking down from on high—a lofty concept that Peart himself might have dismissed were it not for the fact that he's likely playing paradiddles in paradise as I write this—here's smiling at you, Neil.

# TOUR DATES

## MOVING PICTURES TOUR DATES, 1980–1981

Includes prerelease warm-up tour and Exit . . . Stage Left dates

Sources: Rush.com, Concertarchives.org, Setlist.fm, and various magazines and newspapers

## WARM-UP DATES

| Date | Venue | City |
|---|---|---|
| September 11, 1980 | Hampton Coliseum | Hampton, Virginia |
| September 12, 1980 | Charlotte Coliseum | Charlotte, North Carolina |
| September 13, 1980 | Civic Center Coliseum | Charleston, West Virginia |
| September 14, 1980 | Municipal Auditorium | Nashville, Tennessee |
| September 16, 1980 | Riverside Centroplex | Baton Rouge, Louisiana |
| September 18, 1980 | Lee County Arena | Fort Myers, Florida |
| September 19, 1980 | Hollywood Sportatorium | Hollywood, Florida |
| September 20, 1980 | Civic Center Arena | Lakeland, Florida |
| September 21, 1980 | Veterans Memorial Coliseum | Jacksonville, Florida |
| September 23, 1980 | Riverfront Coliseum | Cincinnati, Ohio |
| September 25, 1980 | The Spectrum | Philadelphia, Pennsylvania |
| September 26, 1980 | Capital Centre | Largo, Maryland |
| September 27, 1980 | Cape Cod Coliseum | Cape Cod, Massachusetts |
| September 28, 1980 | Civic Center | Springfield, Massachusetts |
| September 30, 1980 | Allentown Fairgrounds | Allentown, Pennsylvania |
| October 1, 1980 | Cumberland County Civic Center | Portland, Maine |

## MOVING PICTURES TOUR

| February 17, 1981 | Wings Stadium | Kalamazoo, MI |
| February 18, 1981 | Wings Stadium | Kalamazoo, Michigan |
| February 19, 1981 | Wings Stadium | Kalamazoo, Michigan |
| February 20, 1981 | Wings Stadium | Kalamazoo, Michigan |
| February 21, 1981 | Civic Arena | Dubuque, Iowa |
| February 22, 1981 | Palmer College | Davenport, Iowa |
| February 24, 1981 | The Center | La Crosse, Wisconsin |
| February 26, 1981 | International Amphitheater | Chicago, Illinois |
| February 27, 1981 | International Amphitheatre | Chicago, Illinois |
| February 28, 1981 | International Amphitheatre | Chicago, Illinois |
| March 1, 1981 | International Amphitheatre | Chicago, Illinois |
| March 2, 1981 | Mecca Arena | Milwaukee, Wisconsin |
| March 4, 1981 | The Checkerdome (aka St. Louis Arena) | St. Louis, Missouri |
| March 5, 1981 | The Checkerdome | St. Louis, Missouri |
| March 7, 1981 | Louisville Gardens | Louisville, Kentucky |
| March 8, 1981 | Hara Arena | Dayton, Ohio |
| March 10, 1981 | Roberts Stadium | Evansville, Indiana |
| March 11, 1981 | Market Square Arena | Indianapolis, Indiana |
| March 13, 1981 | Cobo Hall Arena | Detroit, Michigan |
| March 14, 1981 | Cobo Hall Arena | Detroit, Michigan |
| March 15, 1981 | Cobo Hall Arena | Detroit, Michigan |
| March 21, 1981 | London Gardens | London, Ontario |
| March 23, 1981 | Maple Leaf Gardens | Toronto, Canada |
| March 24, 1981 | Maple Leaf Gardens | Toronto, Canada |
| March 25, 1981 | Maple Leaf Gardens | Toronto, Canada |
| March 27, 1981 | The Forum | Montreal, Quebec |
| March 28, 1981 | Civic Centre | Ottawa, Ontario |
| April 3, 1981 | Community Center | Tucson, Arizona |
| April 4, 1981 | Veterans Memorial Coliseum | Phoenix, Arizona |
| April 5, 1981 | Tingley Coliseum | Albuquerque, New Mexico |
| April 7, 1981 | Sam Houston Coliseum | Houston, Texas |
| April 8, 1981 | Sam Houston Coliseum | Houston, Texas |

| April 10, 1981 | Reunion Arena | Dallas, Texas |
| April 11, 1981 | Convention Center Arena | San Antonio, Texas |
| April 12, 1981 | Tarrant County Convention Center | Fort Worth, Texas |
| April 14, 1981 | Barton Coliseum | Little Rock, Arkansas |
| April 15, 1981 | Mississippi Coliseum | Jackson, Mississippi |
| April 16, 1981 | Mid-South Coliseum | Memphis, Tennessee |
| April 18, 1981 | Municipal Auditorium | Mobile, Alabama |
| April 19, 1981 | Municipal Auditorium | New Orleans, Louisiana |
| April 21, 1981 | Hirsch Memorial Coliseum | Shreveport, Louisiana |
| April 23, 1981 | Kemper Arena | Kansas City, Missouri |
| April 24, 1981 | Kemper Arena | Kansas City, Missouri |
| April 25, 1981 | The Myriad | Oklahoma City, Oklahoma |
| April 26, 1981 | Tulsa Assembly Center | Tulsa, Oklahoma |
| May 6, 1981 | Civic Arena | Pittsburgh, Pennsylvania |
| May 7, 1981 | Richfield Coliseum | Richfield Township, Ohio |
| May 8, 1981 | Richfield Coliseum | Richfield, Ohio |
| May 9, 1981 | Memorial Auditorium | Buffalo, New York |
| May 11, 1981 | Broome County Arena | Binghamton, New York |
| May 12, 1981 | War Memorial | Rochester, New York |
| May 13, 1981 | War Memorial | Syracuse, New York |
| May 15, 1981 | Cool Insuring Arena (Glens Falls Civic) | Glens Falls, New York |
| May 16, 1981 | Capital Centre | Largo, Maryland |
| May 17, 1981 | Capital Centre | Largo, Maryland |
| May 18, 1981 | Madison Square Garden | New York, New York |
| May 20, 1981 | Nassau Coliseum | Uniondale, New York |
| May 22, 1981 | The Spectrum | Philadelphia, Pennsylvania |
| May 23, 1981 | Boston Garden | Boston, Massachusetts |
| May 24, 1981 | Civic Center | Providence, Rhode Island |
| June 1, 1981 | McNichols Arena | Denver, Colorado |
| June 3, 1981 | Salt Palace Center | Salt Lake City, Utah |
| June 5, 1981 | The Coliseum | Oakland, California |
| June 6, 1981 | The Coliseum | Oakland, California |
| June 7, 1981 | Selland Arena | Fresno, California |

| June 9, 1981 | Sports Arena | San Diego, California |
| June 10, 1981 | Great Western Forum | Los Angeles, California |
| June 11, 1981 | Great Western Forum | Los Angeles, California |
| June 12, 1981 | Convention Center | Anaheim, California |
| June 14, 1981 | Long Beach Arena | Long Beach, California |
| June 15, 1981 | The Aladdin Theater | Las Vegas, Nevada |
| June 16, 1981 | Centennial Coliseum | Reno, Nevada |
| June 18, 1981 | Seattle Center Coliseum | Seattle, Washington |
| June 19, 1981 | Seattle Center Coliseum | Seattle, Washington |
| June 20, 1981 | Veterans Memorial Coliseum | Portland, Oregon |
| June 21, 1981 | The Coliseum | Spokane, Washington |
| June 23, 1981 | Pacific Coliseum | Vancouver, British Columbia |
| June 25, 1981 | Northlands Coliseum | Edmonton, Alberta |
| July 2, 1981 | Met Center | Bloomington, Minnesota |
| July 3, 1981 | Met Center | Bloomington, Minnesota |
| July 4, 1981 | Alpine Valley Music Theatre | East Troy, Wisconsin |
| July 5, 1981 | Alpine Valley Music Theatre | East Troy, Wisconsin |

## EXIT . . . STAGE LEFT TOUR

| October 29, 1981 | New Bingley Hall | Stafford, England |
| October 30, 1981 | New Bingley Hall | Stafford, England |
| October 31, 1981 | Deeside Leisure Centre | Deeside, Wales |
| November 2, 1981 | Brighton Conference Center | Brighton, England |
| November 4, 1981 | Wembley Arena | London, England |
| November 5, 1981 | Wembley Arena | London, England |
| November 6, 1981 | Wembley Arena | London England |
| November 8, 1981 | Royal Highland Exhibition Centre | Edinburgh, Scotland |
| November 9, 1981 | New Bingley Hall | Stafford, England |
| November 11, 1981 | Musikhalle | Hamburg, Germany |
| November 12, 1981 | Hemmerleinehalle | Neunkirchen, Germany |
| November 14, 1981 | Ahoy Sportpaleis | Rotterdam, Holland |
| November 16, 1981 | Circus Krone | Munich, Germany |

| | | |
|---|---|---|
| November 17, 1981 | Walter Kobel Halle | Rüsselsheim am Main, Hesse, Germany |
| November 18, 1981 | Sporthalle | Böblingen, Baden-Württemberg, Germany |
| November 19, 1981 | Sporthalle | Böblingen, Baden-Württemberg, Germany |
| November 20, 1981 | Schwarzwaldhalle | Karlsruhe, Baden-Württemberg, Germany |
| November 21, 1981 | Grugahalle | Essen, Germany |
| November 28, 1981 | Hollywood Sportatorium | Hollywood, Florida |
| November 29, 1981 | Veterans Memorial Coliseum | Jacksonville, Florida |
| December 1, 1981 | Birmingham-Jefferson Civic | Birmingham, Alabama |
| December 2, 1981 | Municipal Auditorium | Nashville, Tennessee |
| December 4, 1981 | Charlotte Coliseum | Charlotte, North Carolina |
| December 5, 1981 | Cumberland County Coliseum | Fayetteville, North Carolina |
| December 6, 1981 | Greensboro Coliseum | Greensboro, North Carolina |
| December 8, 1981 | Civic Auditorium and Coliseum | Knoxville, Tennessee |
| December 9, 1981 | The Omni | Atlanta, Georgia |
| December 11, 1981 | Greenville Memorial Auditorium | Greenville, South Carolina |
| December 12, 1981 | Freedom Hall Civic Center | Johnson City, Tennessee |
| December 13, 1981 | Roanoke Civic Center | Roanoke, Virginia |
| December 15, 1981 | Scope Arena | Norfolk, Virginia |
| December 18, 1981 | Civic Center | Hartford, Connecticut |
| December 20, 1981 | Civic Center | Hartford, Connecticut |
| December 21, 1981 | Brendan Byrne Arena | East Rutherford, New Jersey |
| December 22, 1981 | Brendan Byrne Arena | East Rutherford, New Jersey |

# BIBLIOGRAPHY

## BOOKS

Banasiewicz, Bill. *Rush: Visions: The Official Biography*. London: Omnibus Press, 1988.

Bayles, Martha. *Hole in Our Soul: The Loss of Beauty & Meaning in American Popular Music*. Chicago: University of Chicago Press, 1996.

Berti, Jim, and Durrell Bowman, eds. *Rush and Philosophy: Heart and Mind United*. Chicago: Open Court, 2011.

Bloom, Harold, and Lionel Trilling. *Romantic Poetry and Prose*. New York: Oxford University Press, 1973.

Brown, Blain. *Cinematography: Theory and Practice: Image Making for Cinematographers and Directors*. 2nd ed. New York: Focal Press, 2012.

Carpenter, Humphrey. *Tolkien: The Authorized Biography*. New York: Ballantine Books, 1978.

Collins, Jon. *Rush: Chemistry*. London: Helter Skelter, 2005.

Curtis, Jim. *Rock Eras: Interpretations of Music & Society, 1954–1984*. Bowling Green, OH: Bowling Green State University Popular Press, 1987.

DeRogatis, Jim. *Turn On Your Mind: Four Decades of Great Psychedelic Rock*. Milwaukee, WI: Hal Leonard, 2003.

Dos Passos, John. *The 42nd Parallel*. New York: Signet Classic/Penguin Group, 1979.

———. *Nineteen Nineteen*. New York: Signet Classic/Penguin Group, 1979.

Emerson, Ralph Waldo. *Self-Reliance and Other Essays*. Mineola, NY: Dover Publications, 1993.

Fast, Susan. *In the Houses of the Holy: Led Zeppelin and the Power of Rock Music*. New York: Oxford University Press, 2001.

Gett, Steve. *Rush: Success under Pressure*. Port Chester, NY: Cherry Lane Books, 1984.

Girard, Mike. *Psycho Chicken & Other Foolish Tales*. CreateSpace, 2010.

Goulding, Phil G. *Classical Music: The 50 Greatest Composers and Their 1,000 Greatest Works*. New York: Fawcett/Random House, 1992.

Holm-Hudson, Kevin, ed. *Progressive Rock Reconsidered.* New York: Routledge, 2002.

Katz, Steven D. *Film Directing Shot by Shot.* Studio City, CA: Michael Wiese Publications, 1991.

Lethem, Jonathan. *Fear of Music.* New York: Bloomsbury Academic, 2015.

Macan, Edward. *Rocking the Classics: English Progressive Rock and the Counterculture.* New York: Oxford University Press, 1997.

McDonald, Chris. *Rush, Rock Music and the Middle Class: Dreaming in Middletown.* Bloomington: Indiana University Press, 2009.

Mersereau, Bob. *The History of Canadian Rock 'N' Roll.* Milwaukee, WI: Backbeat Books/Hal Leonard, 2015.

Ott, Chris. *Unknown Pleasures.* London: Continuum, 2004.

Patterson, James, Casey Sherman, and Dave Wedge. *The Last Days of John Lennon.* New York: Little, Brown, 2020.

Popoff, Martin. *Contents under Pressure: 30 Years of Rush at Home & Away.* Toronto: ECW Press, 2004.

Rand, Ayn. *Anthem.* New York: Signet, 1961.

———. *The Virtue of Selfishness.* New York: Signet Classics, 1964.

*Rush Deluxe Anthology.* New York: Core Music Publishers/Warner Bros., 1981.

*Rush: Moving Pictures.* New York: Core Music Publishing/Warner Bros., n.d.

Sharp, Keith. *Music Express: The Rise, Fall & Resurrection of Canada's Music Magazine.* Toronto: Dundurn Press, 2014.

Shaw, Philip. *Horses.* New York: Bloomsbury Academic, 2017.

Smith, Adam. *Powers of Mind.* New York: Random House, 1975.

Twain, Mark. *The Adventures of Tom Sawyer.* New York: Bantam, 1981.

Weinstein, Deena. *Heavy Metal: The Music and Its Culture.* Boston: Da Capo Press, 2000.

Wheeler, Bill, transcriber. *Drum Techniques of Rush.* Secaucus, NJ: Core Music/Warner Bros., 1985.

White, Fred D., ed. *Essential Muir: A Selection of John Muir's Best Writings.* Berkeley, CA: Heyday Books, 2006.

Wiederhorn, Jon, and Katherine Turman. *Louder Than Hell: The Definitive Oral History of Metal.* New York: It Books/HarperCollins, 2013.

# NEWSPAPERS

Atkinson, Terry. "Rush Takes Time, Gets Refined." *Los Angeles Times*, September 19, 1982.

———. "Rush's Sound of Pain." *Los Angeles Times*, March 15, 1981.

Bishop, Pete. "*Moving Pictures* New Look for Rush." *Pittsburgh Press*, March 15, 1981.

———. "Rock Bands Battle, Fans the Winner." *Pittsburgh Press*, April 16, 1975.

Britt, Bruce. "Moving Pictures: Review." *Detroit Free Press*, January 1, 1982.

Cobb, Christopher. "A Rush to the Grass-Roots." *Ottawa Journal*, March 31, 1978.

———. ". . . also Presenting Max Webster: Canadian Group Tipped Most Likely to Succeed." *Ottawa Journal*, March 31, 1978.

Coldstream, John. "Rush at Wembley." *Daily Telegraph*, November 5, 1981.

Cullinane, John S. "Music Not to Dance to." *St. Louis Post-Dispatch*, February 18, 1977.

Deane, Gary. "Rush Worth Encores." *Leader-Post*, June 21, 1975.

Fitzpatrick, Rob. "Rush: Our Fans Feel Vindicated." *The Guardian*, March 24, 2011.

Frohoff, Bob. "Rush Doesn't Need Singles Hits to Sell Albums." *Kansas City Times*, January 22, 1977.

Graff, Gary. "Rush: Neil Peart Doesn't Play for Stardom." *Detroit Free Press*, November 7, 1982.

Griffin, John. "Rush: Pomp-Rock Trio Hot on Tedium." *Montreal Gazette*, March 28, 1981.

Haysom, Ian. "Deaf, Dumb and Blind." *Ottawa Journal*. December 22, 1978.

Hepher, Paul. "Rush: Repertoire of Repetition." *Calgary Albertan*, September 13, 1977.

Hicks, Graham. "The Best of Rush Has Dash of Humor." *Edmonton Journal*, February 18, 1981.

Holden, Stephen. "Rock: Rush, Canada Power Trio." *New York Times*, May 21, 1981.

Holmes, Johnny. "Heavy Metal Is Back." *Corpus Christi Times*, October 25, 1977.

Kaye, Roger. "Even Fans of Rush Don't Know Them." *Fort Worth Star-Telegram*, January 19, 1988.

Konz, Joe. "Heavy Metal 'In Season.'" *Indianapolis Star*, April 26, 1981.

Laycock, John. "In a Rush." *Windsor Star*, February 11, 1977.

Lloyd, Jack. "Sometimes Rush Is in a Hurry." *Philadelphia Inquirer*, May 22, 1981.

McLellan, Don. "Slandering . . . the Sacred Halls of Truth." *Vancouver Sun*, September 14, 1977.

Meyer, Bruce. "Rush Rock is for Thinking Man." *St. Petersburg Times*, June 6, 1977.

Morse, Steve. "Sending New Signals, Rush on the Defense." *Boston Globe*, December 6, 1982.

———. "The Rush: All Flash No Fire." *Boston Globe*, January 12, 1979.

"Moving Pictures/Rush, Review." *Vancouver Sun*, March 20, 1981.

Pond, Steve. "Rush Gets Started with a Bang." *Los Angeles Times*, June 12, 1981.

Provick, Bill. "Rush Feeling Rejuvenated." *Ottawa Citizen*, March 27, 1981.

Provizer, Norman. "A Solid Rush Hits Hirsch." *Shreveport Journal*, April 22, 1981.

Radel, Cliff. "Rush's Rock Gets Bogged Down in Band's Own Aural Quagmire." *Cincinnati Enquirer*, May 15, 1978.

Radz, Matt. "Rush Has Done Its Roadwork." *Montreal Star*, March 30, 1978.

Robicheau, Paul. "Rush Scissors New Sounds." *Boston Globe*, May 10, 1990.

Rockwell, John. "Pop: Rush Plays at Palladium." *New York Times*, January 15, 1979.

Rodriguez, Juan. "Toronto Group Is in a 'Rush' to the Top." *Montreal Gazette*, March 30, 1978.

Ross, Bob. "Rock Fans Get a Rush in Tampa." *St. Petersburg Times*, March 27, 1978.

"Rush: *Fly by Night*: A Review." *Montreal Star*, March 15, 1975.

Snowdon, Annette. "Rush Rock: A Sound to Call Their Own." *Ottawa Citizen*, January 21, 1978.

Sornberger, Joe. "Novocaine Rock: Rush Concert a Boring Affair." *Edmonton Journal*, September 10, 1977.

Von Malder, Tom. "Playback: Graffiti Album Another Winner for Led Zeppelin." *Elk Grove Herald*, March 21, 1975.

Warren, Doug. "Album Catches Rush Power Live." *Miami Herald*, November 28, 1981.

Westbrook, Bruce. "Rush! Crowds Grow in the City." *Daily Oklahoman*, April 19, 1981.

Williams, Robert. "Head East Outshines Rush in Concert." *Abilene Reporter-News*, January 23, 1977.

## MAGAZINES AND PERIODICALS

"1st for Mercury." *Billboard*, December 16, 1978, p. 4.

"Anthem Expands Album Schedule." *Billboard*, January 5, 1980, p. 69.

"Anthem Records: Success Spawns New Label." *RPM*, June 4, 1977, p. 5.

"Anvil's Hard and Heavy Released on Attic Label." *RPM*, June 20, 1981, p. 3.

Barton, Geoff. "Rush Judgement: Tired of the Stress of the City, the Canadian Power Trio Take to the Wilds of Wales—Rush Drummer Neil Peart Talks." *Sounds*, July 16, 1977.

Basche, Philip. "Rush's Simpler 'Signals.'" *Circus*, November 30, 1982.

Basche, Philip, and Steve Weitzman. "Rock on Tour: Got Live if You Can Find It." *Circus*, August 31, 1981, p. 41.

"*Billboard* Album Radio Action." *Billboard*, November 4, 1978, p. 28.

———. *Billboard*, November 18, 1978, p. 30.

———. *Billboard*, February 28, 1981, p. 26.

Blackett, Matt. "Back in the Limelight: Alex Lifeson and Rush Reignite after a Five-Year Hiatus; the Lifeson Chronicle: The Guitarist's View of Rush's Famous Tunes." *Guitar Player*, August 2002.

Considine, J. D. "Rush Screwing Up Pop on Purpose." *Musician*, April 1990.

"Double Gold: Rush." *Billboard*, December 18, 1976, p. 59.

Farrell, David. "Canada: Domestic Acts Score in Sales & Airplay." *Billboard*, October 17, 1981, p. 74.

———. "Canadian Disk, Tape Sales Down, but Year-End Hot." *Billboard*, February 7, 1981, p. 17.

———. "Fledgling Label Sets Sights on LP Action." *Billboard*, December 9, 1978, p. 74.

———. "Rush Ready to Push Latest LP." *Billboard*, February 14, 1981, p. 62.

"50 Albums." *RPM*, April 4–25, 1981.

———. *RPM*, April 25–May 23, 1981.

Foster, Richard S. "A Nice Morning Drive," *Road & Track*, November 1973, p. 148.

Fricke, David. "Power from the People: Ignored by Critics and Radio, This Hard-Rock Trio Went Straight to the Fans." *Rolling Stone*, May 28, 1981.

"Gold Rush." *Record World*, December 3, 1977, p. 56.

Harris, Mike. "Rush: Keepin' the Faith." *Record World*, April 24, 1976, p. 36.

"Hits of the Week." *Record World*, January 26, 1980, cover.

"Hits of the World." *Billboard*, May 9, 1981, p. 63.

———. *Billboard*, May 23, 1981, p. 78.

———. *Billboard*, June 6, 1981, p. 87.

Hogan, Richard. "Vital Signs from Rush." *Circus*, December 31, 1981, p. 42.

Horowitz, Is. "RIAA: Shipment $ Up, Units Continue Decline." *Billboard*, April 4, 1981, p. 1.

"Hot 100." *Billboard*, December 26, 1981, p. 85.

Kordosh, J. "Rush: But Why Are They in Such a Hurry?" *Creem*, June 1981, p. 32.

Kozak, Roman. "Yule Sales Prospects Judged a 'Tough Call.'" *Billboard*, December 5, 1981, p. 1.

McIver, Joel. "Geddy Lee: What a Rush." *Bass Guitar*, April 2011.

Miles, Barry. "Is Everybody Feelin' All Right? (Geddit . . . ?): The Gist of This Being That Heavy Metal Tourists Rush Are All Right-er Than Most." *New Music Express*, March 4, 1978.

Mitchell, Mark. "Magic Man." *Guitar School*, May 1990.

"New on the Charts." *Billboard*, January 15, 1977, p. 33.

Peart, Neil. "Notes on the Making of *Moving Pictures*." *Modern Drummer*, December 1982, January 1983, February 1983.

Peart, Neil. "Rush—Counterparts." *Rush Backstage Club Newsletter*, January 1994.

"Pop: Rush-Mercury 76060, 'Entre Nous.'" *Record World*, May 3, 1980, p. 16.

Ponting, Tim. "Neil Peart: Mystic Rhythms." *Rhythm* magazine August 1988.

Quill, Greg, and Keith Sharp. "Inside Rush's *Moving Pictures*." *Music Express*, January 1981.

"RIAA Counts More Singles, but Fewer Albums in '80." *Billboard*, April 11, 1981, p. 3.

"Rock Albums & Top Tracks." *Billboard*, March 21, 1981, p. 32.

———. *Billboard*, May 23, 1981, p. 41.

———. *Billboard*, December 26, 1981, p. 40.

"RPM Feature Album: Rush: All the World's a Stage." *RPM*, October 16, 1976, p. 9.

*RPM* magazine ad: Anthem Records and Tapes. May 14, 1977, p. 20.

"Rush Forsakes Canada???" *RPM*, November 13, 1976, p. 5.

"Rush Rates First Merc Picture LP." *Billboard*, October 28, 1978, p. 100.

"Rush Return for 3-Nighter." *Billboard*, April 4, 1981, p. 87.

"Rush Rocks the Garden." *Record World*, June 6, 1981, p. 40.

"Rush's Exit Stage Left Features Concert Dates." *RPM*, October 31, 1981, p. 3.

"Rush's *Moving Pictures* Provides Another Single." *RPM*, September 5, 1981, p. 17.

Sciabarra, Chris Matthew. "Rand, Rush and Rock." *Journal of Ayn Rand Studies* 4, no. 1 (2002): 161–85.

"Signings." *Billboard*, November 14, 1981, p. 15.

Sippel, John. "Late Buying Surge Buoys Holiday Sales." *Billboard*, January 9, 1982, p. 1.

"Sold Out Notices for Mercury's Rush." *RPM*, January 22, 1977, p. 3.

Stix, John. "Alex Lifeson of Rush: Still in School." *Guitar for the Practicing Musician*, July 1984.

"Talent Scene." *RPM*, August 24, 1974, p. 14.

Tatrrie, Boyd. "Max Webster—The New Breed." *RPM*, August 28, 1976, p. 4.

Taylor, Peter. "Nuts & Bolts." *RPM*, October 20, 1973, p. 7.

"The Great Platinum Rush of 1981." Ad. *Billboard*, June 13, 1981, p. 9.

"Top Album Picks." *Billboard*, September 27, 1975, p. 84.

"Top Boxoffice." *Billboard*, May 23, 1981, p. 35.

———. *Billboard*, June 6, 1981, p. 36.

———. *Billboard*, July 4, 1981, p. 53.

"Top LPs & Tape." *Billboard*, November 18, 1978, p. 88.

———. *Billboard*, December 23, 1978, p. 124.

———. *Billboard*, March 14, 1981, p. 79.

———. *Billboard*, March 21, 1981, p. 95.

———. *Billboard*, March 28, 1981, p. 67.

———. *Billboard*, April 4, 1981, p. 95.

———. *Billboard*, April 11, 1981, p. 71.

———. *Billboard*, April 18, 1981, p. 139.

———. *Billboard*, May 2, 1981, p. 79.

———. *Billboard*, May 9, 1981, p. 71.

———. *Billboard*, May 23, 1981, p. 83.

———. *Billboard*, May 30, 1981, p. 71.

———. *Billboard*, June 6, 1981, p. 92.

———. *Billboard*, June 27, 1981, p. 79.

———. *Billboard*, September 5, 1981, p. 69.

"Top 100 Singles." *Cash Box*, April 18, 1981, page 4.

———. *Cash Box*, May 2, 1981, p. 4.

"Twenty-Five Questions: An Interview with Neil Peart by You." *Rush Backstage Club Newsletter*, December 1985.

Waymark, Graeme, and Martin Melhuish. "A Fresh Look inside Performers' Canadian Tax Situation." *Billboard*, September 27, 1975, p. C-6.

Wilding, Philip. "On the Crest of a Wave." *Classic Rock*, May 2020, p. 24.

## DVDS, VHS, AND FILMS CONSULTED

*A Show of Hands* (PolyGram/Anthem, 1989, VHS).

Classic Albums documentary of *2112* and *Moving Pictures* (Eagle Vision, 2010).

*Exit . . . Stage Left* (Anthem Entertainment/Island Def Jam, 2007, DVD).

Grace Under Pressure tour 1984 (taped from broadcast TV, circa 1985, VHS).

*Neil Peart: Anatomy of a Drum Solo* (Hudson Music, 2006).

*Neil Peart: Taking Center Stage: A Lifetime of Live Performance* (Hudson Music, 2011, DVD).

Rush: *R30: 30th Anniversary World Tour* (ZoëVision/Rounder, 2005, DVD).

Rush: *R40* (boxed set) (Anthem/ ZoëVision/Rounder, 2014, DVD).

Rush: *The Rise of Kings* (Rush documentary, Sexy Intellectual, 2014).

Rush: *Rush in Rio* (Coming Home Studios/Anthem/ ZoëVision/Rounder, 2003, DVD).

Rush: *Through the Camera Eye* (PolyGram, RCA/Columbia, 1985,VHS).

*Superman* (4 Film Favorites, Warner Bros., 2008).

## WEBSITES AND WEB PAGES

ASCAP.com

TheAtlasphere.com

History.com/news/what-is-the-oldest-known-piece-of-music

Holtsmithsonfoundation.org/spiral-jetty

Rush.com

Socan.com

Worldradiohistory.com

## OTHER REFERENCES AND SOURCES

Floegel, Mareike, Susanne Fuchs, and Christian A. Kell. "Differential contributions of the two cerebral hemispheres to temporal and spectral speech feedback control." *Nature Communications* 11 (2020), 2839. https://doi.org/10.1038/s41467-020-16743-2.

Mercury Records press release, July 17, 1974.

Rush Tour Books, from *2112* (1976) through *Test for Echo* (1996).

# DISCOGRAPHY

**Selected Releases**

*Moving Pictures* (originally issued in 1981) and related titles:

*Moving Pictures* (LP, 1981) (Mercury/PolyGram, SRM-1-4013, 6337 160).

*Moving Pictures* (LP, 1981) (Anthem ANR-1-1030).

*Moving Pictures* (eight-track, 1981) (Mercury/PolyGram MC-8-1-4013).

*Moving Pictures* (cassette, 1981) (Mercury/PolyGram MCR-4-1-4013).

*Moving Pictures* Remastered (cassette, 1997) (314 534 631-4).

*Moving Pictures* (cassette, U.K., 1981) (Mercury 7141 160) .

*Moving Pictures* (CD) (Mercury/PolyGram 800 048-2) (1984 edition, reissued in 1987).

*Moving Pictures* Original Master Recording (CD, 1992) (Mobile Fidelity Sound Lab/Mercury UDCD569).

*Moving Pictures* Remaster (CD, 1997) (Anthem/Mercury 314 534 631-2).

*Moving Pictures* Remastered/Reissued Digipak CD/DVD video/DVD-Audio (2011) (Mercury/Anthem/Island Def Jam B0015272-00).

*Moving Pictures Live: 2011* (2011) vinyl LP, 180 gram (Anthem/Roadrunner Records 1686-176601).

*Moving Pictures* vinyl 200 gram (2015) (Mercury/Anthem/Universal Music B0022380-01).

*Moving Pictures* vinyl 180 gram Direct Metal Mastering (DMM, 2019). (Mercury/Anthem/Universal Music B0022380-01).

*Moving Pictures* Super Deluxe Edition (2022) (Mercury B09SV9194D).

**_Moving Pictures_–Related Singles**

"Limelight"/"YYZ" (Mercury, 76095).

"Limelight"/"YYZ" (Anthem ANS 031).

"Tom Sawyer"/"Witch Hunt" (Mercury/PolyGram 76109).

"Tom Sawyer"/"Witch Hunt" (Anthem, ANS-034).

"Vital Signs"/"In the Mood" (Mercury/Phonogram Vital 7).

"Vital Signs" and "A Passage to Bangkok"/"Circumstances" and "In the Mood" (twelve-inch 45 rpm) (Mercury/Phonogram Vital 12).

"Rush Live!" (twelve-inch single) (Mercury/PolyGram Exit 12).

"Subdivisions"/"Red Barchetta" vinyl seven-inch 45-rpm picture disk, 1982 (Mercury/PolyGram Rush P9).

"Subdivisions"/"Red Barchetta" and "Jacob's Ladder" (twelve-inch vinyl 45 rpm), 1982 (Mercury/PolyGram Rush 912).

"New World Man"/"Vital Signs" (live) (U.S.), 1982 (Mercury 6170 227).

"New World Man"/"Vital Signs" (live) (U.K.) (Mercury/Phonogram Rush 8).

"New World Man"/"Vital Signs" (live), 1982 (Anthem ANS-046).

# INDEX